VIETNAM
THE DECISIVE BATTLES

VIETNAM
THE DECISIVE BATTLES

John Pimlott

Foreword by Max Hastings

angus

This edition published in 2003 by
Angus Books Ltd
12 Ravensbury Terrace
London
SW18 4RL

Conceived, edited and designed by Marshall Editions

Copyright © 1997 Marshall Editions
The Old Brewery
6 Blundell Street
London N7 9BH
UK

ISBN: 1-904594-23-9

Printed and bound in Thailand by Imago

Editor	James Harpur
Art Director	David Goodman
Picture Research	Anne-Marie Ehrlich
Editorial Coordinator	Lindsay McTeague
Research	Michael Nicholson
Chief Illustrator	Harry Clow
Production	Anna Pauletti
Managing Editor	Ruth Binney
Historical Consultant	Shelby L. Stanton

CONTENTS

Foreword by Max Hastings		7
Introduction		8
Dien Bien Phu *March 13–May 7, 1954*		12
Ap Bac *January 2, 1963*		24
Gulf of Tonkin Incident *August 2, 1964*		32
Operation Starlite *August 18–21, 1965*		40
The Ia Drang Campaign *October 26–November 27, 1965*		48
Long Tan *August 18, 1966*		60
Operation Attleboro *September 14–November 24, 1966*		72
Operation Bolo *January 2, 1967*		84
Operation Junction City *February 22–May 14, 1967*		96
Rach Ba Rai River *September 15, 1967*		108
Khe Sanh *January 21–April 7, 1968*		116
The Tet Offensive *January 30–February 24, 1968*		128
Hamburger Hill *May 11–20, 1969*		140
Operation Lam Son 719 *February 8–April 6, 1971*		148
An Loc *April 8–July 11, 1972*		160
Thanh Hoa Bridge *May 13, 1972*		172
The fall of the South *March 11–April 30, 1975*		180
The continuing war		188
Glossary		192
Bibliography		193
Index		194
Acknowledgments		200

Page 1: U.S. artillerymen fire a quad-50 machine gun across the An Lao valley during Operation Pershing in July, 1967.

Page 2: A wounded Marine is dragged away by his comrades during the battle of Hue in early 1968.

Page 4: Flames engulf Da Nang Air Base after a Communist rocket attack on January 30, 1968.

Page 6 (TOP): A South Vietnamese soldier on guard duty keeps his eyes and ears open for a possible enemy attack. **(BOTTOM)** Armored vehicles patrol Route 19 to deter possible Communist ambushes.

FOREWORD by Max Hastings

The Vietnam war was one of the longest and bloodiest conflicts the world has seen since 1945. It gripped the public imagination in an extraordinary fashion, partly because of the dominant participation of the United States; but chiefly because it was the most extensively filmed and reported war in history. The picture the world sees of most international struggles is patchy and fragmented for a variety of reasons. In sudden, fast-moving, brief campaigns such as the 1971 Indo-Pakistan war, the Turkish invasion of Cyprus, the various Arab-Israeli wars, it is difficult for correspondents and cameramen to follow the action closely. The tight security usually enforced by the combatants further restricts access to the battlefield.

But through thirty years of war in Vietnam, although the focus of strategic and tactical attention frequently shifted from region to region, the length of the struggle and the opportunities for access provided by the United States and its allies gave the world a unique window on the battlefield. Some soldiers and politicians argued that the effects of this were disastrous for the American cause. The injuries and miseries inflicted on both combatants and non-combatants in Vietnam were no different from the sufferings inseparable from all wars. But the vividness with which they were brought into the living rooms of the American public, month upon month, year upon year, contributed mightily to the nation's disillusionment. Likewise, the Americans' cause suffered from the fact that, while their own misfortunes and blunders were lavishly chronicled in the world's media, those of Hanoi were not, just as the Communists' atrocities were barely publicized.

Yet I believe that those American commanders and politicians who seek to argue that their own media cost them victory in Vietnam are mistaken. The simple truth is that the North Vietnamese eventually prevailed in their long struggle because, on a thousand battlefields from the Demilitarized Zone in the north to the Mekong Delta in the south, they wore down and finally broke the will of the Americans and their South Vietnamese clients.

First the French colonial power in the 1950s, and then the Americans over the ensuing decade and a half, sought to conduct a Western war supported by Western technology, against an Asian peasant army. Had they studied the difficulties encountered by the United Nations fighting the Chinese People's Liberation Army in Korea in 1950–53, they might have saved themselves great grief. Against lightly-armed guerrilla forces, armour, artillery and air power are of only limited value. The decisive factors are the ability of ground forces to operate effectively in alien jungle or waterlogged terrain in extreme climatic conditions; and even more important, the creation of a local government and society as strongly motivated as those of the Communist enemy. On both these counts, first the French and later the Americans failed.

The technique of explaining and interpreting campaigns through computer-assisted maps and artworks, featured in this book and others in the series, has now become familiar, and widely admired by military historians. Both the French and the South Vietnamese were finally defeated in conventional battles. The Americans in Vietnam prevailed in most of the major setpiece actions they fought, above all in the 1968 Tet Offensive. But the losses they suffered, and their inability to achieve a decisive victory over the North Vietnamese, at last caused them to withdraw from the war, leaving the Saigon regime to suffer defeat in the final spring campaign of 1975. The tragedy the war inflicted upon Vietnam, and the injury to the confidence of the United States in its own ability to achieve its foreign policy objectives by force of arms, left scars which remain unhealed, even a generation later.

Max Hastings, author of many military history books, including *Bomber Command*, *Overlord*, and *The Korean War*, visited Vietnam for BBC TV and the London *Evening Standard* every year between 1970 and 1975. He was flown out of the American Embassy compound in Saigon in April, 1975, during the final evacuation of the city. He is today editor of *The Daily Telegraph*.

INTRODUCTION

"One becomes a revolutionary because one is oppressed."

HO CHI MINH, *THE ROAD TO REVOLUTION* (1926)

SINCE 1945, THE COUNTRIES OF Indochina—Vietnam, Laos, and Cambodia—have enjoyed little peace. What began as a nationalist/Communist revolutionary struggle against French colonial rule in the 1940s evolved into a civil war between North and South Vietnam after the French defeat in 1954.

This was exacerbated by the involvement of outside powers, either directly (as in the case of the United States) or indirectly (China and the Soviet Union), reflecting the far wider confrontation of the Cold War. Nor did the violence end with the Communist victories of 1975; instead, it developed into local conflicts based on territorial and nationalist rivalries. All the signs indicate that these controversies are far from settled.

The reasons for this appalling record are many and varied. To the French, the need to retain control of Indochina was based on a mixture of prestige and economic gain; to the Americans, it was a case of stopping what they saw as a global spread of Communism; to the indigenous peoples, it was always a question of nationalism and self-determination, overlaid in more recent years by the influence of rival forms of Communism.

One factor, however, is common to all—the desire to control an extremely important region of the world in terms of strategic position and actual or potential wealth. Under both the French and the Americans, it was manifested in a desire to prevent Communist control of an area linking China and the Indian subcontinent or western Pacific; to the Communist superpowers of more recent times, it was, and still is, a question of who controls Southeast Asia. If the Soviets increase their influence, China is hemmed in; if China dominates the scene, Soviet access to the Indian Ocean and beyond is denied.

The effects of all this have been profound. In Indochina itself, the social, economic, and ecological damage has been enormous, leading (among other things) to a mass exodus of people desperate to escape political persecution or to find a better life elsewhere in the world. On an international level, both France and the United States have had to face the reality of defeat in Indochina at the hands of a comparatively unsophisticated enemy, resulting in periods of deep soul-searching and affecting national self-confidence.

Between 1945 and 1954, for example, there was little public support in France for the war, leading to political crises and even attempted military coups as a similar nationalist threat emerged in Algeria (1954–62). The situation was never that extreme in the United States, but the same pattern of public opposition and political strain was apparent between 1965 and 1973, the echoes of which were still being heard as late as the 1980s.

In considering the military side of the Indochina wars, a number of general points emerge which help to explain the Western defeats. There is little doubt, for example, that the Western or Western-style armed forces deployed in Vietnam were ill-suited to the nature of the threat. The Communists' methods of warfare—which were based on a mixture of political subversion, guerrilla action, and open

A Frenchwoman and her Vietnamese servant in a typical colonial scene in the 1880s.

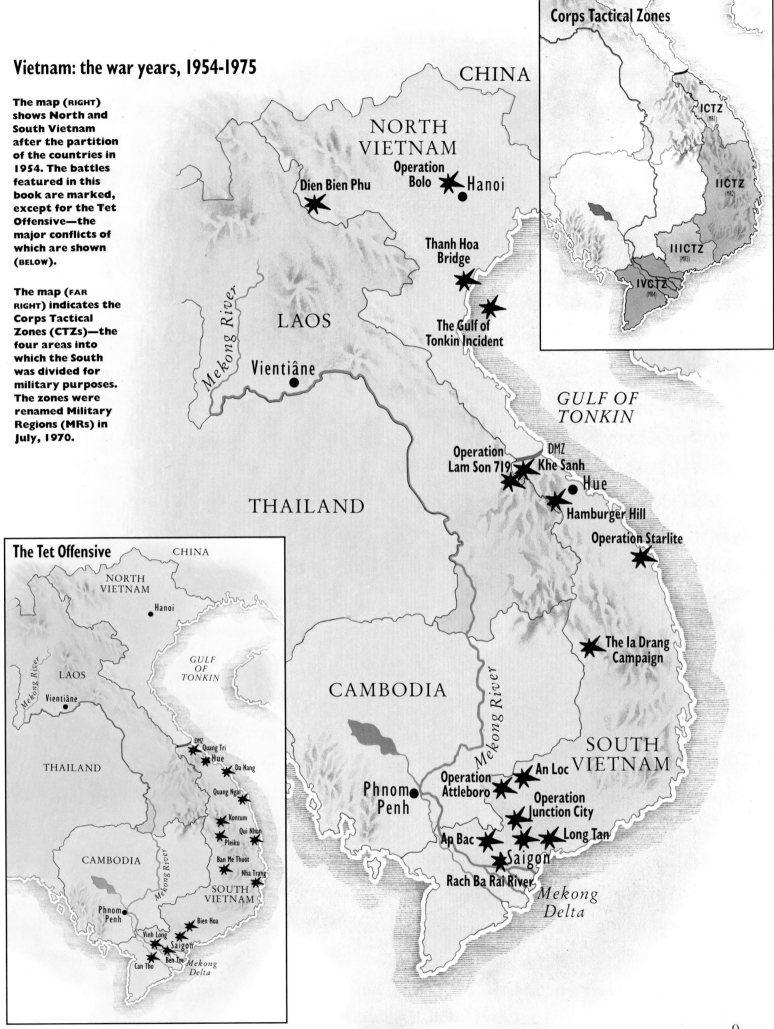

Vietnam: the war years, 1954-1975

The map (RIGHT) shows North and South Vietnam after the partition of the countries in 1954. The battles featured in this book are marked, except for the Tet Offensive—the major conflicts of which are shown (BELOW).

The map (FAR RIGHT) indicates the Corps Tactical Zones (CTZs)—the four areas into which the South was divided for military purposes. The zones were renamed Military Regions (MRs) in July, 1970.

Corps Tactical Zones

ICTZ (MR1)

IICTZ (MR2)

IIICTZ (MR3)

IVCTZ (MR4)

CHINA

NORTH VIETNAM

Operation Bolo

Hanoi

Dien Bien Phu

Thanh Hoa Bridge

LAOS

Mekong River

The Gulf of Tonkin Incident

Vientiâne

THAILAND

GULF OF TONKIN

DMZ

Operation Lam Son 719

Khe Sanh

Hue

Hamburger Hill

Operation Starlite

CAMBODIA

Mekong River

The Ia Drang Campaign

Phnom Penh

An Loc

Operation Attleboro

Operation Junction City

SOUTH VIETNAM

Ap Bac

Long Tan

Saigon

Rach Ba Rai River

Mekong Delta

The Tet Offensive

CHINA

NORTH VIETNAM

Hanoi

Mekong River

LAOS

GULF OF TONKIN

Vientiâne

THAILAND

DMZ

Quang Tri

Hue

Da Nang

Quang Ngai

Kontum

Qui Nhon

Pleiku

Ban Me Thuot

Nha Trang

CAMBODIA

Mekong River

SOUTH VIETNAM

Phnom Penh

Bien Hoa

Vinh Long

Saigon

Ben Tre

Can Tho

Mekong Delta

battle—were poorly understood or, in the case of the Americans, whose Special Forces had made detailed studies of revolutionary and counterrevolutionary warfare, deliberately misconstrued.

The consequence was the deployment of conventional forces using standard military techniques against initially unconventional Communist armies. U.S. commanders strongly believed that the North Vietnamese Army posed the greatest threat to the South after 1964. As a result, many battles were fought on the borders; although the majority were successful for the allies in military terms they failed to prevent the final outcome.

What mattered throughout were the people of Indochina, for if they could be persuaded or intimidated into supporting the revolutionaries, no amount of military success by itself could prevent a Communist victory. This was not recognized by the French, who saw the Viet Minh as a purely military organization and reacted accordingly; it was ignored by many Americans, who showed little understanding of the needs of the people and who, through such techniques as search-and-destroy or massive firepower, often alienated the peasants from the Saigon government; it was even disregarded by the South Vietnamese, whose actions after the Americans had gone did nothing to heal social wounds or create a unified, anti-Communist society.

But the allied forces did not fight badly. French soldiers, from the Red River Delta in 1951 to Dien Bien Phu three years later, operated with bravery and skill within the parameters laid down by their government; the Americans, whether patrolling in the Ia Drang valley or flying over the North, proved their courage on countless occasions.

In addition, the Americans displayed great technological innovation, introducing methods of war which were to affect future concepts. The idea of airmobility and the processes of electronic surveillance used in Vietnam have become part of AirLand Battle, the fighting doctrine designed to see the Americans and their allies into the 21st century.

The Indochina wars therefore continue to fascinate, not least because of the apparent conundrum that military success for the West did not lead to political victory. One lesson above all stands out: when facing a revolutionary threat—or, indeed, a threat of any description—it is essential to combine political and military efforts. Neither the French nor the Americans did this satisfactorily. In both cases, it led to defeat.

The spirit and determination of the Vietnamese Communist forces, who defeated first the French and then the might of the United States and her allies, were fueled by a fierce nationalism. Even before the French took control of what was then called Indochina in the second half of the 19th century, the Vietnamese people's sense of identity had been forged by the struggle to shake off Chinese domination throughout much of their recorded history.

The French captured Saigon in 1859 and soon extended their control over Tonkin, Annam, and Cochin China—areas that make up what is now Vietnam.

French rule, which finally ended at Dien Bien Phu in 1954, was repressive. Over the years, it created a powder keg of resentment of which Ho Chi Minh, the most famous Vietnamese nationalist this century, would light the fuse.

French colonials (OPPOSITE PAGE, BELOW) strike domineering poses, while Vietnamese peasants (OPPOSITE PAGE, ABOVE) toil in the fields. Street scenes of Saigon (LEFT, BELOW LEFT, and BELOW) show everyday life in a French colonial town. Saigon was to fall in 1975 to victorious Communist troops and begin a new era under the name Ho Chi Minh City.

DIEN BIEN PHU

March 13–May 7, 1954

THE FRENCH RULED INDOCHINA for less than 70 years. During that time they had created a *Union Indo-Chinoise* to administrate the colonies of Tonkin and Cochin China and the protectorates of Laos, Cambodia, and Annam. However, many of the indigenous people saw the French simply as foreign oppressors. Plots, guerrilla attacks, and even open rebellions were common, and as each was ruthlessly suppressed, the depth of hatred increased. By the mid-1920s, a Vietnamese Nationalist Party had been formed, principally in Tonkin and northern Annam. Although the party was destroyed after an abortive uprising at Yen Bay in 1929, it helped to establish a pattern of resistance, centered on the northern area of Vietnam.

This pattern was inherited and exploited by the Indo-Chinese Communist Party (ICCP), founded by the Annamese revolutionary Nguyen ai Quoc ("Nguyen the Patriot") in 1930. This man, who would become known to the world as Ho Chi Minh, supervised the establishment of clandestine political cells, primarily in Tonkin and Annam, "awaiting a hatchet blow to the existing order from outside, which would give [the ICCP] the opportunity to seize power." As long as the French remained strong, that opportunity seemed remote.

The situation changed dramatically in 1940, when France fell to the Germans. For, although the administration of Indochina remained in French hands, it now came under the collaborationist regime in Vichy. This in turn enabled the Japanese—Germany's Axis partners in the Far East—to put pressure on Hanoi to close the supply route through Tonkin to China, with whom Japan had been at war since 1937. When, in June, 1940, the French obliged, it was clear that their authority was waning.

Perceptible French weakness boosted the Vietnamese nationalists, and in March, 1941, Ho Chi Minh drew them all together under Communist control, creating the *Viet Nam Doc Lap Dong Minh Hoi* ("League for the Independence of

"We're blowing up everything. Adieu."

THE LAST FRENCH RADIO MESSAGE FROM DIEN BIEN PHU.

Vietnam")—or, in short, the Viet Minh. Resistance activities were increased, attracting the support of Allied powers in the Far East. When the Japanese seized control of Indochina in March, 1945, ousting French forces which now owed allegiance to General de Gaulle's new government in Paris, the Viet Minh were ideally placed to fill the power vacuum in the countryside. Ho and his military commander, Vo Nguyen Giap, expanded the area of Communist control, setting up "safe bases" of peasant support, and prepared to assume political power. Their chance came when the Japanese surrendered to the Allies. On September 2, 1945, Ho entered Hanoi and, with U.S. backing, declared the establishment of a Democratic Republic of Vietnam.

But his success was short-lived. As early as the Potsdam Conference in July, the Allied powers had decided that, in the event of a sudden Japanese surrender, Indochina would be liberated by Nationalist Chinese troops from the north and by British troops from the south, meeting on the line of the 16th parallel. Despite an American reluctance to see the French return, the arrival of the British in Saigon in September, coupled with the weakness of Ho's hold over the south, made a re-establishment of French control difficult to prevent. By early 1946, French units had arrived from Europe, most of the towns south of the 16th parallel had been cleared of opposition by the British, and both Laos and Cambodia had been entered.

Meanwhile in the north, the Chinese had swept forward. Although they did not interfere with Ho's government, their actions weakened Communist credibility in the eyes of the people. In February, 1946, Ho approached the French for help, agreeing to restricted independence for Vietnam within a French-controlled Indochinese Federation, in exchange for pressure to force a Chinese withdrawal. A month later, as the Chinese departed, French troops entered Hanoi, inevitably confronting the Viet Minh. On November 20, a minor clash between

French paratroopers watch their comrades descend from the skies on November 20, 1953, near the village of Dien Bien Phu. The operation, codenamed Castor, brought six battalions of the French 1st and 2d Airborne Battle Groups to this remote valley, close to the Laotian border.

The colors of the 13th Demi-Brigade of the French Foreign Legion list this famous unit's battles, from Camerone in 1863 to "Indochine," 1946 to 1954.

A group of French soldiers share a moment of relaxation during the early stages of Dien Bien Phu. By the end of the battle, the French had suffered more than 8,000 casualties, with at least 9,500 taken prisoner. The cream of France's army in Indochina had been wiped out.

Ho Chi Minh:
"He Who Enlightens"

As founder and political leader of the Indo-Chinese Communist Party, Ho Chi Minh (an alias meaning "He Who Enlightens") occupies a central place in the Vietnam War. Born Nguyen Tat Thanh in the Annamese province of Nghe An in 1890, he left Vietnam in 1912, traveling to France where he first discovered the attractions of Communism. After further study in the Soviet Union, he founded the ICCP in Hong Kong in 1930 (by which time he was known as Nguyen ai Quoc, or "Nguyen the Patriot"); and, 11 years later, he formed the Viet Minh as a revolutionary group dedicated to the seizure of political power.

A follower of the teachings of Mao Tse-tung, Ho conducted a politico-military campaign of subversion, guerrilla attacks, and open battle against the French between 1946 and 1954. By the latter date he had achieved his goal in northern Vietnam and from then until his death in September, 1969, he strove to complete the process in the South. Like many revolutionary leaders, he could be ruthless—in 1956 he committed troops to put down a revolt in Nghe An in which over 6,000 peasants died—but he was (and continues to be) an inspiration to his people.

Paratroopers hug the ground as one of their comrades hurls a grenade at a concealed enemy position at Dien Bien Phu. The hills in the background give an idea of the commanding position held by the Viet Minh over the French.

A black plume of smoke rises over the Dien Bien Phu battlefield as two French soldiers run for cover. In April, 1954, the monsoons turned the ground into a sea of mud, further discomforting the exhausted and hungry defenders.

French customs officials and Viet Minh soldiers in Haiphong led to a French ultimatum for the port to be handed over. Eight days later French forces took Haiphong by force and, as Giap withdrew his men to safe bases in the countryside, they overthrew Ho's government in Hanoi on December 19/20. The First Indochina War had begun.

Initially the French held the advantage, seizing control of the major towns and lines of communication throughout the north. From October to November, 1947, they even mounted large-scale search operations to the north of Hanoi to capture the Communist leaders. When these raids failed, the French reverted to colonial policing, setting up garrisons and outposts throughout the affected area. For just over a year, the strategy seemed to work, but in fact Giap was rebuilding his forces and spreading Communist control in remote villages, chiefly in the Viet Bac, an area in northeast

Vietnam. By April, 1949, he commanded about 300,000 guerrilla fighters and was ready to strike.

Giap chose to hit isolated outposts first, concentrating superior manpower against each in turn and gradually forcing the French onto the defensive. In the so-called "War of the Posts," French losses were substantial; but the real blow came in 1950 when Giap shifted his attention to more significant garrisons close to the Chinese border. By then, the French were facing a strategic dilemma, for victory by Mao Tse-tung's Communists in China had opened up the border to the Viet Minh, providing them with a safe haven and virtually unlimited supplies. If the French tried to block the border, they would leave Vietnam stripped of protection against Communist subversion; if they concentrated on Vietnam they faced an unstoppable buildup of Viet Minh strength. In the event, they chose the latter, with predictable consequences.

The opposing commanders: de Castries and Giap

Born of aristocratic parentage in 1902, Christian Marie Ferdinand de la Croix de Castries entered the French Army as a private soldier in 1922, and rose through the ranks by virtue of his bravery and skill. Wounded and captured by the Germans in 1940, he escaped to join the Free French, seeing hard service in Italy. He was posted to Indochina for the first time in 1946, and soon gained a reputation as a fighter (as well as a womanizer and gambler). Despite being badly wounded in an ambush in 1952, he seemed a natural choice to command the Dien Bien Phu garrison a year later. During the siege, however, he showed command

weakness and was virtually ousted by his para subordinates. After release from Viet Minh captivity, he continued to serve until 1969 and then retired.

Vo Nguyen Giap was born in the Annamese province of Quang Binh in 1912 and educated at French-run schools and at

Colonel de Castries, second from left, studies a map of Dien Bien Phu before the battle.

In a mountain cave, General Giap gives instructions for an attack at Dien Bien Phu.

the University of Hanoi before becoming a teacher. He was a dedicated Communist and joined the Viet Minh, where he soon displayed remarkable military skills, organizing and commanding the Communist forces that gained victory over the French, culminating in the battle of Dien Bien Phu in 1954. As North Vietnam's Minister of Defense, he committed North Vietnamese Army (NVA) troops to the South in the 1960s; and, although his major offensives in 1968 and 1972 failed to achieve military victory, the political gains were substantial. Eased from office in the 1970s, he now lives in virtual retirement.

The French strongholds at Dien Bien Phu were linked by trenches and protected by minefields and barbed wire. Clustered around the command bunker (**9**) near the end of the airstrip (**10**) were strongpoints "Huguette" (**5**), "Francoise" (**6**), "Claudine" (**7**), and, to the east of the Nam

Yum River (**8**), "Eliane" (**11**) and "Dominique" (**12**). Beyond the central area lay "Gabrielle" (**2**), "Anne-Marie" (**4**), and "Beatrice" (**13**). Four miles to the south was the isolated "Isabelle."

On March 13, 1954, General Giap mounted

a major offensive on the French positions. After a heavy barrage, Viet Minh infantry (**14**) overwhelmed "Beatrice." Giap then bombarded the Algerian defenders of "Gabrielle" before unleashing human-wave assaults (**1**). By March 15, "Gabrielle" had capitulated. Three days later, the Viet Minh (**3**) stormed "Anne-Marie."

On May 1, 1954, General Giap ordered his final assault on the French positions at Dien Bien Phu, which, by this time, were concentrated around de Castries's command bunker (**6**). Two new strongpoints had been created, protecting the north and south sides of the bunker: "Sparrowhawk" (**5**) and "Juno" (**7**).

Over the next three days, the Viet Minh (**1**, **9**, and **12**) overran large parts of "Dominique" (**11**), "Eliane" (**8**), and "Huguette" (**2**), leaving "Claudine" (**4**) precariously vulnerable. Then, late on May 6, a massive barrage hit the

demoralized French troops, while, in the hills to the east, Viet Minh troops massed for the *coup de grâce*.

Next day, Giap's men (**3** and **10**) crushed the remaining resistance. At 1730 they reached de Castries's bunker, holding their red and gold flag in triumph.

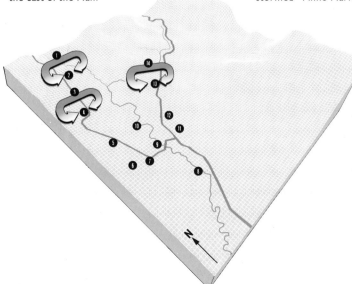

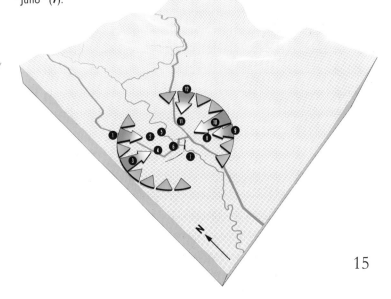

On November 20, 1953, elements of the 1st and 2d French Airborne Battle Groups parachuted into the valley around the village of Dien Bien Phu in an operation codenamed Castor. Within weeks, interlocking strongpoints (reputedly named after the mistresses of the French commander, Colonel de Castries) had been established.

The Viet Minh commander, General Giap, responded to the French challenge by developing a supply route and moving 55,000 men and heavy artillery into the hills overlooking the valley.

At 1700 on March 13, 1954, the siege of Dien Bien Phu began with a massive Viet Minh barrage, followed by human wave assaults on the French positions. Strongpoint "Beatrice" was soon taken. "Gabrielle" fell on March 15, "Anne-Marie" three days later.

By the time Giap's final assault was launched on May 1, the French defensive perimeter had shrunk with the relentless Viet Minh pressure. Now much of "Dominique," "Eliane," and "Huguette" were overrun. Five days later an intense Viet Minh bombardment pounded the exhausted French defenders as Giap's infantry massed in the hills, preparatory to the next day's grand assault.

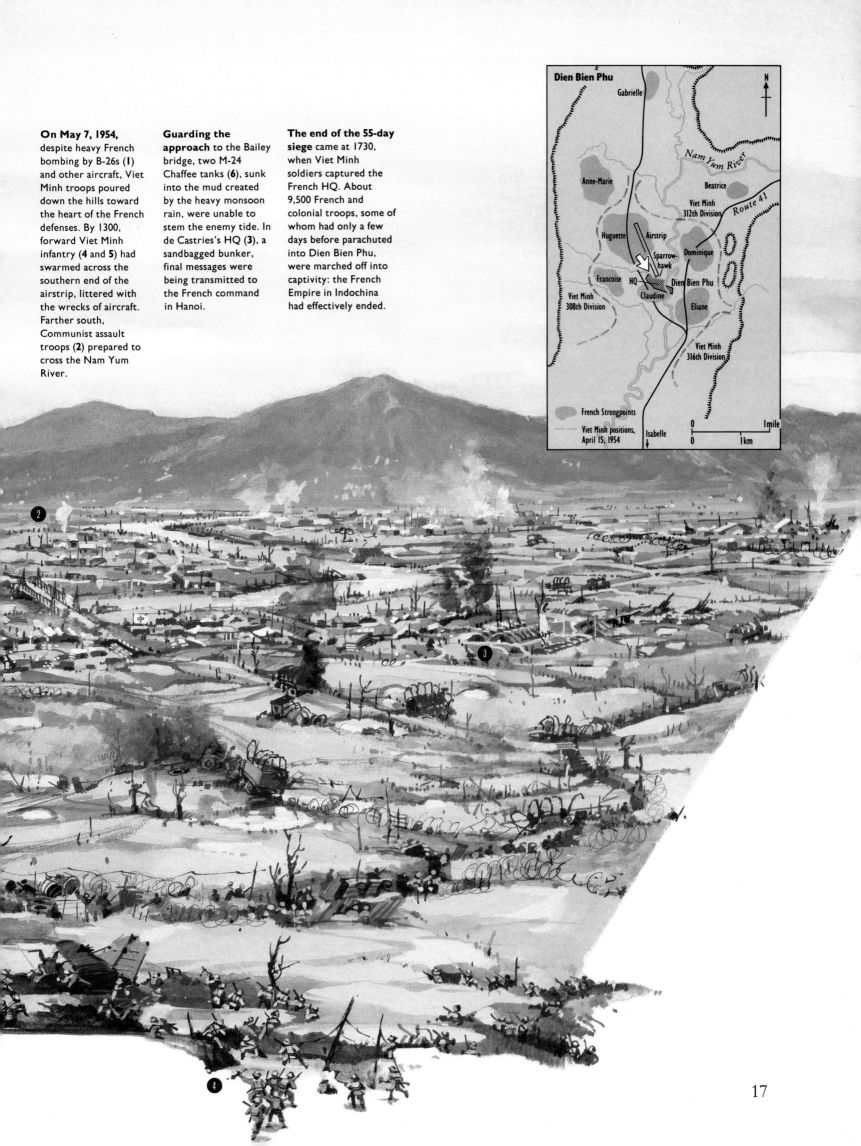

On May 7, 1954, despite heavy French bombing by B-26s (1) and other aircraft, Viet Minh troops poured down the hills toward the heart of the French defenses. By 1300, forward Viet Minh infantry (4 and 5) had swarmed across the southern end of the airstrip, littered with the wrecks of aircraft. Farther south, Communist assault troops (2) prepared to cross the Nam Yum River.

Guarding the approach to the Bailey bridge, two M-24 Chaffee tanks (6), sunk into the mud created by the heavy monsoon rain, were unable to stem the enemy tide. In de Castries's HQ (3), a sandbagged bunker, final messages were being transmitted to the French command in Hanoi.

The end of the 55-day siege came at 1730, when Viet Minh soldiers captured the French HQ. About 9,500 French and colonial troops, some of whom had only a few days before parachuted into Dien Bien Phu, were marched off into captivity: the French Empire in Indochina had effectively ended.

Dien Bien Phu

Gabrielle

Nam Yum River

N

Anne-Marie

Beatrice

Viet Minh 312th Division

Route 41

Huguette

Airstrip

Sparrow-hawk

Dominique

Francoise

HQ

Dien Bien Phu

Viet Minh 308th Division

Claudine

Eliane

Viet Minh 316th Division

French Strongpoints

Viet Minh positions, April 15, 1954

Isabelle

0   1 mile
0   1 km

17

A French patrol (RIGHT) sets up a mortar in an outlying position at Dien Bien Phu.

With his 9mm MAT-49 sub-machine gun at the ready, a member of Colonel Godard's relief column, heading for Dien Bien Phu, crouches in the jungle. The column had set out to reinforce the defenders in an operation codenamed Condor. However, poor management and ambiguous orders led to the men being stalled in the Laotian jungle.

Giap began his offensive in February, 1950, seizing the vulnerable garrison of Lao Khe, close to the Chinese border. He then moved east to attack the Cao Bang-Lang Son ridge in northeastern Tonkin. Dong Khe, an outpost midway between the garrisons of Cao Bang and That Khe, was taken on May 25, but had to be abandoned when a French parachute battalion intervened. As soon as the monsoon ended, Giap tried again, overwhelming Dong Khe for a second time. Cao Bang, isolated from its support farther south, was evacuated by the French on October 3.

It was a disastrous decision. The retreating garrison, strung out along Route 4, was attacked by guerrilla forces and, together with a relief force moving north from That Khe, was dispersed. The French dropped a parachute battalion to act as a diversionary focus, only to see it annihilated and, amid scenes of chaos, Lang Son was abandoned. By the time the last remnants of the ridge garrisons had reached the safety of the Red River Delta (around Hanoi and Haiphong), 6,000 French troops had been lost.

The British in Vietnam

On September 11, 1945, nine days after the formal surrender of Japan to the Allies, advance parties of Major-General Douglas Gracey's 20th Indian Division flew into southern Vietnam. Their instructions, as part of the British-administered Allied Land Forces French Indochina, were "to ensure civil order in the area surrounding Saigon [and] enforce the Japanese surrender." No specific orders were given to guarantee a restoration of French rule.

The British entered a political nightmare. Although the Viet Minh had seized public buildings in Saigon in support of Ho Chi Minh's declaration of independence for Vietnam, anarchy and murder were rife, and fully armed Japanese still roamed the streets. Gracey, shown (ABOVE) presenting the sword of a captured Japanese to an Indian army officer, had little choice but to declare martial law. He rearmed French detainees and even deployed Japanese Marines to restore order. In the process, the French ousted the Viet Minh from the center of Saigon.

The result was more violence and an attempt to lay siege to the city by the thwarted nationalists. Viet Minh reinforcements were rushed down from the north, and key installations were assaulted. British-Indian troops fought to keep the Viet Minh at bay and, as they did so, the French brought in fresh units from Europe. Gracey finally withdrew in late January, 1946. He left behind an uneasy calm, policed by French forces intent on a restoration of colonial rule. Four decades of war were to follow.

Convinced that the French were close to defeat, Giap moved swiftly to attack Hanoi, transforming his guerrilla units into a regular army ready for battle. But the French, under the command of General Jean de Lattre de Tassigny, were equally swift to recover, manning a series of defended positions around Hanoi (known as the "De Lattre Line"), backed by artillery, aircraft, and an airborne reserve. When Giap's 308th and 312th Divisions debouched from the mountains and tried to take Vinh Yen, 40 miles to the northwest of Hanoi, on January 13, 1951, they entered a trap. De Lattre concentrated his forces in response and inflicted substantial losses on Viet Minh fighters caught, for once, in the open. By January 16, Giap had been forced to withdraw.

In late March he tried again, sending three divisions, each of about 11,000 men, against Mao Khe, 20 miles to the north of Haiphong. In hand-to-hand fighting, with French fighter-bombers screaming down to deliver napalm and rockets, the Viet Minh lost 3,000 men in five days. A third assault, to the south of Hanoi in late May, fared no better.

De Lattre then went onto the offensive. On November 14, 1951, French paratroops seized Hoa Binh, 25 miles to the west of the De Lattre Line, and were quickly reinforced. But Giap was not finished. Deploying forces to cut the French off from Hanoi, he inflicted such damage that General Raoul Salan—de Lattre's successor—ordered a withdrawal from Hoa Binh on February 22, 1952. The war was far from over.

Giap concentrated on guerrilla attacks to wear down French resolve, assaulting garrisons along the Nglia Lo ridge, northwest of Hanoi, on October 17, 1952. Once again, French paratroops were committed to save retreating columns of garrison troops and, as Giap now controlled most of northern Vietnam beyond the De Lattre Line, the situation seemed critical. Salan responded by mounting a strong attack—Operation Lorraine—along the Clear River, to force Giap to take the pressure off the remaining Nglia Lo outposts. On October 29, 30,000 French troops advanced toward Viet Minh supply dumps at Phu Doan and Phu Yen.

At first, Giap did not react to the French, who found that they were overextended. Salan ordered a withdrawal on November 14, upon which Viet Minh guerrillas hit the exposed columns: 1,200 French troops failed to reach the safety of the De Lattre Line. By the end of the year Giap seemed to hold the initiative.

Warfare according to Mao

Ho Chi Minh's successful campaign against the French followed a pattern of revolutionary war laid down by the Chinese Communist leader Mao Tse-tung (1893–1976), shown (BELOW) in 1947, riding a mule. Mao's seizure of political power in Peking in October 1949 was the culmination of 22 years of struggle, based on the conviction that the mobilization of peasant support was the key to victory.

Mao's revolution followed three distinct, overlapping phases. In Phase One, Communist cadres infiltrated remote villages, offering education, justice, and better taxation as well as propaganda and the destruction of "class enemies." Each village became a "safe base," out of which new cadres spread the word elsewhere.

Phase Two began when the government reacted by sending in troops: guerrilla groups were formed to protect the safe bases. Exploiting local knowledge and local support, the guerrillas mounted pinprick attacks to undermine the morale of government units. Eventually, as the guerrillas gained in strength, they were transformed into regular armies capable, in Phase Three, of confronting and defeating a weakened enemy in open battle.

This pattern of revolution not only presented three different threats simultaneously—subversion, guerrilla attack, and open battle—but also proved to be flexible. If, for example, the revolutionaries were defeated in battle (as Giap was in 1951), they could revert to guerrilla attacks to wear down the enemy still more, before returning to Phase Three.

The Viet Minh

A revolutionary organization dedicated to the seizure of political power in Vietnam, the Viet Minh, despite their military framework, were first and foremost a political group. They were controlled by the Indo-Chinese Communist Party (ICCP), the politburo of which, chaired by Ho Chi Minh, was secure in the Viet Bac after 1946. The ICCP divided Vietnam into six regions (or "interzones"), each with its own political hierarchy, chosen and controlled by the politburo.

Viet Minh military organization began in the villages, where local militia units were raised. In November, 1949, Ho Chi Minh ordered a general mobilization of all males and females between the ages of 18 and 45 in Communist-controlled areas, creating a vast reservoir of support. These people were unarmed, but they could be trained in rudimentary political and military tasks, information gathering, and manual labor. By 1954, an estimated 350,000 militia existed, many of whom, equipped with nothing more sophisticated than bicycles, kept Giap's divisions supplied around Dien Bien Phu.

Once trained, members of the militia could be transferred to the regional forces controlled by the interzone committees. Regional troops were usually armed, acting as a "home guard" to protect the interzone and carrying out small-scale attacks on enemy outposts. Using their local knowledge and local support, they mounted classic guerrilla attacks that wore down enemy resolve. About 75,000 regional troops were available by 1954.

But they could not defeat the French on their own; for that, Giap needed conventional, main-force units known as the Chu Luc. In 1950 he reorganized his existing battalions into five full divisions—the 304th, 308th, 312th, and 316th in the Viet Bac, and the 320th in the South Delta Base—to form the cutting edge of Viet Minh military strength. By the end of the year, a sixth division—the 351st Heavy, equipped primarily with artillery—had been added; and, by 1954, a seventh, the 325th, was being formed. By then, the Chu Luc was made up of over 125,000 well-armed and disciplined men. They were more than a match for the French.

The Viet Minh drew on vast numbers of militia to aid the war effort. Here, women carry ammunition boxes to the front.

At Dien Bien Phu, the French were outgunned by Viet Minh artillery, which was dragged to the front by human labor.

Despite committing troops to besiege the French garrison at Na San, close to the Laotian border, in late 1952, Giap was able to build up his strength for an invasion of northern Laos. This began on April 9, 1953, widening the war and forcing the French to commit reserves to the Plain of Jars to protect the Laotian capital. As air-supplied "hedgehog" positions were established, the Viet Minh pulled back, having secured the annual opium crop and strengthened the resolve of the local Pathet Lao guerrillas.

Ironically, the French interpreted this response as a victory, concluding that any renewed Viet Minh invasion could be blocked by air-supplied centers of resistance. Salan's successor, General Henri Navarre, went further and argued that such centers could be established at key points, tempting the Viet Minh to attack. Looking at the map, he chose the village of Dien Bien Phu, close to the Laotian border, as an ideal target.

Dien Bien Phu had a number of advantages. It was on a Viet Minh supply route into Laos and had an old French airstrip. Also, it was situated in the T'ai Mountains, where native T'ai units with French officers still operated; indeed, the original plan of attack on the valley envisaged a link-up with such units, chiefly from the T'ai capital of Lai Chau, after which Dien Bien Phu would be turned into a "guerrilla anchoring point" for attacks on Viet Minh supply lines. With this in mind, Operation Castor was ordered and, on November 20, 1953, six battalions of the French 1st and 2d Airborne Battle Groups dropped into the valley, sweeping aside the local Viet Minh garrison.

The paras found themselves in possession of a heart-shaped valley, 12 miles long and 8 miles wide, surrounded by low, heavily wooded hills. In the center was Dien Bien Phu and the vital airstrip, the only link with Hanoi, 170 miles away. Patrols pushed into the hills, encountering little opposition, and orders were issued for the T'ai withdrawal from Lai Chau. The operation seemed a success.

Things soon began to change. In early December most of the T'ai units were destroyed in Viet Minh ambushes, and Giap was moving substantial forces toward Dien Bien Phu. The French, convinced that they could inflict a crushing defeat on the enemy in a set-piece battle, transformed their "anchoring point" into a fortress, building a series of strongpoints, which were reputedly named after the mistresses of the garrison commander, Colonel Christian de Castries.

A French paratrooper (LEFT) at the time of Dien Bien Phu. He wears a U.S.-made steel helmet, a camouflage uniform, and rubber jungle boots. He is armed with grenades, a bayonet, and a U.S. 30-caliber M1 carbine.

A Viet Minh main-force infantryman (RIGHT), equipped with a 7.62mm submachine gun. He carries his utility blanket bandolier-style and wears light, practical open sandals. A Viet Minh star adorns his helmet and belt buckle.

Triumphant Viet Minh (BELOW) stand atop de Castries's command bunker after the French capitulation on May 7, 1954.

Finally defeated by overwhelming odds, the French had held out at Dien Bien Phu for 55 days.

In the center of Dien Bien Phu was the command headquarters, with strongpoints "Huguette" to the west, "Claudine" to the south, "Eliane" to the east, and "Dominique" to the northeast, connected by trenches and protected by minefields and barbed wire. Similar posts existed outside the central "hedgehog," protecting approaches from the north-

A French machine-gun unit (BELOW LEFT) prepares to lay down covering fire for an advancing squad of soldiers at Dien Bien Phu.

French prisoners (BOTTOM) begin the march into captivity. Few would survive both the journey and subsequent imprisonment.

west ("Anne-Marie"), northeast ("Beatrice"), and north ("Gabrielle"), while four miles farther south "Isabelle" covered a small auxiliary airstrip. Artillery was dug in, six Bearcat fighters were stationed on the main airstrip, and ten M-24 light tanks provided more mobile firepower. To many observers, Dien Bien Phu seemed impregnable; in reality the French had committed 10,800 men to the defense of an isolated, monsoon-affected valley, surrounded by hills that had not been secured.

Giap responded by deploying a total of five divisions—about 55,000 men—into the hills around Dien Bien Phu, constructing a supply road, and dragging artillery pieces (including antiaircraft

U.S. Policy in Vietnam, 1945–54

Official United States policy toward the Viet Minh changed dramatically in the late 1940s. While the war with Japan continued, Ho Chi Minh was regarded as a resistance fighter, tying down the enemy forces far from the battle zone in the Pacific. U.S. advisers and arms were provided and, when Ho declared the independence of Vietnam on September 2, 1945, American uniformed officers were present. By then, the future strategic value of Indochina in terms of rice, rubber, and tin had persuaded President Harry Truman's administration that a restoration of French colonial rule—and the crises it would create—was not advisable.

This policy began to alter as the world entered the Cold War. By late 1949, with a growing confrontation between East and West in Europe, Mao's seizure of power in Peking, and a series of Communist-inspired uprisings in Southeast Asia, the United States was facing a global threat. The Communist-backed North Korean invasion of the South in June, 1950, merely reinforced the belief that Peking was orchestrating the attacks, especially when the Chinese Army reinforced the North Koreans in October, 1950.

In such circumstances, the French were rapidly transformed from colonial oppressors to front-line fighters in the West's efforts to stop Communist-inspired revolutions, now firmly believed to be controlled by Peking. U.S. supplies poured into Saigon, controlled by the Military Assistance Advisory Group (MAAG). By 1954, U.S. aid amounted to a staggering $1,063,000,000, equivalent to 78 percent of the French war effort. The French defeat could not be avoided (an offer of U.S. air support around Dien Bien Phu was rejected), but the Americans were already deeply committed.

guns) into camouflaged positions overlooking the valley. On January 31, 1954, the French came under fire for the first time and, over the next few weeks, patrols encountered Viet Minh forces in all directions. The valley was under siege.

Viet Minh strategy was familiar—aiming for the isolated strongpoints first, then mounting a major assault on the main position. The offensive began at 1700 hours on March 13, with a barrage that blew up French artillery bunkers, smashed trenches, and destroyed aircraft on the runway. It was followed immediately by human-wave infantry assaults against "Beatrice," catching the defenders by surprise.

After heavy fighting, the strongpoint was overwhelmed and over 550 French troops were killed or captured. Almost without pausing, Giap subjected "Gabrielle" to a ceaseless barrage of artillery and infantry attacks. French artillery could not relieve the pressure and, by mid-morning on March 15, "Gabrielle" was in Viet Minh hands. Three days later "Anne-Marie" went the same way, leaving the airstrip exposed and impossible to use. From now on, no wounded would be evacuated, and all re-supply would be by paradrop, made hazardous by intense antiaircraft fire.

The Viet Minh renewed their attacks on March 30/31, concentrating on "Dominique," "Eliane," and "Huguette," but costs were heavy. As the French mounted desperate counterattacks, fighting for strongpoints which had been transformed into blood-soaked piles of rubble strewn with the dead of both sides, Giap pulled back to recuperate, enabling de Castries to reorganize his defenses. He concentrated his forces into an area little more than a mile in diameter, taking in "Claudine," "Eliane," and parts of "Dominique" and "Huguette" but leaving "Isabelle" isolated to the south. Two new strongpoints, "Sparrowhawk" to the north of the command bunker and "Juno" to the south, completed the new perimeter.

Between April 4 and May 1, Giap switched from massed assaults to a steady encroachment, constructing an elaborate web of trenches which, under continuous artillery support, slowly closed in around the French positions. French airstrikes failed to have much effect and, to top it all, on April 22 the monsoon began, flooding many of the French positions.

Giap mounted his final assault on May 2, squeezing in from all sides. Over the next three days, amid some of the fiercest fighting so far, large areas of "Domini-

que," "Eliane," and "Huguette" were overrun, leaving the central defensive area exposed. The defenders were desperately short of ammunition—over 30 percent of their paradropped supplies had landed on Viet Minh territory—the hospital on the banks of Nam Yum River was overflowing, and morale had begun to crack. Some units, notably the Foreign Legion and paras, continued to fight with a bravery born of desperation; but the end was near. Late on May 6, a massive barrage swept the remaining strongpoints and, as Viet Minh reinforcements massed in the hills to the east, de Castries faced defeat.

Early on the 7th, the infantry attacks began again, overwhelming defenders shattered by 55 days of siege. By midday, most of the positions east of the river had fallen; at 1730 hours a Viet Minh forward unit, holding their red and gold flag aloft in triumph, entered the command bunker. De Castries surrendered and, although "Isabelle" was to survive for a further 24 hours, over 9,500 French troops began a captivity that few would survive. With the 8,200 casualties suffered during the siege, this meant the cream of the French Army in Indochina had been wiped out.

Although Giap had not escaped lightly, losing an estimated 20,000 men in the battle, he had destroyed the last vestiges of French colonial rule. Wearied by a war that had become increasingly unpopular at home, the French government thankfully accepted an international settlement hammered out in Geneva in July. The First Indochina War was over.

On May 8, 1954, France-soir *proclaims the grim news—"Dien Bien Phu has fallen."*

The Geneva Accords

Signed on July 20/21, 1954, by the French and Viet Minh, the Geneva Accords established the independence of Laos and Cambodia, while splitting Vietnam along the line of the 17th parallel. A demilitarized zone (DMZ) was created and a ceasefire agreed, to be monitored by an International Armistice Commission. The French were to withdraw from north of the DMZ, where Ho Chi Minh would be free to set up a Democratic Republic, and elections would be held throughout Vietnam within two years to finalize its future status. As the U.S. refused to sign any of the agreements because of uncertainties governing the "freedom" of such elections, the chances of a permanent settlement were poor.

THE WAR YEARS

May 10, 1941	*Viet Nam Doc Lap Dong Minh Hoi* (Viet Minh) formed by Ho Chi Minh to coordinate resistance activities.
Sept. 2, 1945	Japan formally surrenders to the Allies; Ho Chi Minh declares the independence of Vietnam in Hanoi.
Dec. 19/20, 1946	French troops oust the Viet Minh from Hanoi; First Indochina War begins.
Oct. 1, 1949	Mao Tse-tung declares the People's Republic of China in Peking.
Feb. 27, 1950	NSCM 64 outlines U.S. policy to contain the spread of communism in Southeast Asia.
June 25, 1950	North Korean invasion of South Korea; United Nations' troops committed to support the South (war ends July, 1953).
Aug. 3, 1950	U.S. Military Assistance Advisory Group (MAAG) set up in Vietnam to coordinate U.S. aid to the French.
Nov. 4, 1952	Dwight D. Eisenhower elected President of the U.S.
May 7, 1954	Dien Bien Phu falls to the Viet Minh after a 55-day siege.
July 7, 1954	Ngo Dinh Diem appointed Prime Minister of (South) Vietnam under the Emperor Bao Dai.
July 20/21	Geneva Accords grant independence to Laos, Cambodia, and a divided Vietnam; First Indochina War ends.

AP BAC

January 2, 1963

THE GENEVA ACCORDS NEVER stood much chance of success. Designed to allow the French to withdraw from Indochina in the aftermath of Dien Bien Phu, they created more problems than they solved, particularly in Vietnam. After years of struggle, Ho Chi Minh was unlikely to accept as permanent the division of his country along the 17th parallel, while the United States was equally unlikely to sanction unification if there was the slightest chance of Communist domination.

To begin with, Ho's Democratic Republic of North Vietnam was in no condition to continue the conflict. A period of recovery and consolidation was essential. At the same time, the promise of free elections throughout Vietnam two years after Geneva offered the prospect of a peaceful Communist victory, based on Ho's popularity as a nationalist leader. He could afford to wait.

This gave the United States the opportunity to support a strong government in the South that would act as a bastion against Communist expansion. President Dwight D. Eisenhower, elected to the White House in 1952 at the height of the Cold War, was convinced that the countries in Southeast Asia were like a row of dominoes—if one fell to Communism, others would follow. Consequently, he was not willing to allow "free elections" if Ho stood any chance of victory. What was needed was an alternative to Ho in the South—a leader whose strength (backed by the U.S.) would appeal to the people of "Free Vietnam" and provide a non-Communist focus for their nationalism. Such a man seemed to be available in Ngo Dinh Diem, appointed prime minister by the pro-French puppet president Bao Dai on July 7, 1954, even before the Geneva Accords had been signed.

Diem had distinct advantages. He had chosen exile rather than collaboration with the French, so was untainted by "colonialism," and his Roman Catholicism made him a natural opponent of

"I predict to you that you will, step by step, be sucked into a bottomless military and political quagmire."

PRESIDENT DE GAULLE TO PRESIDENT KENNEDY, MAY, 1961

Communism. He was also susceptible to American ideas, fed to him through the Central Intelligence Agency (CIA) in the person of Colonel Edward Lansdale, a renowned expert on counterinsurgency. In April, 1955, Diem moved against his main rivals in the South—the quasi-religious Cao Dai and Hoa Hao sects, as well as the powerful Binh Xuyen pirates—and when he held a plebiscite in October, it was claimed that 98 percent of the people supported him. Diem declared himself president and refused to accept the projected "free elections."

In reality, Diem proved a disaster. In a country that was predominantly Buddhist, his Catholicism isolated him from the people, while his obsession with power and constant fear of a coup led him to distrust all but his own family, who gradually assumed positions of excessive influence. His brother Nhu became his chief political adviser as well as head of the secret police, while Nhu's wife—known always as Madame Nhu—was effectively the "First Lady" to the bachelor president. Two other brothers, Can and Thuc (the latter an archbishop), enjoyed similar power, helping to spread a web of corruption throughout the country.

Catholics were openly favored for political posts, and land confiscated from the French was given to those who were loyal to the regime. Since many of the Catholics were northerners who had fled south in 1954, their presence was particularly resented by a peasant class whose support was essential. By the late 1950s, South Vietnam had degenerated into a repressive, undemocratic state in which the broad mass of the people felt isolated and angry.

Trouble began as early as 1957, with guerrilla attacks on government agencies in rural areas; there is little doubt that the attacks were organized by "stay behind" parties of Viet Minh (now known as Viet Cong, or Vietnamese Communists), who had gone underground in 1954. In response, the Vietnamese Workers' Party in

An Army UH-1A helicopter (LEFT) recovers the remains of a UH-1 Iroquois gunship, one of five helicopters shot down by the VC during the battle of Ap Bac. The gunship had tried to rescue the crews of two CH-21 Shawnees immobilized by VC antiaircraft fire.

U.S. advisers (RIGHT) inspect the battle gear of ARVN casualties at Ap Bac.

An M-113 armored personnel carrier (TOP) splashes into a river during an ARVN exercise in early 1963. These APCs, capable of crossing rivers and paddy fields, spearheaded a number of attacks on the VC positions at Ap Bac, but were repelled each time.

the North pledged support and, starting in 1959, began a policy of large-scale infiltration of armed cadres into the South along what would soon be called the Ho Chi Minh Trail. A National Liberation Front was established in late 1960, dedicated to the reunification of Vietnam by the familiar combination of subversion, guerrilla attacks, and open war. Exploiting the resentment created by Diem, the Communists quickly gained control of substantial parts of the South.

This was the situation facing President John F. Kennedy when he took office in January, 1961. He was convinced that renewed insurgency in South Vietnam was part of a Sino–Soviet campaign to ensure the spread of Communism and, although he was aware of Diem's shortcomings, felt forced to bolster up the Saigon regime. Helicopters and aircraft were provided, together with U.S. pilots and mechanics to train the South Vietnamese in their use; U.S. Special Forces (Green Beret) and Army advisers were deployed to boost the capability of the Army of the Republic of Vietnam (ARVN). By late 1961, more than 3,160 U.S. service personnel were in the South; two years later, this number had risen to 16,000, administered through the Military Assistance Command, Vietnam (MACV).

The impact on the guerrillas was noticeable. On September 25, 1962, for example, an ARVN unit equipped with U.S.-supplied M-113 armored personnel carriers (APCs) inflicted a rare defeat on Viet Cong (VC) forces in the Plain of Reeds to the southwest of Saigon. Coming under fire, the ARVN commander ignored U.S. advice to dismount his men and literally charged across flooded paddies, crushing the guerrillas beneath his tracks and inflicting over 150 casualties. Similar victories were gained as U.S.-piloted helicopters gave the ARVN enhanced mobility and Vietnamese Air Force (VNAF) fighter-bombers (with active assistance from U.S. Air Force officers) increased the weight and availability of firepower.

But these advantages were short-lived. The VC learned to operate despite the new equipment and, as U.S. advisers soon discovered, ARVN unit commanders—many of them political appointees—often lacked resolve, allowing VC to escape rather than risk heavy ARVN casualties. In addition, new techniques now being developed (despite U.S. Special Forces' warnings), ranging from the relocation of villagers in especially fortified "Strategic Hamlets" to the indiscri-

"God has gone South"

Clause 8 of the "Final Declaration of the Geneva Conference on the problem of restoring peace in Indo-China," agreed on July 21, 1954, laid down clearly that "everyone in Viet Nam" had the right "to decide freely in which zone he wishes to live." It was an agreement that was to lead to a mass movement of people within Vietnam over the next 12 months, as over 850,000 northerners traveled south, and about 80,000 southerners went north.

The majority of the northerners were Catholics from villages in the Red River Delta, where French missionary activity had been strong. Most chose to move rather than face persecution, but the Americans, under CIA operative Colonel Edward Lansdale, did all they could to boost the exodus, recognizing that a ready-made anti-Communist population would do much to guarantee Diem's survival in Saigon. Diem made his contribution by announcing that "God has gone South," and promising land grants in the Mekong Delta for those villagers who made the move.

Included among these people were undoubtedly Communist agents, ordered to create "cells" among the southern population. At the same time, although most of the Viet Minh activists in the south moved north in 1954–55, special "stay behind" parties remained. When the revolution resumed, these people played a key role.

South Vietnamese soldiers cross a wooden bridge during a five-day mission against the VC five months before Ap Bac.

In an operation against the VC in 1963, ARVN troops storm ashore from U.S. landing craft (LEFT). The influx of U.S. equipment at this time made an immediate, but temporary, impact on the VC.

minate use of air and artillery strikes in rural areas, were alienating the very people Diem needed on his side—the ordinary peasants. In such circumstances military operations, fought in a political vacuum among an apathetic population, often failed.

This was shown on January 2, 1963, when the ARVN 7th Division was

ordered to destroy a VC transmitter in the hamlet (Ap) of Tan Thoi, on the eastern boundary of the Plain of Reeds. The plan, suggested by U.S. advisers under Lieutenant Colonel John Paul Vann, was for ARVN infantry to be landed by helicopter to the north of the hamlet, while two Civil Guard (militia) battalions, supported by a company of M-113s,

The "Domino Theory"

On January 19, 1961, the outgoing U.S. President, Dwight D. Eisenhower, briefed his successor, John F. Kennedy, on the current priorities of American foreign policy. According to Clark Clifford, presidential adviser and future Secretary of Defense, the first item on Eisenhower's agenda was Southeast Asia: "He had in mind that if we let South Vietnam fall . . . Laos, Cambodia, Burma, and on down into the subcontinent would go, the Philippines would go and possibly even Australia and New Zealand." It was a clear exposition of the "Domino Theory."

Eisenhower had always been a strong advocate of the theory—in April, 1954, he used the analogy at a press conference: "You have a row of dominoes set up, you knock over the first one, and what will happen to the last one is the certainty that it will go over very quickly." But the theory had its origins even earlier than his presidency. On February 27, 1950, National Security Council Memorandum 64 had laid down that "all practicable measures should be taken to prevent further Communist expansion in Southeast Asia." As Mao Tse-tung consolidated his power in China and the North Koreans invaded the South, the concept of a "wall of containment" against further expansion became an act of faith. Presidents Eisenhower, Kennedy, and John-son all believed in the theory, tying U.S. foreign policy firmly to the survival of South Vietnam—the first and most important of the "dominoes." It was a policy that was eventually to lead to U.S. main-force commitment in 1965.

President John F. Kennedy meets with his foreign policy advisers in New York in 1961. Sitting on the President's right are Dean Rusk, Arthur Dean, and John McCloy. Like presidents Eisenhower and Johnson, Kennedy was a firm believer in the "Domino Theory."

By 1963, the Army of the Republic of Vietnam (ARVN) had been bolstered by 16,000 U.S. service personnel and an array of modern equipment. However, despite initial successes during this period, the ARVN were unable to keep up the momentum. Poorly led, and faced with an apathetic civilian population, ARVN troops were often hard pressed to defeat numerically inferior—but highly motivated—VC guerrillas.

Such was the case on January 2, 1963, in the Mekong Delta, 65 miles southwest of Saigon. Acting on a plan drawn up by Lieutenant Colonel John Vann and his field advisers, the ARVN 7th Division was ordered to destroy a VC radio transmitter located in the hamlet (Ap) of Tan Thoi.

Here, dug in along an irrigation dike that ran along to the neighboring hamlet of Bac, the VC waited for the assault. Their foxholes were so well concealed that it was almost impossible to spot them by aerial reconnaissance. And when the ARVN did attack, they found that the VC, for once, were ready to stand their ground.

The fighting on January 2 began at 0745 when two South Vietnamese Civil Guard battalions, advancing from the south, ran into VC positioned along a treeline to the south and west of Ap Bac. As the Civil Guard units stalled, reinforcements were ordered in by helicopter.

The VC, undeterred by artillery shells and napalm, which had set on fire both Tan Thoi (4) and Bac (6), waited for their chance. As the CH-21 Shawnees ("Flying Bananas") came in too close to the enemy positions, the VC opened fire: one CH-21 was disabled—as were two other helicopters sent to rescue the first. In the end, two CH-21s (3) and one UH-1 gunship (2) lay helpless in the paddy fields.

As the ARVN reserves (1) took shelter behind paddy dikes, Vann, observing the battle from his L-19 spotter plane (5), coerced the M-113 Armored Personnel Carriers (APCs) into the attack. After a delay, the M-113s launched a couple of half-hearted sorties. The VC were entrenched along a zigzagging dike wall that enabled them to lay down a withering crossfire, beating off the attacks.

At about 1430, three M-113s (8) charged the enemy with more determination. However, the VC stood their ground and, inspired by a squad leader named Dung, rose from their positions (7) and hurled grenades at the APCs. The assault was stopped in its tracks, and the APCs were compelled to retreat.

Vann tried to salvage something out of the battle which had gone so wretchedly for the ARVN. He therefore "suggested" that an airborne reserve should be dropped to the east of Ap Bac to cut off the likely VC escape route. Instead, the reserve was placed to the west of the hamlet, and, as a result, the VC made their escape under cover of darkness.

The battle of Ap Bac was won by the courage and determination of the VC, who, for their efforts, were grudgingly praised by Vann. The guerrillas, numbering about 350 men, had fought off a force four times more numerous and equipped with modern APCs, artillery, and airpower.

VC losses were light, with 18 killed and 39 wounded, while the ARVN suffered 80 killed and more than 100 wounded. The Americans lost 3 men killed, with 8 wounded. More alarming for the Americans was the indecisiveness shown by the ARVN commanders, a factor that would haunt them throughout the war.

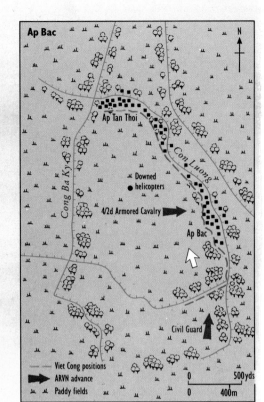

29

Strategic Hamlets

Introduced officially by President Diem in March, 1962, the Strategic Hamlets program involved concentrating the rural population of South Vietnam in secure locations, away from Viet Cong pressure. The aerial view (RIGHT) shows the layout of a typical Strategic Hamlet. Based on a similar idea used by the British in Malaya in the 1950s—and already tried experimentally within Vietnam through the "agroville" scheme of 1959—the program was, in reality, a disaster, helping to drive a deep wedge between the ordinary peasants and the government. It contributed in no small measure to the successes of the VC in the early 1960s—something the U.S. Army Special Forces tried, without success, to point out.

There were many reasons for its failure. For a start, most South Vietnamese peasants were deeply attached to their villages, so any attempt to remove them forcibly was resented. In addition, Diem's brother Nhu, who masterminded the scheme, showed more interest in statistics than "hearts and minds": when he announced in September, 1962, that 4,322,034 people (33.9 percent of the population) were already settled in Strategic Hamlets, he ignored the fact that many of the new locations were badly built and that the people had often been moved so quickly that VC cadres already in their midst had moved with them. Finally, the endemic corruption of South Vietnam meant that much of the money earmarked

for irrigation work, seed, fertilizer, and medical care disappeared into the hands of local officials. In the end, the ordinary people saw no advantages to the program and "voted with their feet," ignoring the scheme or joining the VC in protest.

The M-113 APC

Designed as a "battlefield taxi," the M-113 armored personnel carrier (APC) could transport a squad of infantrymen to the battle area and provide machine-gun fire support once they had dismounted. It was manufactured in response to a U.S. Army call in 1956 for an air-transportable, cheap, reliable, and adaptable APC and entered service in 1960. Two years later it was issued to ARVN armored cavalry units in Vietnam.

A slab-sided, tracked APC of all-welded aluminum construction, the basic M-113 was powered originally by a Chrysler V8 gasoline engine, although Vietnam-issue M-113A1s had the more reliable Model 6V53 diesel fitted. The M-113 had a crew of two (driver and commander) and could carry ten infantrymen in a poorly ventilated compartment entered through a hydraulically operated rear ramp. A single 0.50-cal heavy machine gun, housed in a rotating cupola, provided firepower. The vehicle also had a degree of water-crossing capability.

By 1965–66, the main machine gun had been given a shield, and pintles had been added for two M60s, one on each side: this helped to transform the APC into an armored cavalry assault vehicle (ACAV). Although its armor proved susceptible to mines or rocket-propelled grenades the M-113 was dependable, cheap to manufacture, and mobile, representing a good investment in military terms.

approached from the south, through the neighboring hamlet of Bac. It was thought that the transmitter was guarded by about 120 VC.

In reality, the VC commander had three times that number, deployed in Tan Thoi as well as in expertly camouflaged foxholes along an earthen bank, topped by trees, to the west of Bac. Farther south, where another bank jutted out, a section of VC covered the Civil Guard approach route. It was an ideal ambush position.

The ARVN attack went wrong from the start. Although an infantry company was landed to the north at 0703 hours, ground fog was so thick that further helicopter operations had to be postponed until 0930. This meant that the first clash took place in the south, where the Civil Guard blundered into the VC section across their route at 0745. The South Vietnamese, having lost their commanding officer, went to ground and, after a desultory firefight, called for urgent reinforcements. Unknown to Vann, who was flying over the battle area in an L-19 spotter plane, the ARVN

divisional commander ordered two reserve companies to be helicoptered in.

As soon as Vann was aware of this move, he directed the helicopters—ten CH-21 Shawnees (known as "Flying Bananas")—to land 300 yards to the west of Bac, while their escort of five UH-1 Iroquois gunships raked the earthen bank. The U.S. pilots, according to Vann's version of events, ignored him, landing only 200 yards from the hamlet. It was just what the VC had been waiting for: as the helicopters came in at 1020 hours, they were hit by machine-gun and rifle fire from the hidden foxholes. One of the CH-21s was disabled and, as the ARVN reserve took shelter among the paddy dikes, their momentum stalled. Another CH-21 came in to pick up the aircrew, only to be shot down; a similar fate awaited a UH-1 on an identical mission.

Vann called Captain Jim Scanlon, the U.S. adviser with the M-113s, ordering him to "suggest" an immediate advance on Bac, but the APCs were away to the west, beyond a series of canals. Moreover,

the ARVN commander initially refused to move, even when Vann screamed over the radio for Scanlon to "shoot that rotten, cowardly son-of-a-bitch"; when he finally advanced, it was 1300 before the first of the APCs reached the battle area. They arrived in small groups, one of which, spearheaded by an APC with a flamethrower that proved faulty, charged VC positions at 1430. The VC, against all expectations, stood their ground, showering the vehicles with grenades. The M-113s withdrew in confusion.

An airborne reserve was now made available to the 7th Division, but when Vann suggested it be dropped to the east of Bac to cut off the VC escape, the divisional commander prevaricated. He finally committed them at 1800, just before dusk, to the west of the hamlet. The VC, leaving 18 dead, pulled back under the safety of darkness, having inflicted 80 ARVN and 3 American fatalities. It was, in Vann's words, "a miserable performance [by the ARVN], just like it always is."

Operations such as this deeply worried

An ARVN M-113 (BOTTOM) pulls a sister APC from a paddy field in Kien Giang Province.

M-113A1

Weight	11.8 tons
Powerplant	Six-cylinder water-cooled Model 6V53 diesel engine
Range	300 miles
Speed	42mph
Protection	1.5in
Armament	One 0.5in and two 7.62mm machine guns

The life and death of Diem

Jean-Baptiste Ngo Dinh Diem was born into a well-established Roman Catholic family in Annam in 1901. An involvement in politics led to his appointment as Minister of Justice under the French in 1933, but his growing nationalism soon forced his dismissal; he declined offers first from the Viet Minh, then the returning French to resume office after 1945. Instead, he traveled to the United States, and later to Belgium, where he lived for a while in a Benedictine monastery. He returned to Vietnam in 1954 to take up the post of prime minister in the Bao Dai government in the last days of French rule.

As prime minister and later president of South Vietnam, he must bear some of the blame for the escalation of conflict with the Communists. His policies, culminating in campaigns against the Buddhists in the summer of 1963, led to his isolation, while his overt favoring of his own family gave his regime an aura of nepotistic corruption. When, on November 1, 1963, his generals carried out a coup, he fled with his brother Nhu to the Chinese district of Cholon in Saigon. Pursued by the rebels, the two men were captured early on November 2 and subsequently murdered. Photographs of their bodies shocked the Kennedy administration in Washington, which had not expected such violence; but the demise of the dictator—who had become an embarrassment to the United States—was privately seen as a source of hope for the future.

---

the Americans, particularly as the oppressive nature of Diem's rule intensified. By summer, 1963, the CIA in Saigon was aware that ARVN generals were plotting a coup and, although Kennedy refused to give them his blessing, he made it clear that unless Diem introduced reforms, American aid would have to be reassessed.

Diem, confident that the Americans could not afford to pull out of Vietnam at this stage, ignored the signs, putting into effect anti-Buddhist policies that created a major crisis. As Buddhist priests set fire to themselves in public and Diem responded by attacking their pagodas, it was obvious that he was set on a course of self-destruction.

On November 1, 1963, the generals, backed by the CIA, struck, seizing the presidential palace and establishing a military government. Diem and Nhu, to the dismay of the Americans, were killed. Now there was no going back. As the politics of South Vietnam degenerated into chaos, the slide to full-scale U.S. force commitment was inexorable.

THE WAR YEARS

Sept. 8, 1954	South East Asia Treaty Organization (SEATO) formed to coordinate protection of the area against Communism.
Oct. 9, 1954	The last French troops leave Hanoi; Ho Chi Minh takes over on the 11th.
Oct. 26, 1955	Ngo Dinh Diem declares himself President of the Republic of (South) Vietnam.
Oct. 1957	First guerrilla attacks against President Diem's government.
Sept. 21, 1961	U.S. Army 5th Special Forces Group activated at Fort Bragg, North Carolina.
Feb. 8, 1962	Military Assistance Command, Vietnam (MACV) replaces MAAG in Saigon.
June 11, 1963	Buddhist monk Quang Duc burns himself to death in Saigon.

In protest against President Diem's anti-Buddhist policies, Quang Duc sets fire to himself in June, 1963.

Diem (LEFT) was later overthrown and murdered by ARVN generals on November 1/2, 1963.

GULF OF TONKIN INCIDENT

August 2, 1964

TWENTY-TWO DAYS AFTER THE murder of President Diem in Saigon, President John F. Kennedy fell victim to an assassin's bullets in Dallas, Texas. In such a short period, two of the key players in the developing drama of Vietnam had been plucked from the stage, leaving uncertainty and disruption in their wake.

In the United States, Lyndon B. Johnson was sworn in as Kennedy's successor with a minimum of fuss, but within 48 hours he was having to face the reality of Vietnam. National Security Action Memorandum (NSAM) 273, dated November 24, 1963, confirmed U.S. commitment to Saigon and optimistically predicted an end to insurgency by late 1965. But it could not disguise a growing concern in Washington that the situation in South Vietnam was spiraling out of control.

The coup in Saigon that toppled Diem had brought to power a military junta under General Duong Van ("Big") Minh, but the demise of Diem had done nothing to stabilize South Vietnamese society. Factional fighting re-emerged and, as the administration was purged of Diem supporters, a dangerous vacuum was created, especially in rural areas, where Minh replaced 35 out of 44 provincial governors and countless other key officials down to village level. Those who remained, as well as many of the new appointees, were wary, and this inevitably affected the ability of the ARVN to cope with increasing levels of VC violence.

The politburo in Hanoi, always prepared to exploit weakness, decided in December to boost their aid to insurgents in the South, going so far as to prepare North Vietnamese Army (NVA) regular units for deployment. It was to take almost a year before complete NVA regiments crossed the border, but the decision to escalate had been made.

America's concern for the future of the South grew as it became obvious that ARVN success under Diem had been exaggerated. Over Christmas 1963, Johnson's Secretary of Defense, Robert

S. McNamara, visited Saigon; he came away voicing the gloomy opinion that "the Vietcong now control very high proportions of the people in certain key provinces, particularly those south and west of Saigon."

Almost immediately, the situation deteriorated further, for on January 30, 1964, another coup occurred: the junta was overthrown and replaced by another. Minh was still titular head of the government, but effective power was now in the hands of General Nguyen Khanh. The United States had to accept the new government, even though by now all pretense of democracy had disappeared.

South Vietnam devolved into political chaos—1964 was to see five more coups or attempted coups and a total of seven different governments—and, as Communist pressure grew, the United States began to prepare contingency plans in case of imminent collapse. These included preparations for U.S. bombing of selected targets in the North to deter the politburo from continuing its support of aggression in the South, put forward in NSAM 288 on March 17, 1964. As a "carrot" to this evolving "stick," diplomatic channels were opened with the North. Also, because it was a presidential election year, Johnson was desperate to receive his own mandate from the American people. But all the time the airpower option was being explored: the chance to use it soon came.

By 1964, the CIA was helping the South Vietnamese to carry out secret attacks on coastal targets north of the DMZ, under the codename Operations Plan (OPLAN) 34A using Special Forces-trained agents. At the same time, U.S. naval units were conducting regular surveillance patrols, known as De Soto, in international waters off the North Vietnamese coast in the Gulf of Tonkin. Officially, there was no connection between the two, but in the eyes of the North (and subsequent historians) they were intimately linked.

On July 28, the destroyer USS *Maddox* left Taiwan on a De Soto mission,

"Being approached by high-speed craft with apparent intent to conduct torpedo attack."

COMMANDER HERBERT L. OGIER , USS *MADDOX*, 1645 HOURS, AUGUST 2, 1964

increased speed, but the boats continued to close. At 1645 he reported the situation to his superiors in Hawaii and requested air support from the carrier USS *Ticonderoga*, farther south. Four F-8E Crusaders took off in response.

At 1705 Ogier ordered warning shots to be fired and, when these were ignored, the *Maddox* opened continuous fire with its 5in guns. The North Vietnamese answered with 12.7mm machine guns but were out of range; as they did so the second boat in the column of three was hit, veering sharply to the left and launching two torpedoes. As the *Maddox* turned to avoid them, the third boat passed astern of the destroyer and sped away. The first boat in the column received a direct hit and stopped dead in the water. By then, the F-8s had arrived, but the engagement was over. Only one machine-gun bullet had hit the *Maddox*, and no U.S. casualties had been suffered.

In Washington, Johnson exercised restraint, refusing to authorize retaliation. Instead, he ordered the De Soto mission to continue, with the destroyer USS *Turner Joy* joining *Maddox* in the Gulf. Together, they resumed the patrol only to report, late on August 4, that another attack was taking place, this time some 60 miles offshore.

This second incident is still full of controversy. Although the ships' crews were adamant that they were under attack, reporting a total of 22 incoming torpedoes and hits on at least three enemy boats in an action lasting nearly four hours, no concrete evidence could be produced in its aftermath—no wreckage, no bodies and no damage to the U.S. warships. The action took place, in the words of the official naval report, during a "very dark night with no moon and thunderstorm activity in the area."

The radar and sonar operators were relatively inexperienced and, in retrospect, it could be argued that the destroyers reacted to their own echoes: indeed, Johnson described it as "those dumb stupid sailors . . . just shooting at flying fish." But it was enough to suggest that the North Vietnamese were deliberately escalating the war; even if the *Turner Joy* and *Maddox* had overreacted, both captains believed they were under attack. Combined with the undeniable evidence of August 2, it was sufficient to merit an American response.

This reaction took two forms. As reports of the second incident came in, Johnson authorized retaliatory airstrikes, codenamed Pierce Arrow. At 1315 (local time) on August 5, F-8s from the *Ticonder-oga* hit a North Vietnamese patrol boat base at Quang Khe; two and a half hours later, aircraft from the USS *Constellation* carried out a similar raid against Hon Gai. Altogether, 25 patrol boats were reported destroyed.

Of far more significance, however, was Johnson's call for Congressional approval of his action: on August 7, the Senate voted overwhelmingly in favor of the "Gulf of Tonkin Resolution." Endorsed unanimously by the House of Representatives on the 8th, it allowed the President, "as commander in chief, to take all

America's new commander

On June 20, 1964, General William Childs Westmoreland was officially appointed Commander, Military Assistance Command Vietnam (MACV) in Saigon. He inherited a deteriorating military and political situation in South Vietnam: the ARVN, despite increasing levels of U.S. advisory support, were losing the village war against the VC; North Vietnamese troops were poised on the border, ready to intervene; Saigon was gripped in an endless round of coup and counter-coup. Westmoreland's task was to help reverse this decline, marshalling and using American resources to the best possible advantage.

Westmoreland, shown (BELOW) being cheered by men of the 25th Infantry Division, brought with him a wealth of relevant experience. Born in March, 1914, in South Carolina, he had attended West Point in the mid-1930s. Like many of his contemporaries, he received accelerated promotion during World War II, eventually commanding a field artillery battalion in the Northwest Europe campaign of 1944–45. After the war, he transferred to the airborne forces, commanding an airborne combat team in Korea in the early 1950s, before carrying out a series of staff appointments in Washington. By 1964, he could claim to be an experienced military commander, a first-rate manager—and could hold his own in the corridors of political power.

But his job at MACV was intensely difficult, especially once the decision had been made to commit U.S. main-force units to Vietnam in 1965, for he enjoyed remarkably little control over the war. Although in command of U.S. Army troops, he could not direct U.S. naval or air force elements, nor could he influence the activities of the CIA.

Nevertheless, by the end of 1967, he could claim to have blunted the cutting edge of the VC in rural areas by a combination of helicopter mobility and massive firepower. However, the Tet Offensive of 1968 undermined his credibility in the eyes of many Americans who had come to believe his promises of victory. Replaced as MACV commander in June, 1968, he went on to serve as U.S. Army Chief of Staff. He retired in 1972.

In 1964, a year in which South Vietnam was afflicted with severe political instability, the CIA was working with South Vietnamese forces on secret raids on the North Vietnamese coast. This military pressure on Hanoi was reinforced by U.S. Navy De Soto patrols off the North's coast in the Gulf of Tonkin.

On the night of July 30, 1964, the North Vietnamese islands of Hon Me and Hon Ngu were raided, provoking a Communist reaction. The USS *Maddox*, which had left Taiwan for the Gulf of Tonkin two days before, picked up enemy messages about the future defense of the islands and the presence of the *Maddox*.

In the early afternoon of August 2, the *Maddox* tracked five North Vietnamese P4 patrol boats, which disappeared behind the island of Hon Me. At 1600, three boats reappeared and began to close with the U.S. destroyer.

Herbert L. Ogier, commander of the

Maddox, increased speed and, at 1645, requested air support from the carrier USS *Ticonderoga*. In response, four F-8E Crusaders were dispatched to assist. At 1705, the *Maddox* fired three warning shots at the boats, and, three minutes later, began continuous firing.

At 1715, the *Maddox* (4) hit the second boat (1) of the column, which swerved to the right having launched two torpedoes. Altering course to avoid the torpedo tracks (5), the *Maddox* scored a direct hit on the first boat (2).

The third P4 boat (3), which was also believed to be hit, headed north astern of the destroyer. The battle had been short and decisive, with the *Maddox* being hit by only a single 12.7mm machine-gun bullet.

Two days later, the U.S. sailors were again on full alert. During a stormy night on August 4, the crews of both the *Maddox* and the USS *Turner Joy* believed they were under attack. However, no conclusive evidence was subsequently produced to prove the reality of this second "incident."

Gulf of Tonkin Incident

CHINA

Hon Gai

NORTH VIETNAM

Hon Me

Maddox, August 2

Hon Ngu

Maddox
August 4
Turner Joy

Quang Khe

LAOS

DMZ

N

necessary measures to repel any armed attack against the forces of the United States and to prevent further aggression." It was a virtual *carte blanche* for Johnson to increase the level of U.S. involvement in Vietnam as he saw fit. One of the few critics of the Resolution, Senator Ernest Gruening, described it as "a predated declaration of war"; Johnson likened it to "Grandma's nightshirt—it covered everything."

To Johnson's supporters, the Resolution came not a moment too soon. Although Pierce Arrow had boosted South Vietnamese morale, a new political crisis soon wiped out the advantage. On August 16, Khanh tried to introduce a new constitution—the Vung Tau Charter—that would have given him full presidential power without an election. Students and Buddhists took to the streets in protest and, inevitably, a coup was staged. In the event, it was put down by a group of officers known as the "Young Turks," who included General Nguyen Van Thieu and Air Marshal Nguyen Cao Ky. Even so, political unrest continued until late October.

By then, the VC had shifted their

A U.S. helicopter flies on patrol over the hilly jungle near Pleiku on February 19, 1965, soon after the VC attack on the U.S. base there. Eight Americans were killed and more than 100 wounded in the surprise assault.

attention to American targets in South Vietnam. On October 31, four U.S. servicemen were killed at Bien Hoa, probably as part of a Communist ploy to put pressure on Johnson as Americans went to the polls. If so, it had little direct effect—on November 3, Johnson won an unprecedented 61 percent of the vote—but it did increase calls for more sustained retaliation against the North.

These calls grew more strident as the year turned. On December 24, two people were killed and over 100 injured in a bomb attack on the Brink Hotel in Saigon, used as U.S. bachelor officers' quarters, and on February 6, 1965, more than 300 VC hit Camp Holloway at Pleiku, in the Central Highlands, killing eight Americans. Johnson was rapidly losing patience; in an attempt to persuade the politburo in Hanoi to alter their policy of support for the VC, he ordered another

airstrike on the North, codenamed Flaming Dart. At the same time, he authorized the deployment of U.S.-manned surface-to-air missiles around Da Nang, a particularly vulnerable airbase close to the DMZ.

It was not enough. On February 10, the VC hit Qui Nhon, killing 21 Americans (and triggering more airstrikes under Flaming Dart II); three days later Johnson decided "to execute a program of measured limited air action" against the North, to be known as Rolling Thunder. Extra urgency was given to this plan by yet another attempted coup in Saigon, for although it, too, was put down by the "Young Turks," they later celebrated by ousting Khanh themselves.

Rolling Thunder, delayed by bad weather, began on March 2; it immediately raised problems, not least that of the security of U.S. airbases in the South. On March 7, following representations from the Joint Chiefs of Staff as well as the U.S. ambassador in Saigon, Maxwell Taylor, and the MACV commander, General William C. Westmoreland, the President ordered U.S. Marines to go ashore to protect Da Nang. It was an historic and far-reaching decision.

We Sink 2 Attacking Red PT Boats

By JACK METCALFE

Washington, Aug. 4 (NEWS Bureau)—Communist North Viet Namese PT boats, making their second unprovoked attack in three days on American warships, fired torpedoes at two U.S. destroyers off the coast of North Viet Nam today. At least two PT boats were believed sunk and two damaged in the night battle.

There was no damage to the destroyers or injury to their crews.

The Defense Department announced that the "second deliberate" attack developed suddenly while the destroyers Maddox and C. Turner Joy were patrolling international waters about 65 miles from shore in the Gulf of Tonkin.

The destroyers and fighter planes from the carriers Ticonderoga and Constellation fired back at the attackers in more than three hours.

"The attackers," said the Defense Department, "were driven off with no U.S. casualties or hits and no damage to either destroyer. It is believed that at least two of the PT boats were sunk and two are damaged."

As dispatches streamed in from the Far East, President Johnson summoned members of the Na-

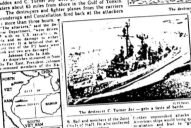

He's a Cardiovascular Wizard
By MICHAEL O'NEILL
(First article of a series)

THE DOCTORS crowded along the railing in the darkened observation gallery above Operating Room 3 in Houston's Methodist Hospital. One was from Spain, two from Sweden, one from Italy, another from New Jersey. They had come to see one of the world's great surgeons in action.

officials said no enemy planes would continue to use international waters and will take "whatwere involved. (Continued on page 18, col. 1)

INDEX TO FEATURES

The New York Daily News (ABOVE and RIGHT) proclaims the news of the second Gulf of Tonkin incident and the U.S. airstrikes. According to the News, "At least two PT boats were believed sunk and two damaged in the night battle." The second incident is still shrouded in controversy, with the possibility that no contact at all was made with the PT boats.

DAILY NEWS — FINAL — 7¢
NEW YORK'S PICTURE NEWSPAPER

U.S. PLANES BLAST BASES IN NORTH VIET

LBJ Announces Retaliatory Action for Gunboat Attacks
TAKING ISSUE TO UN
'We Will Seek No Wider War,' Says Johnson; Meets Security Chiefs

THE WAR YEARS

Nov. 22, 1963 President John F. Kennedy assassinated in Dallas, Texas; Lyndon B. Johnson sworn in as his successor.

U.S. newspapers announce Kennedy's death

Jan. 30, 1964 General Nguyen Khanh seizes power in Saigon.

June 20, 1964 General William C. Westmoreland assumes command of MACV in Saigon.

Aug. 2, 1964 U.S. destroyer Maddox attacked by three North Vietnamese patrol boats in the Gulf of Tonkin.

Aug. 4 Confused four-hour action in the Gulf of Tonkin; U.S. destroyers report they are under attack.

Aug. 7 U.S. Senate votes in favor of the Gulf of Tonkin Resolution.

Oct. 31, 1964 VC guerrillas attack U.S. airbase at Bien Hoa.

Feb. 6, 1965 VC attack on U.S. base at Pleiku; Johnson orders retaliatory airstrikes (Flaming Dart).

March 2, 1965 Sustained U.S. bombing of North Vietnam begins under the codename Rolling Thunder.

The second incident: myth or reality?

On August 24, 1964, Commander Herbert L. Ogier, captain of the destroyer USS Maddox, compiled a report on recent incidents in the Gulf of Tonkin for the U.S. Chief of Naval Operations. In it, he described the controversial action of August 4 (all times are local):

"1945: Maddox detected a contact at 070, 36.4 miles . . . evaluated as a probable patrol craft due to its high speed. Considered to be a threat. . . . Soon after, two other contacts were picked up to the northeast . . . at approximately 40 miles, also closing.

2007: Maddox observed that contacts . . . merged on the radar at about 32 miles.

2139: Turner Joy opened fire . . . range 7,000 yards.

2142: Maddox sonar reported hydrophone effects bearing 051, which was classified torpedo. . . .

2211: Turner Joy obtained a contact . . . at a range of 3,600 yards and closing with a speed of 48 knots.

2224: Firing commenced at this time . . . the contact disappeared from all radars and was believed sunk at 2228.

2304: Maddox acquired an intermittent radar contact close-up astern.

2306: Maddox released a depth charge. . . . No apparent results.

2319: Maddox sonar reported torpedo bearing 200. . . . Validity of contact: poor.

2321: A contact bearing 005, was obtained by Turner Joy at 1,300 yards and taken under fire. . . . Firing ceased at 2322 . . . no hits were observed. . . . No other surface contacts were observed. . . .'"

39

OPERATION STARLITE

August 18–21, 1965

AT PRECISELY 0903 HOURS ON March 8, 1965, 11 LVTPs (Landing Vehicle Tracked, Personnel) of the U.S. Marine Corps, each with 34 fully armed Marines on board, growled ashore on Red Beach 2, a few miles to the northwest of Da Nang. Part of Battalion Landing Team (BLT) 3/9th, the men conducted an assault landing, complete with battle tanks and with self-propelled antitank vehicles, in difficult "high-surf" conditions. But their arrival was something of an anticlimax: instead of encountering armed opposition, they were met by a crowd of pretty Vietnamese girls distributing garlands of flowers.

By 0918 all of BLT 3/9th was ashore and, somewhat self-consciously, the Marines boarded trucks and tracked vehicles to take them to the airbase at Da Nang. Joined later in the day by elements of the 1st Battalion, 3d Marines (1/3d Marines), airlifted from Okinawa, they were deployed to safeguard the airbase against guerrilla attack, freeing ARVN units for more mobile operations. The Marines were expected by the White House to do no more than this—the orders to Brigadier General Frederick J. Karch, commander of the 9th Marine Expeditionary Brigade (9MEB), were crystal clear: "The U.S. Marine Forces will not, repeat will not, engage in day to day actions against the Viet Cong."

General William C. Westmoreland, MACV commander, was upset at the scale of the Marine landing, having expected a "low-profile" deployment. However, as he was convinced that a North Vietnamese attack was imminent, he soon decided to take advantage of such a strong Marine combat presence. As early as April 1 he persuaded President Johnson to authorize increased force levels in Vietnam—up to 33,000 U.S. troops—and to allow elements of 9MEB to protect a top-secret Army Security Agency communications complex at Phu Bai, farther up the coast from Da Nang.

Two weeks later, after sustained

Marine pressure for latitude in combat activity, Westmoreland issued a "concept of operations" that was clearly designed to permit more aggressive action in certain defined circumstances. Although close defense of the Da Nang and Phu Bai "enclaves" remained top priority, Marines were also to conduct "protective" reconnaissance patrols around their locations and, if necessary, cooperate with local ARVN units. On April 22 a patrol from the Marines' 3d Reconnaissance Battalion clashed with a force of 105 VC near Binh Thai, nine miles southwest of Da Nang. Only one guerrilla was killed, but America's "main-force" shooting war had begun.

This encounter reinforced a feeling that the coastal enclaves, which now included one at Chu Lai, farther south around a new airbase, were too defensive, doing nothing to prevent a buildup of Communist strength in the surrounding countryside. As General Wallace M. Greene, the Commandant of the Marine Corps, drily observed during a visit to 9MEB: "You don't defend a place by sitting on your ditty box."

Two days before Binh Thai, a high-level conference at Honolulu had recommended further Marine reinforcement, and Westmoreland took the opportunity to refine his concept of operations. Although base security and patrolling remained, the Marines could now conduct clearing missions to break up suspected enemy concentrations. The war was escalating rapidly.

Such a shift of emphasis seemed justified when, in June, Communist attacks concentrated on ARVN units that showed little heart for fighting. As defeat followed defeat, the ARVN lost the equivalent of a battalion a week in battle and South Vietnam appeared close to collapse. Johnson felt he had no choice but to commit additional U.S. forces. On July 1, more Marines landed at Qui Nhon and, as this coincided with renewed guerrilla assaults on Da Nang (implying a shift of Communist attention to U.S.

The first U.S. Marines in Vietnam (RIGHT and BELOW) storm ashore onto a beach a few miles to the northwest of Da Nang on March 8, 1965. However, the assault landing was not met by enemy fire but by a welcoming party of Vietnamese girls bearing garlands.

The Marines brought to Vietnam the unusual Ontos (RIGHT), an antitank weapon with an armament of six recoilless rifles and one 50-caliber machine gun.

The U.S. Marines, whose insignia is shown (ABOVE), were sent to Vietnam initially to bolster the defenses of Da Nang airbase, thus allowing ARVN units to mount more mobile operations.

Da Nang in flames

A small group of North Vietnamese sappers crept toward the dim outlines of U.S. aircraft parked alongside the airstrip at Da Nang. Suddenly a Marine sentry, alerted by a slight noise, threw an illumination grenade. As it bathed the area in a burst of light, the attackers rushed forward, throwing satchel charges, while their VC supporters laid down a barrage of rifle and mortar fire. It was 0130 on July 1, 1965; within seconds two C-130 transports and an F-102 fighter-bomber were in flames.

The guerrillas were part of an 85-man team that had approached the southern perimeter of the airbase late the previous evening. Infiltrating ARVN lines, they tunneled beneath the wire around the U.S. compound, setting up a 57mm recoilless rifle and four 81mm mortars to cover their attack. As the sappers withdrew, leaving the aircraft burning, the mortars laid down fire to disrupt an American pursuit.

Major General Lewis W. Walt, commanding the Marines, was further delayed in his response by a stream of phone calls from MACV headquarters in Saigon, CinCPac in Hawaii, and even the White House in Washington, all wanting, in his own words, "to know all about the attack and what I was doing about it."

A joint Marine/ARVN sweep later on July 1 captured one of the attackers, but the real significance of the incident lay in its impact elsewhere. As press reports of the infiltration spread, pressure began to grow to allow the Marines to adopt a more aggressive posture in case this was a prelude—as many imagined—to a full-scale NVA invasion. It was part of the slide toward full-scale U.S. military involvement.

A Marine mans a machine gun on Hill 327, situated near, and providing protection for, Da Nang. After the VC attack on the airbase on July 1, 1965, the Marines were encouraged to adopt a more aggressive role against the enemy.

Infiltration of the NVA

According to U.S. intelligence, by 1964–65 elements of the North Vietnamese Army (NVA) were entering the South in support of VC guerrillas. They came by a variety of ways. A few traveled by sampan down the coast; others moved across the DMZ. But the vast majority made use of a growing network of pathways (the Ho Chi Minh Trail) that wound their way through Laos and Cambodia to exit avenues into South Vietnam. These areas included the A Shau and Ia Drang valleys in the north and center, and War Zone C farther south, close to Saigon. The common denominator was that all were extremely difficult to block, although Army Special Forces had been patrolling and ambushing the areas with some success since 1964.

A North Vietnamese soldier dashes forward grasping his AK-47 Kalashnikov assault rifle during a training exercise. The infiltration into the South of NVA troops presented a daunting problem to the Americans.

targets), the concept of simply defending enclaves ceased to be a viable one.

In fact, Westmoreland had already received permission (on June 26) to use the forces under his command as he saw fit, giving him the green light for more offensive action. This should have led to counterinsurgency operations (already set up by Army Special Forces under Kennedy's guidelines), persuading the people to support the government rather than the Communists by offering social reform and military protection.

The Marines around Da Nang, following the Special Forces "pattern" had already paved the way: as early as May, elements of the garrison had pushed northwest to occupy the village complex of Le My, clearing it of VC infiltrators and offering social aid to the people. This action was followed in June by a remarkably successful operation north of the Cu De River in which other villagers agreed to leave their homes and seek Marine protection in Le My.

But such policies took time and seemed too low key to cope with the problem of a possible Communist invasion on the pattern of the North Korean attack on South Korea in 1950. What was needed—and was in fact ordered on July 20—was an expansion of existing Marine bases to dominate likely NVA invasion routes or guerrilla concentration areas.

At Da Nang, this meant Marine activity around the airbase (hitherto an ARVN responsibility) and in village complexes known to contain VC forces. A successful operation had been carried out in this region on July 12, when Marines had cleared Duong Son (1) (the number distinguishing the village from others with the same name); it acted as a model for renewed activity in early August.

On August 3, as part of Operation Blastout I, men of the 9th Marines approached the hamlet of Cam Ne (1), traveling down the Cau Do River in LVTPs to landing zones about 1,200 yards from their objective. Coming under VC fire, they advanced cautiously into the hamlet, only to encounter booby traps, sniper fire, and civilian hostility. Searches revealed a network of spiderholes and tunnels.

As VC opposition continued, some Marines (under orders) set fire to huts in an effort to deny the VC shelter or

Marines (LEFT) retrieve the dead commander of an LVTP during Operation Starlite.

A Marine M-48 tank (ABOVE) searches a riverbed 16 miles south of Chu Lai during Operation Starlite. The search party found several holes along the bank which might have been hiding spots for the VC. The operation was conducted in energy-sapping heat, which contributed to the Marines' discomfort. Nevertheless, despite suffering 45 men killed, the Americans claimed victory against the VC, counting 614 enemy bodies.

supplies, before being forced to pull back. A television crew was on hand and, on August 5, viewers around the world watched U.S. servicemen burning peasant dwellings for no apparent reason. The commentary made light of VC opposition, creating a public image of U.S. actions in Vietnam that proved impossible to alter in succeeding months. It was a propaganda windfall for the Communists, which they were quick to exploit.

Cam Ne (1) was finally cleared on August 20, but by then the escalation to full-scale U.S. involvement in the war was complete. Earlier in the month, another conference in Honolulu had called for an increase in U.S. force levels in Vietnam to 125,000 men and outlined a new strategy of large-scale offensive action. For the Marines it heralded the first of the "big battles" of the war—Operation Starlite.

Since July, information had been coming in to suggest a major VC assault on Marine bases. This report was confirmed on August 15, when a Communist deserter revealed that about 1,500 members of the 1st VC Regiment had established a base in the Van Tuong village complex, 12 miles south of their intended target—Chu Lai. The Marines were authorized to attack them.

The plan—complex and prone to confusion as Marines unused to combat tried to put it into effect—was to surround the VC. One company of the 3/3d Marines was to move from Chu Lai to set up blocking positions along the Tra Bong River, about two miles north of Van Tuong, while the rest of the battalion landed by sea farther south, opposite the hamlet of An Cuong (1), to prevent escape in that direction. The whole of the 2/4th Marines would then land by helicopter on three landing zones (LZs) roughly a mile inland, before advancing (with the sea-landed force) to the northeast, clearing Van Tuong, and trapping the VC with their backs to the sea.

At first, all went well. Blocking positions on the Tra Bong River were

In early August, 1965, a conference in Honolulu confirmed that U.S. forces in Vietnam should be increased to 125,000 men and that a new offensive strategy should be adopted to counter VC guerrilla activity.

For the U.S. Marines, who had arrived in Vietnam only five months before, this new aggressive stance took the form of Operation Starlite, the first major encounter in the war between U.S. troops and the Communists.

On August 15, information from a VC defector confirmed the presence of 1,500 troops of the 1st VC Regiment at a base at Van Tuong, 12 miles south of the U.S. coastal enclave of Chu Lai. The operation, in simple terms, was to destroy the VC before they could attack Chu Lai.

Starlite began promisingly on August 18, 1965, a hot sunny day, with the Marines coming ashore and clearing the hamlet of An Cuong (1). At the same time, helicopters dropped off Marines at LZs inland.

To the west of An Cuong (1), however, in an area of woods and paddy fields, Company H, 2/4th Marines, landing at LZ Blue, came under intense VC fire from Hill 43 (1).

By 1130, the men of Company H had broken out and were advancing northeast when they again came under automatic-weapon and mortar fire, which effectively pinned them down (2) in paddy fields.

The battle developed further as a U.S. supply column of LVTs and flame-thrower tanks, sent out to aid Company H, got lost between An Thoi (2) and Nam Yen (3). The column (3) was then ambushed by VC positioned around An Cuong (2) (4), which had been set on fire by grenade and mortar fire.

In response to frantic radio appeals from the beleaguered supply column, Major Andrew G. Comer at the Command Post (6) rapidly assembled a relief force made up of a flame-thrower tank, an M-48 tank, three Ontos, and LVTs. However, before it had progressed very far, this unit was also ambushed—on Hill 30 (5), to the north of An Cuong (2).

The M-48 was hit as it crested the small hill, causing the other vehicles to bunch together and the infantry to dismount under fire: the Marines suffered casualties within minutes.

The Marines held on until nightfall when the VC, subdued by a U.S. naval bombardment, broke off the fight. Next day, the sweep to the sea continued: it was to take another five days, in energy-sapping heat, and at a cost of 45 Marine lives, before the operation officially ended.

The VC had fought stubbornly, inflicting substantial casualties on the Americans. Until U.S. units later gained skill through combat experience, the VC—as Operation Starlite showed—had the ability to trade punches before melting away, ready to fight another day.

Operation Starlite

SOUTH CHINA SEA

Phuoc Thuan Peninsula

Tra Bong River

Nho Na Bay

Van Tuong (1)

LZ Red

An Thoi (2)   Hill 30

LZ White   An Cuong (2)   Command Post

Nam Yen (3)   An Cuong (1)

LZ Blue

N

Hill 43

0   1mile
0   1km

45

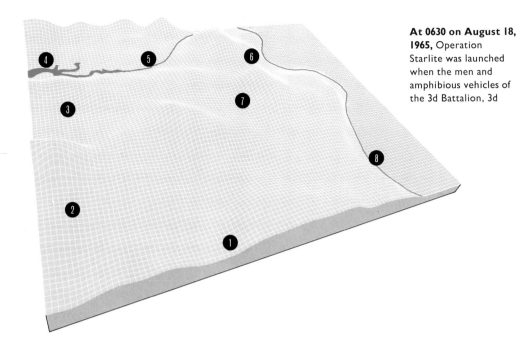

At 0630 on August 18, 1965, Operation Starlite was launched when the men and amphibious vehicles of the 3d Battalion, 3d Marines, landed on Green Beach (**8**), at the southern end of Phuoc Thuan Peninsula (**6**).

Joining the 3/3d Marines in the planned sweep up toward the village of Van Tuong (1) (**7**), was the 2d Battalion, 4th Marines. At 0645, Companies G and E were helilifted into LZs Red (**3**) and White (**2**), respectively, and Company H was dropped into LZ Blue north of Hill 43 (**1**).

Meanwhile, Company M, 3/3d Marines, having moved south from Chu Lai the previous day, maintained their blocking position (**5**) on the Tra Bong River (**4**).

As the action developed on the morning of the 18th, Company G (**2**) moved out northeastward and joined up with Company M (**1**) without incident. From LZ White, Company E (**3**) overcame VC opposition to the east and northeast before continuing its advance. Over by the coast, Company K (**12**), 3/3d Marines, advanced northward and, with the support of Company L (**13**), 3/3d Marines, they attacked and overwhelmed VC entrenched on high ground.

At LZ Blue, Company H (**4**) was fiercely engaged on Hill 43 (**5**) by the VC 60th Battalion, who were eventually subdued with the help of air support and tanks. Later, Company H came under fire to the east of Nam Yen (3) (**6**) and, by 1400, was bogged down and ready to retreat to LZ Blue.

From Green Beach (**11**), Company I (**10**), 3/3d Marines, advanced to An Cuong (2) (**8**), cleared it, and was then ordered north to join Company K. Meanwhile, an LVT resupply column, sent to the aid of Company I, got lost and was ambushed (**7**) to the west of An Cuong (2) (**8**). A rescue force made up of an M-48 tank, a flame-tank, an Ontos column, and some LVTs was dispatched, but it, too, was ambushed on Hill 30 (**9**).

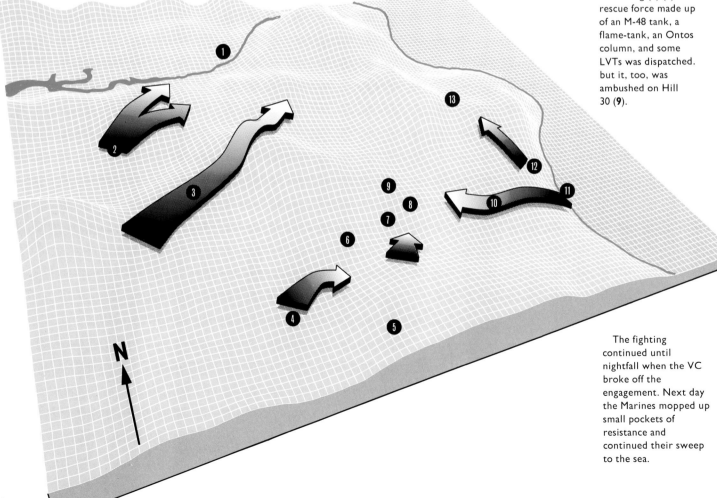

N

The fighting continued until nightfall when the VC broke off the engagement. Next day the Marines mopped up small pockets of resistance and continued their sweep to the sea.

LVTPs: transport and assault vehicles

In 1965, the U.S. Marine Corps was still using the LVTP (Landing Vehicle Tracked, Personnel) Model 5 for its amphibious assaults. Developed in 1951 to update the tracked landing vehicles ("Amtracs") used so successfully in the Pacific "island-hopping" campaign of 1943–45, the LVTP5 could carry 34 Marines or up to 12,000 pounds of cargo from transport ships offshore to the assault beach, with the advantage of being able to continue onto land without unloading. In Vietnam, the LVTP5 —and its successor the LVTP7—were also used as armored personnel carriers.

LVTP5

Carrying capacity	34 Marines or 12,000 lb of cargo afloat; 8,000 lb on land
Powerplant	One Continental LV-1790-1 V12 gas engine
Range	233 miles on land
Speed	30mph on land; 12mph on water
Armament	Single 7.62mm machine gun, mounted in a turret on the forward part of the troop/cargo compartment

THE WAR YEARS

March 8, 1965	U.S. Marines go ashore at Da Nang: the first Marine combat ground troops to be deployed to Vietnam.
April 1, 1965	General Westmoreland persuades President Johnson to increase U.S. force levels in Vietnam to 33,000 men.
April 22	First clash between U.S. Marine ground troops and VC guerrillas, at Binh Thai.
April 24	Johnson officially designates Vietnam a "combat zone" for U.S. forces.
May 7, 1965	3,500 men of the 173d Airborne Brigade arrive in Bien Hoa.
June 10/13, 1965	Battle between Army Special Forces, U.S. sailors, native mercenaries and VC at Dong Xoai; U.S. airpower crucial.
June 18	Air Marshal Nguyen Cao Ky appointed premier of South Vietnam.
July 1, 1965	U.S. Marines land at Qui Nhon in Binh Dinh province.
July 12	U.S. Marine Lieutenant Frank S. Reasoner killed in action; later awarded the first Medal of Honor of the Vietnam War.
July 28	Johnson promises to increase U.S. force levels in Vietnam to 125,000 men (confirmed at Honolulu, early August).

established late on August 17, and, at 0630 on the 18th, after air and artillery strikes, the Marines came ashore, clearing An Cuong (1) and moving inland. As they did, the helicopter landings took place. In the north, at LZ Red, no enemy opposition was encountered and the Marines quickly linked up with the company on the Tra Bong River. Farther south at LZ White, a brief firefight developed but, by midmorning, the VC had been pushed to the northeast according to plan. Only on LZ Blue, west of An Cuong (1), was heavy fighting experienced. It was here, in an area of paddy fields, hedgerows, and hamlets, that the real battle developed. It was a confused affair.

Company H, 2/4th Marines, commanded by First Lieutenant Homer K. Jenkins, landed at LZ Blue at 0730, coming under intense fire from Hill 43 to their south and the hamlet of Nam Yen (3) to the north. Airstrikes enabled Jenkins's men to take the hill, but confused reports about supporting attacks from the sea-based companies to the east, which had encountered trouble in An Cuong (2), led him to believe that Nam Yen (3) had been cleared. At 1130 he advanced northeast, away from the LZ, only to come under heavy automatic-weapon and mortar fire. He quickly set up a defensive position in paddies close to Nam Yen (3); his men were effectively pinned down until 1630, when they pulled back to the relative safety of LZ Blue.

Jenkins should have been reinforced from the beachhead to the east, but this proved impossible, chiefly because of a breakdown of battlefield control. At noon a supply column of five LVTs and three flame-thrower tanks had managed to get lost in a maze of trails between Nam Yen and the neighboring hamlet of An Thoi (2). Ambushed as they crawled between paddies and thick hedges, they screamed for help over the radio. In response, Major Andrew G. Comer, 3/3d's executive officer, hastily assembled a relief column made up of an M-48 tank, a flame tank, three Ontos antitank vehicles, and some LVTs. As they pushed forward over Hill 30, just to the north of An Cuong(2), they too were attacked. The column bunched up and, within minutes, casualties were suffered with at least 5 Marines dead and 17 wounded.

There were now three separate engagements taking place in an area little more than two-thirds of a mile square. A U.S. naval bombardment relieved the pressure, and a reserve company was helicoptered in from the fleet offshore; but as night fell on August 18, Starlite still hung in the balance. It was only when the VC, unnerved by U.S. naval firepower, made the mistake of withdrawing that the Marines could gain the upper hand.

The operation was to continue for five more days, with Marines advancing through Van Tuong in brain-boiling heat. They claimed victory—counting 614 VC bodies and suffering 45 dead in exchange—but in reality a pattern that was soon to become familiar had been established: regardless of U.S. firepower and tactical skill, the VC had the ability to melt away, avoiding annihilation.

Premier Ky of South Vietnam watches villagers digging a defensive trench.

THE IA DRANG CAMPAIGN

October 26–November 27, 1965

B Y THE TIME OF OPERATION Starlite, the Marines were not the only American ground combat troops in Vietnam. U.S. Army Special Forces, the Green Berets, had been fighting their own unconventional operations since 1957, and advisers had been attached to the ARVN for even longer. But in the aftermath of the Marine commitment to Da Nang, President Johnson had authorized the deployment of entire army formations.

On April 14, 1965, the 173d Airborne Brigade—the army's rapid response force for the western Pacific—was ordered to move to Vietnam, and, three months later, they were joined by the 1st Brigade, 101st Airborne Division. The latter was initially slated to relieve the 173d, but ended up fighting alongside it. The steady escalation of U.S. force levels had begun.

Both formations found the transition to war frustrating, acting as heliborne infantry in a country-wide "firefighting" role. For much of the time, the troopers were involved in repetitive, tiring, and mundane "walks in the sun," chiefly in War Zone D north of Saigon and around Pleiku in the Central Highlands. The VC were initially reluctant to engage U.S. troops.

One of the reasons for Communist caution lay in the enhanced mobility displayed by the Americans. Helicopters had been used before in Vietnam, as both Ap Bac and Starlite showed, but both airborne brigades were now using them on a much more regular basis, lifting troops over difficult terrain to landing zones (LZs) in the enemy rear. It was an idea that had been explored as early as 1962, when Secretary of Defense Robert McNamara had set up the U.S. Army Tactical Mobility Requirement Board under the leadership of Lieutenant General Hamilton Howze.

By 1965, "airmobility" had been taken much further than that displayed by the 101st and 173d, who used helicopters only for movement: the newly activated 1st Cavalry Division (Airmobile) used

"We are in heavy contact. These guys are good!"

CAPTAIN ROBERT H. EDWARDS, LZ X-RAY, NOVEMBER 14, 1965

them for all aspects of battle—reconnaissance, air attack, transport, and logistic support—to produce a self-contained and potentially devastating force.

On July 28, 1965, President Johnson announced the commitment of the 1st Cavalry to Vietnam. The division had formally come into existence only a month before, absorbing personnel from the experimental 11th Air Assault Division (Test) and reassigned units from the 2d Infantry Division (now given cavalry designations), but the commanding officer, Major General Harry W. O. Kinnard, was eager for action. More than 400 helicopters—OH-13 Sioux for reconnaissance, UH-1 Hueys for assault and infantry lift, CH-47 Chinooks and CH-54 Flying Cranes for heavy lift—were loaded on transports; these, together with 16,000 personnel and 1,600 vehicles, were shipped across the Pacific, approaching Vietnam in early September.

General Westmoreland's first reaction was to split the division, sending each of its three brigades to a different part of the country; but Kinnard was adamant: the whole point of airmobility, he argued, was to keep the closely integrated force together to maximize its impact.

Kinnard's view prevailed, and he was ordered to deploy his division to An Khe, 35 miles inland from Qui Nhon in the central provinces. An immense heliport (soon to be dubbed "the Golf Course") was constructed, and the 101st Airborne was drafted in to clear Route 19. On September 14, the first Regular Army helicopters flew in to An Khe.

The central provinces were not chosen at random, for, by the summer of 1965, it was becoming apparent that the area was under attack, not just from the VC but also, more significantly, it was believed, from elements of the North Vietnamese Army. Infiltration of NVA regulars down the Ho Chi Minh Trail in Laos and Cambodia had been recognized for some time, but intelligence sources were now painting a much more menacing picture. They were not mistaken: a special Field

48

An engineer of the 1st Cavalry comes under fire near Chu Pong Mountain by the Ia Drang Valley. On November 14, 1965, the entire 1st Battalion, 7th Cavalry, was helilifted into this area at LZ X-Ray and immediately ran into two NVA regiments.

Men of the 1st Air Cavalry Division (Airmobile) unload their Huey in the Chu Pong Mountain area during the campaign.

Shoulder sleeve insignia of the 1st Cavalry Division (Airmobile). This unit's hard fighting in the Ia Drang Campaign won a Presidential Unit Citation.

The origins of airmobility

The U.S. Army used helicopters for medical evacuation and light transportation duties as early as the Korean War (1950–53). Indeed, while that war was still going on, in August, 1952, a decision was taken to create 12 helicopter battalions which would be used for ferrying infantry units into combat over difficult terrain. But technology lagged behind: it was not until the development of the gas turbine engine in the mid-1950s that helicopters could be given the power to lift heavy loads. The Army was slow to capitalize on this potential, even though a few officers were already discussing the possibility of self-contained heliborne units.

In January, 1960, recognizing the need for rationalization, the Chief of Staff set up the Army Aircraft Requirements Review Board under Lieutenant General Gordon B. Rogers. This Board made a number of recommendations regarding the design and procurement of helicopters, but said little about how they could be used beyond observation and transportation. It was not until April, 1962, that a wider perspective emerged. Secretary of Defense Robert

McNamara, exasperated by the Army's apparent inability to think beyond such unimaginative possibilities, set up the Army Tactical Mobility Requirements Board under Lieutenant General Hamilton Howze (ABOVE LEFT). The concept of airmobility, with its emphasis on the full range of military capability within one heliborne formation, came out of the Howze Board. It led to the creation of the 11th Air Assault Division (Test) under Brigadier General Harry W.O. Kinnard (ABOVE RIGHT): the formation that would enter Vietnam in 1965 as the 1st Cavalry Division (Airmobile).

By 1100 on November 14, 1965, the first elements of the 1st Battalion, 7th Cavalry, had been helicoptered from their base at Plei Me to Landing Zone X-Ray (**7**) just east of Chu Pong Mountain (**4**). A major U.S. search and destroy operation in the valley of the Ia Drang (**1**) had begun.

Shortly after setting down, Company B (**6**) moved off to the west and north toward a spur of the massif. Waiting for them in positions on the mountain and in the valley were elements of the NVA 66th and 33d Regiments (**2** and **3**), diverted from an intended attack on Plei Me. Company B was soon pinned down by fierce enemy fire; so, too, was Company A (**5**), which had been dispatched to provide support for Company B on its left flank.

As the battle developed, Company C (**8**), providing security for the LZ, probed to the east and was charged, unsuccessfully, by two NVA companies (**9**). With Company D reinforcing Company C around the LZ's south and southwest perimeter, the cavalrymen held on until 1800, when Company B, 2d Battalion, 7th Cavalry, was helilifted in to bolster the defenses.

Next day, November 15, the NVA mounted spirited attacks against X-Ray, but with artillery and helicopter gunship support, the Americans repelled their attackers. By the time the 2d Battalion, 5th Cavalry (**10**), arrived overland at about 1300, the threat had subsided. The NVA had melted away.

N

50

Force under NVA Brigadier General Chu Huy Man was preparing to seize Kontum and Pleiku provinces, before thrusting toward the coast and splitting South Vietnam in two.

For this to succeed, the NVA had to destroy other, more westerly, Special Forces camps at Plei Me and Duc Co, opening up the main routes to Pleiku City. In late July, 1965, the NVA 32d Regiment began the campaign by surrounding Duc Co, threatening to overwhelm its defenders, who were a mixture of South Vietnamese Special Forces and Montagnard and Nuong tribesmen, all under U.S. Special Forces control. An ARVN mechanized column was committed to relieve the base, but was caught in an ambush four miles east of Duc Co. The NVA, under heavy U.S. air attacks, eventually withdrew, having inflicted significant casualties.

The NVA 32d Regiment was joined by the 33d in early September, linking up with the local VC main-force battalion to establish a base on the eastern slopes of Chu Pong Mountain. This was a 174-square-mile massif that straddled the border south of the Ia (River) Drang; it rose more than 500 meters above the floor of a rolling plateau of jungle that stretched the 37 miles to Pleiku City. Unknown to the Americans, General Man was about to receive a third regiment—the 66th—that would increase his command to the equivalent of a division (nine infantry battalions, each of 550 men, backed by artillery and support units). It was the first time the NVA had operated in the South at a multi-regimental level.

Camp Plei Me was attacked early on October 20, and the ARVN responded predictably: as the defenders of the base fought for survival, a mechanized column was prepared in Pleiku City. But local ARVN commanders, scared of committing their troops, stalled. It was not until Westmoreland agreed to send the 1st

1st Cavalry Division troopers are pinned down by enemy fire as they fight to establish an LZ in the Ia Drang valley in November, 1966. By their action, the Cavalry were able to preempt a major NVA attack in the Central Highlands.

Brigade, 1st Cavalry, to Pleiku to guard against possible envelopment that the relief column set out, on October 22.

As the column approached Plei Me, however, it was ambushed and, despite heavy U.S. air support, the commander insisted on caution. Only when Kinnard, in an early display of airmobility, helicoptered artillery forward to LZs close to the ambush point did the column begin to move. Plei Me was finally relieved late on October 25, having survived only through the courage and fighting skill of its Green Beret garrison.

Westmoreland was impressed by the rapid response of 1st Cavalry, and on October 26 he agreed to "give Kinnard his head," changing the role of the division from one of reaction/reinforcement to unlimited offense within a particular area of Vietnam. Kinnard was given responsibility for most of Pleiku, Kontum, and Binh Dinh provinces in II Corps Tactical Zone and was ordered to seek out, fix, and destroy any enemy forces in the region. He gave the task to his 1st Brigade, which immediately began widespread aerial searches, hoping to find the

By the summer of 1965, U.S. intelligence was aware that a combined force of NVA regulars and local VC was threatening Special Forces camps at Plei Me and Duc Co in the central provinces. NVA Brigadier General Chu Huy Man's apparent plan was to drive east across the country to the sea, cutting South Vietnam in half.

Countering this threat were units of the 1st Cavalry Division (Airmobile) under Major General Harry W. O. Kinnard, stationed at An Khe. The 1st Air Cavalry were soon in action, helping to relieve the besieged Special Forces camp at Plei Me in late October, 1965. This success led to their being sent on the offensive in an area near the Chu Pong massif and Ia Drang valley, where there were signs of a major Communist base.

52

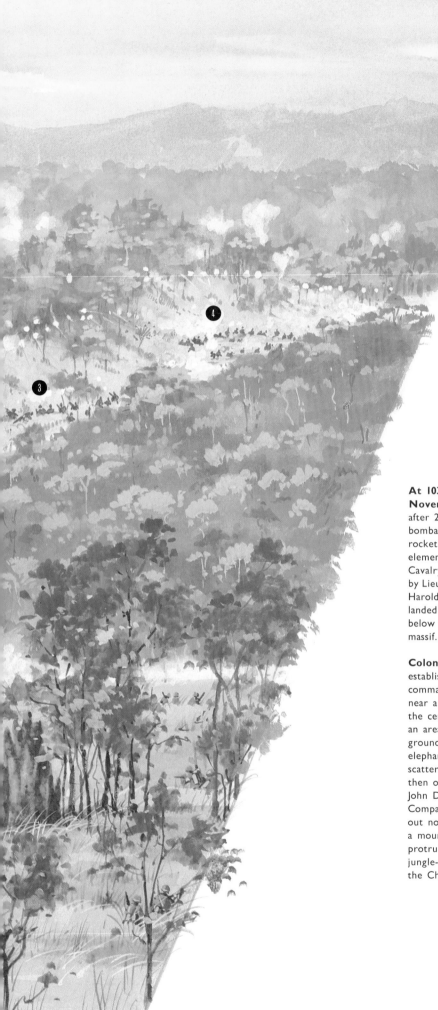

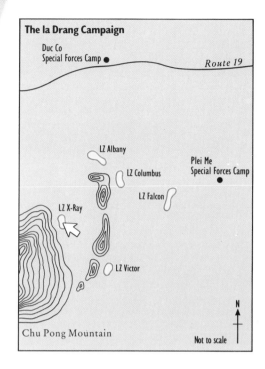

The Ia Drang Campaign

Duc Co
Special Forces Camp ●

Route 19

LZ Albany

LZ Columbus

Plei Me
Special Forces Camp ●

LZ Falcon

LZ X-Ray

LZ Victor

Chu Pong Mountain

N

Not to scale

At 1037 on November 14, 1965, after 20 minutes of bombardment and rocket fire, the first elements of the 1/7th Cavalry, commanded by Lieutenant Colonel Harold G. Moore, landed at LZ X-Ray below the Chu Pong massif.

Colonel Moore established his command post (**5**) near a large anthill in the center of the LZ, an area of level ground covered with elephant grass and scattered trees. Moore then ordered Captain John D. Herren's Company B to strike out northwest toward a mountain spur protruding from the jungle-covered wall of the Chu Pong (**1**).

As another wave of Huey helicopters (**6**) came in to land at 1245, Herren's 1st Platoon (**3**) ran into enemy fire. On its right flank, 2d Platoon (**4**) also came under fire and was then rapidly surrounded. Captain Herren responded by moving 3d Platoon (**2**) to cover the left flank of 1st Platoon, but it too was soon to become mired in the firefight.

Meanwhile, back at the command post, Colonel Moore called up artillery and air support which eventually succeeded in subduing the enemy fire. This allowed the rest of the 1/7th Cavalry to be lifted in to LZ X-Ray at 1500 hours. As a result, Moore was able to set about reorganizing his defenses.

On the night of the 14th, 2d Platoon, reduced to seven unwounded men, was left to fend for itself as Communist forces tried to overrun the LZ. But by 0900 on the 15th, reinforcements were lifted in to X-Ray and, with 2/5th Cavalry approaching overland, the NVA began to break off the fight.

It was not until 1030 on November 16, however, after another night of fighting, that Moore was finally relieved. The battalion had sustained 79 killed and 121 wounded against an enemy body count of 634.

Creating LZs and FSBs

For airmobility to be effective, helicopters had to be able to land inside enemy-held territory to bring in the men, weapons, and supplies needed for offensive operations. Natural landing zones (LZs), such as jungle clearings, were likely to be defended, so quite often they had to be created.

Once a location had been chosen, pathfinders and combat engineers would descend through the jungle canopy by rope rappel or on special "Jacob's Ladders" from hovering helicopters, while other aircraft "prepped" the area to disrupt any enemy response. On the ground, the advance engineers would begin to clear the undergrowth and trees with chain saws, axes, and explosives, creating as quickly as possible an area into which the helicopters could descend to disgorge assault platoons. In some cases, a rough, defensive perimeter would be set up by reconnaissance troops. The LZ was then ready for actual landings.

The same techniques would often be employed to create a Fire Support Base (FSB), usually located on a hilltop so that emplaced artillery could provide support to infantry on patrol in the surrounding countryside. As such bases needed to be fairly substantial, the initial clearance might be done by dropping special "Daisy Cutter" bombs, primed to explode just above ground level to topple trees. A stake would then be positioned at the center of the site and a 131-foot rope attached to mark out the main bunker line—the bunkers being 15 feet apart.

A similar rope, 246 feet long, marked the outer perimeter. Bulldozers would be brought in by helicopter to dig command bunkers and artillery pits, followed by a battery of 105mm medium howitzers. Dug in and protected by barbed wire, mines, air support, and infantry, the FSB would be ready for action.

U.S. Army UH-1 helicopters (RIGHT) fall into a tight landing formation at an LZ near Phuoc Vinh, some 40 miles north of Saigon.

On a hilltop base (BELOW) men of the 1st Cavalry Division wait to hook a 155mm howitzer to the hoist of a CH-54 Tarhe Flying Crane.

troops responsible for the Plei Me attack. The 1st Brigade was spearheaded by the 1st Squadron, 9th Cavalry, whose task it was to fly light scout helicopters at treetop height, calling in "aero-rifle platoons" in UH-1s whenever contact was made. The brigade's main body was made up of three heliborne infantry battalions as well as artillery and aerial-rocket fire support, the latter delivered by specially adapted UH-1 "gunships."

Unaware that the Plei Me attack and ambush had been carried out by NVA regulars, the Cavalry concentrated on areas to the north and east of the camp, hoping to spot VC guerrillas returning to their home villages. Little was found, chiefly because General Man had ordered the 32d and 33d Regiments back to the Chu Pong base in the west, where they would link up with the 66th Regiment before renewing their attack on Plei Me.

It was not until 0720 hours on November 1 that contact was made, when 9th Cavalry helicopters, ranging far and wide, spotted movement about seven miles west of Plei Me. Aero-rifle support was called up and, at 0808 hours, a group attack was made on what turned out to be an NVA field hospital. In less than 30 minutes, 15 NVA had been killed and 43 captured, along with a mound of documents and medical equipment. Isolated

firefights continued throughout the day, at the end of which Kinnard could claim a "body count" of 99 NVA for 11 of his own men killed. Airmobility was beginning to bite.

It soon became obvious from the captured documents that the Cavalry were looking in the wrong place for the wrong enemy. On November 2, Kinnard shifted his search pattern to the west, where 9th Cavalry scouts had already reported jungle trails between the Chu Pong and the Ia Drang. They started sweeping the area on November 3, setting up a temporary LZ south of the river from which infantry patrols could be mounted. Late on the same day, one of these patrols ambushed elements of the NVA 66th Regiment and then helped to defend the LZ against attacks that cost the Communists a further 72 confirmed dead.

Kinnard now suspected that the Chu Pong area was a major NVA base. On November 9, he relieved the 1st Brigade of his division with the 3d ("Garry Owen") Brigade, commanded by Colonel Thomas W. Brown, and ordered it to prepare for an assault into the Communist-held area. An entire battalion of heliborne troops—the 1/7th Cavalry—was to be lifted on November 14 onto an LZ at the foot of the Chu Pong and then patrol out, searching for contacts.

Bell AH-1G Huey Cobra (Gunship)

Max speed	219mph	Max weight	9,500lb	Range	357 miles
Armament	One 7.62mm minigun, one 40mm grenade launcher or 20mm or 30mm cannon, plus stub-wing pylons for 76 2.75in rockets or minigun pods or 20mm guns.				

Hughes OH-6A Cayuse Loach (Light observation)

Max speed	150mph	Max weight	2,700lb	Range	380 miles
Armament	One 7.62mm minigun, mounted on the left side; one 40mm grenade launcher (optional).				

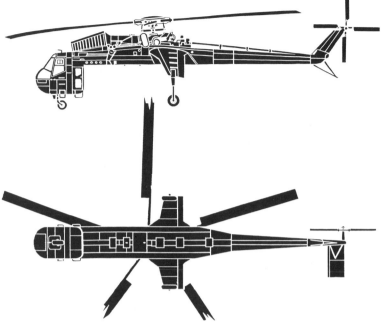

Sikorsky CH-54A Tarhe Flying Crane (Heavy lift)

Max speed	126mph	Max weight	42,000lb	Range	230 miles
Armament	None carried. Could lift up to 20,000lb of cargo externally, including bridge sections and bunker units.				

The 1/7th was commanded by Lieutenant Colonel Harold G. Moore and, at first light on the 14th, he led an air reconnaissance of the eastern edge of the Chu Pong (the western side was in Cambodia and therefore "off-limits"), looking for likely LZs. He chose a clearing on the edge of the massif, later designated LZ X-Ray. After a 20-minute artillery bombardment, followed by rocket fire from support helicopters, the battalion would be trans-ported in a series of lifts to the LZ, spearheaded by Captain John D. Herren's Company B. Once landed, they would secure the LZ and, as soon as Company A arrived, patrols would be sent out, initially to the north and northeast, where a mountain spur jutted out from the Chu Pong. Companies C and D, brought in by subsequent airlifts, would defend the LZ perimeter and move west toward the mountain itself.

Artillery fire crashed down on X-Ray at 1017 hours and, 20 minutes later, 16 lift helicopters came in at treetop height. They landed amid shattered tree stumps and waist-high grass on an LZ dominated by the immense wall of green of the Chu Pong: one sergeant looked up at the mountain and was heard to mutter in a Georgia drawl: "My Gawd, that son of a bitch is big." Moore set up his command post around a large anthill in a clump of

The role of the helicopter

The helicopter is widely associated with the war in Vietnam. Although not all U.S. units were heliborne, it was a rare operation that did not involve helicopters in some guise—carrying troops over difficult terrain in or out of the combat zone, providing gunship support, observing the enemy, evacuating the wounded, or transporting supplies. Because of this wide range of tasks, different helicopter designs had to be introduced, from the wasplike light observation machines to huge "flying cranes" capable of lifting artillery pieces or even armored cars. The result was an impressive degree of mobility—essential if an elusive enemy was ever to be brought to battle.

(Note: all figures for range and weight were modified by Vietnam's tropical atmosphere.)

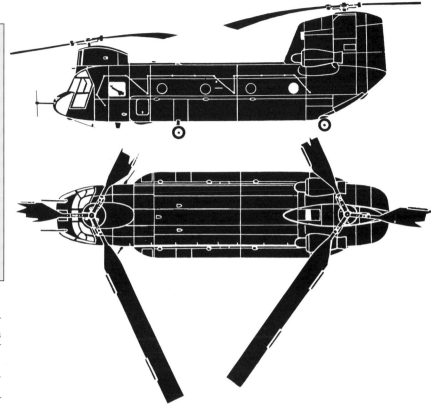

Boeing-Vertol CH-47A Chinook (Medium transport)

Max speed	189mph	Max weight	33,000lb	Range	115 miles
Armament	Two 40mm grenade launchers; 2.75in rockets; two 20mm cannon; five 0.50in machine guns (all fitted locally in Vietnam). Could carry up to a platoon of troops (about 20 to 25 men).				

Bell UH-ID Iroquois Huey (Troop carrier and close support)

Max speed	127mph
Max weight	9,500lb
Range	248 miles

Armament
Four 7.62mm machine guns (two fixed, forward firing; two on pintles in the doorways); 38 2.75in rockets. Could carry a light squad of infantry (6 to 8 men).

Medevac: rescuing the wounded

Between April, 1962, when the first five medical evacuation UH-1As of the 57th Medical Detachment (Helicopter Ambulance) arrived in Vietnam, and the end of American involvement in 1973, about a half-million Allied wounded were lifted from the combat zone to an appropriate medical facility. The work was extremely dangerous: hundreds of aviators were killed and wounded in what were known as "Dust-Off" missions—in the one shown (BELOW), a wounded Marine is lifted into a medevac Huey south of Da Nang. But the certain knowledge that a medevac chopper would appear if it was humanly possible acted as a valuable morale-booster to the troops on the ground. On average, a wounded man would be in surgery less than 100 minutes after being hit: the fact that the vast majority of the wounded who arrived at a hospital survived speaks volumes for the bravery and skill of the medevac crews.

trees near the center of the LZ and ordered Herren to start patrolling. Within minutes, his 1st Platoon had captured an NVA deserter, who willingly confirmed that the area was a major Communist base. As elements of Company A came in by the second lift, Moore directed Herren to probe toward the mountain spur in the north.

Company B went forward in textbook fashion, with 1st Platoon on the left, 2d Platoon on the right, and 3d Platoon trailing in reserve. At 1245 hours, 1st Platoon encountered an enemy force and, as a firefight developed, called for aid. Herren ordered the 2d Platoon, 27 men

U.S. Special Forces and the CIDGs

The American Special Forces, known as the Green Berets, played a unique and valuable part in the Vietnam War. Committed throughout South Vietnam in 1962 after six years of advisory involvement, their primary role was one of countering VC subversion and movement using ethnic minorities such as the Montagnards. The Montagnards' homeland in the Central Highlands straddled the border with Cambodia and Laos. Beginning in the village of Buon Enao, northeast of Ban Me Thuot, Special Forces volunteers offered a mixture of military protection together with civic action ("hearts and minds") in a determined attempt to persuade the tribes to oppose Communist activity.

The experiment worked well, and the Montagnards, now given advantages they felt were worth defending, willingly formed a local militia, under U.S. or ARVN Special Forces command. This initiative, known officially as the Civilian Irregular Defense Group (CIDG) program, was gradually extended to other areas and different ethnic minorities all along the borders of South Vietnam. From late 1964, the CIDGs came under MACV control through the 5th Special Forces Group (Airborne), consolidated at Nha Trang.

But the CIDGs were more than just a village guard unit. Exploiting the Montagnards' local knowledge of jungle survival and local population support, Special Forces teams transformed them into counterguerrilla groups, establishing camps in border areas or astride infiltration routes to monitor or even stop Communist move-

ment. At the same time, long range patrols operated deep inside enemy territory, gathering intelligence or, as mobile strike ("Mike") forces, attacking NVA/VC bases. As long as the U.S. Special Forces were in

command the advantages were high, but when they withdrew in early 1971, leaving the CIDGs to South Vietnamese who distrusted ethnic minorities, the program quickly collapsed.

A U.S. Special Forces team poses for the camera at a camp in IICTZ in 1968.

A Green Beret patrol crosses a bridge near Dak To in the Central Highlands.

strong, to move across to make contact. As they did so, they bumped into a squad of NVA and started to pursue them, only to come under a hail of fire from their right flank. In seconds, the platoon was surrounded. Herren responded by ordering his 3d Platoon forward, but it soon became obvious that he was up against a large, well-disciplined enemy force.

Moore, monitoring these developments, called in airstrikes and artillery strikes before sending the newly arrived Company A to reinforce Herren. As Company A's lead platoon advanced across a dry creek bed to make contact, it, too, came under heavy fire and, as NVA mortar rounds began to hit the LZ, Moore had to suspend helicopter operations. By 1445 hours, with fewer than three companies on the ground, he was in a perilous situation. In response, Colonel Brown assigned a company of 2/7th Cavalry to fly in from An Khe as soon as possible; he then ordered 2/5th Cavalry to move to LZ Victor, five miles to the southeast of X-Ray, and to prepare to reinforce overland.

Fortunately for the Americans, enemy fire slackened under the weight of air and artillery attack, enabling the rest of 1/7th to be lifted into X-Ray at 1500 hours. This allowed Moore to reorganize his defense, leaving Companies C and D to hold the LZ while A and the remains of B regrouped for another attack to relieve the surrounded platoon. Behind a storm of artillery and rocket fire, the attack began at 1620, only to be halted after an advance of less than 150 yards. Moore had no choice but to pull his men back, leaving the trapped platoon, commanded by Sergeant Clyde E. Savage, to survive as best it could. By 1900, Company B, 2/7th, had arrived, and Moore had set up a rudimentary perimeter.

The NVA spent the night trying to wipe out Savage's platoon—in the event, three separate attacks were held off—and to move forces around to encircle the LZ. Just after dawn on November 15, they struck from the south, inflicting heavy casualties on Company C, 1/7th, before repeating the process to the east against Company D. Fire swept the LZ, and it was not until 0900 hours that more reinforcements could be helicoptered in. By then, the 2/5th Cavalry were approaching from LZ Victor and the NVA began to melt away.

Moore ordered all his companies to push out from the perimeter, searching for American wounded and NVA stragglers. The latter were still capable of causing casualties—during a second

night of battle, they tried to mount harassing attacks—but with Savage's platoon finally relieved and more reinforcements flying in, the crisis had passed. At 1030 on November 16, Moore's battalion was relieved. By then, the Cavalry had lost 79 killed and 121 wounded; the confirmed number of enemy dead was 634, but the figure may have been over 1,000.

But the Ia Drang Campaign was not yet over. On November 17, LZ X-Ray was abandoned (preparatory to B-52 bombing strikes on the Chu Pong), and the units that had replaced Moore's battalion—2/5th and 2/7th Cavalry—were ordered to pull back to LZs Columbus and Albany to the east. The move to Columbus went without a hitch, but as 2/7th approached the clearing known as Albany, they triggered an NVA attack that caught them squarely on the flank. Company C bore the brunt, losing 41 men killed; the fighting went on through the afternoon and evening. Reinforcements were rushed in from Columbus and An Khe, but the final NVA body count of 403 was overshadowed by an American loss of 151 killed and 121 wounded.

Despite this tragedy there could be no doubt that the 1st Cavalry had fought well in the Ia Drang. Sweeps continued until November 27, when the operation was officially called off: in 33 days, Kinnard's men, in a stunning display of airmobility, had blunted a major NVA attack in the Central Highlands, killing a confirmed 1,519 NVA, wounding an estimated 1,178, and capturing 157. It had cost the 1st Air Cavalry Division 304 dead and 524 wounded, but the NVA had, for the time being, been forced back over the border into Cambodia.

THE WAR YEARS

July 29, 1965	1st Brigade, 101st Airborne Division (Separate) arrives at Cam Ranh.
Sept. 14, 1965	1st Cavalry Division (Airmobile) arrives at An Khe.
Oct. 15, 1965	At a protest rally in the U.S., David Millar becomes the first man to burn his draft card. He is arrested.
Oct. 15/16	Relatively minor antiwar protests held in over 40 U.S. cities and various western European capitals.
Oct. 20	NVA attack on Plei Me Special Forces camp, Central Highlands.
Nov. 14, 1965	1/7th Cavalry assault LZ X-Ray, Ia Drang valley.
Nov. 27	Pentagon calls for a troop buildup in Vietnam in 1966 to nearly 400,000 men.
Dec. 25, 1965	President Johnson suspends Rolling Thunder air attacks on the North to induce negotiations. Bombing resumes January 31, 1966.
Jan. 19, 1966	President Johnson asks Congress for an additional $12.8 billion for the war in Vietnam.
Jan. 24	Operation Masher/White Wing begins in IICTZ (ends March 6).
Feb 6/8, 1966	Honolulu Conference: President Johnson reaffirms U.S. support to South Vietnam.

The 1st Brigade, 101st Airborne Division (Separate), arrived in Vietnam on July 29, 1965, and was immediately deployed in IICTZ. In early 1966, the brigade was involved in clearing Phu Yen province and, in the summer, saw action near Kontum.

LONG TAN

August 18, 1966

ON APRIL 23, 1964, PRESIDENT Johnson called for "more flags" to be represented in South Vietnam, hoping that America's allies would rally round to aid "a beleaguered friend." The response was by no means universal. Great Britain, for example, refused to send military forces, chiefly because of a crisis in Borneo; but, by the end of the year, the Philippines, the Republic of (South) Korea, Thailand, Australia, and New Zealand had all indicated a willingness to contribute some form of military aid. It enabled Johnson to portray the developing war as an international, rather than purely an American, problem.

In the event, the size and nature of allied aid varied considerably. The Republic of Korea, for instance, deployed two infantry divisions and a Marine brigade (about 48,000 men), while the Philippines preferred to concentrate on "civic action," sending only 2,000 personnel to help rural development and pacification. Between these two extremes were the Australians (with New Zealand backing), deploying about 7,000 combat troops, chiefly to the province of Phuoc Tuy, southeast of Saigon. They were to fight with an effectiveness, relative to their strength, that was virtually unrivalled in Vietnam.

Australian involvement actually predated Johnson's "more flags" appeal; 20 months earlier, in August, 1962, an Australian Army Training Team Vietnam (AATTV) of 30 officers and NCOs had arrived in ICTZ to advise the ARVN. By 1964, the AATTV had been increased to 80 personnel, many of whom worked with U.S. Special Forces and accompanied the ARVN on operations. For purposes of command, the Australians were integrated into the U.S. advisory framework, although they were allowed to develop their own ideas. But the real change came in April, 1965, when the Australian government agreed to deploy the 1st Battalion, Royal Australian Regiment (1RAR), as a complete combat unit.

"Aggressiveness, quick reaction, good use of firepower, and old-fashioned Australian courage have produced outstanding results."

GENERAL WILLIAM C. WESTMORELAND, AUGUST 19, 1966

Sent to Bien Hoa outside Saigon, 1RAR joined the newly deployed U.S. 173d Airborne Brigade, gaining invaluable experience in a series of heliborne operations in War Zone D.

In September, 1965, the Australian force was augmented by a battery of 105mm artillery (joining a similar battery provided by New Zealand two months earlier) and a squadron of U.S.-supplied M-113 APCs. The growing effectiveness of what was now known as 1RAR Group helped to persuade the government in Canberra to form a Task Force of two infantry battalions, backed by APCs, engineers, artillery, and logistic support—a total of about 1,500 men. The decision was announced in March, 1966, and 5RAR and 6RAR were earmarked for deployment when 1RAR returned home.

No one in Australia was keen to see these forces acting merely as an adjunct to the Americans. So pressure was brought to bear to have them transferred to a self-contained area of South Vietnam, ideally on the coast and away from international borders, where the 1st Australian Task Force (ATF) could conduct its own, semi-independent operations. Phuoc Tuy was chosen—a coastal province close to Saigon that was relatively small (about 1,500 square miles) but under Communist control. The ATF went to Vung Tau, on the coast of Phuoc Tuy, in May, 1966.

The province was not a jungle area: small patches existed, but most of the terrain was scrubland interspersed with low hills and French-owned rubber plantations. The population (about 100,000 people) was concentrated near the coast, and was either pro-VC or neutral, having been subject to Communist subversion since the 1940s. A VC main-force division—the 5th—was known to be hiding in the May Tao hills to the northeast, while the D445 VC Battalion (a locally raised guerrilla unit) operated in the peasant villages. Neither the ARVN nor the Americans had made any serious attempt to clear the province.

Brigadier O.D. Jackson, the ATF

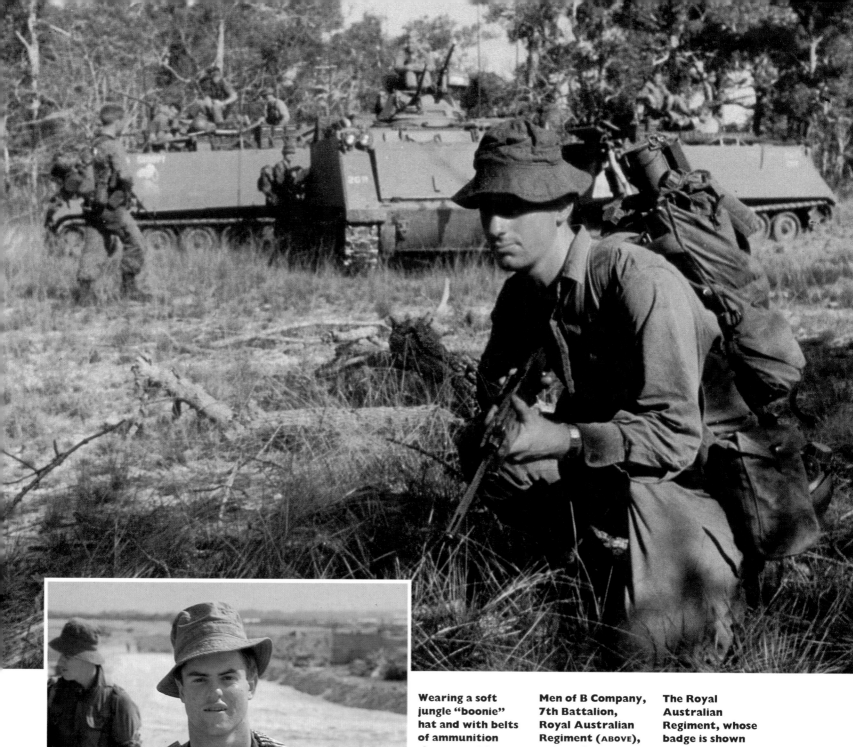

Wearing a soft jungle "boonie" hat and with belts of ammunition slung over his shoulders, an Australian infantryman (LEFT) strides forward clutching a 7.62mm machine gun.

Although a small number of Australian advisers had been in Vietnam since 1962, it was only in 1965 that a more substantial presence was established with the arrival of the 1st Battalion, Royal Australian Regiment.

Men of B Company, 7th Battalion, Royal Australian Regiment (ABOVE), return from patrol in Bien Hoa province, an area lying to the east of Saigon.

The Royal Australian Regiment, whose badge is shown (BELOW), fought with distinction in Vietnam from 1965 to 1972.

commander, decided to set up a forward base at Nui Dat, a small hill less than 20 miles north of Vung Tau, from which his artillery batteries, backed by a unit of American-manned 155mm self-propelled guns, could dominate a wide radius of land. Under this cover, his infantry would conduct "aggressive patrolling," clearing nearby villages of VC and driving a wedge between the VC 5th Division and the main population centers in the south. On May 24, 5RAR joined the 173d Airborne in an operation to secure Nui Dat; three weeks later 6RAR arrived, allowing the Americans to pull out. The Australians were on their own.

Nui Dat had few facilities: the infantry lived under canvas and the artillery had to be dug in, all in monsoon conditions. Nevertheless, patrolling began immediately. Australian Special Air Service (SAS) teams pushed deep into Phuoc Tuy, leaving the ordinary infantry to clear a buffer zone around the base in order to push local VC beyond mortar range. In the process, the villages of Long Phuoc and Long Tan, to the south and east, respectively, were searched and their inhabitants were then moved to more secure locations.

But the ATF had problems. Equipment was in short supply, helicopter support was insufficient and, most important of all, intelligence collation was poor. In retrospect, it seems obvious that the VC would try to hit Nui Dat as quickly as possible, moving battalions across from the May Tao hills. At the time, however, the Australians found it difficult to distinguish good intelligence from the welter of information coming in.

The Australian SAS

Insignia of the Australian SAS

The first members of the Australian Special Air Service (SAS) to serve in Vietnam did so as part of the Australian Army Training Team in 1962, acting as advisers to the ARVN. However, in July, 1966, when the 1st Australian Task Force moved into Phuoc Tuy province, a complete squadron of SAS went in with it to act as its eyes and ears beyond the immediate vicinity of Nui Dat, conducting deep-penetration patrols to gather information about the Communist enemy.

Organized into five-man teams, made up of a lead scout, patrol leader, second-in-command, signaller, and medic, the SAS proved to be extremely effective. Most of the troopers had seen recent service in the jungles of Borneo, preventing Indonesian incursions during a period known as "Confrontation" (1963–66), and this experience was invaluable. Committed to the remoter areas of Phuoc Tuy, each team was selected for its compatibility and kept together for the duration of its one-year tour. The men would be dropped in by helicopter, dressed to blend in with the surrounding countryside, and heavily armed to mount (or survive) ambushes.

Moving over the worst possible terrain to avoid accidental clashes with the enemy, the team would adhere to a strict operational schedule, traveling and observing by day, but hiding by night. This did not mean that they were not prepared to fight, for the Australian SAS had the highest kill ratio of any similar unit in Vietnam. They accounted for at least 500 enemy killed in action while losing none of their own men to hostile fire. It was an impressive record.

As a helicopter descends to drop off more troops (OPPOSITE PAGE), a member of the 5th Battalion, Royal Australian Regiment, takes cover in the LZ's elephant grass on May 23, 1966.

The Australians were taking part in Operation Pin Feather in the Vung Tau Peninsula. It was the battalion's first operation since setting up base near Vung Tau, 45 miles southeast of Saigon.

Lieutenant David Sabben (ABOVE) surveys the rubber plantation which was the scene of bitter fighting during the battle of Long Tan, a day after the action. Branches and twigs, shot off the trees during the battle, are strewn on the ground. In the background is a VC 7.62mm machine gun.

A soldier of 5RAR, armed with an Owen submachine gun, watches Long Tan village burn.

In 1966, the 1st Australian Task Force (ATF) was deployed in the Communist-controlled province of Phuoc Tuy southeast of Saigon, where it was to mount its own semi-independent operations. In May, a forward base was set up on a small hill named Nui Dat and patrolling of the area began at once.

On August 17, the VC mounted a surprise attack on Nui Dat. The next day, D Company, 6RAR, was sent out to sweep the area lying to the east of the base.

D Company, commanded by Major Harry Smith, was split into three platoons: 10, 11, and 12. Shortly after 1540, 11 Platoon surprised a group of VC and pursued them into a rubber plantation. Here, however, the Australians were met by a withering wall of fire. By early evening, 11 Platoon (**3**) was pinned down in mud created by driving torrential rain. Waves of VC (**4** and **5**) tried to outflank the Australians, who also had to contend with enemy snipers (**1**) who were concealed in the rubber trees.

About 100 yards to the north of 11 Platoon, the men of 10 Platoon (**2**) also came under intense enemy fire and were unable to come to the rescue of their comrades. However, the Australians' precarious position was strengthened by 105mm artillery pieces back at Nui Dat, whose shells exploded with bright blue flashes of light among the attacking VC.

With restrained and accurate use of fire, the Australians managed to hold on until a relief column arrived at dusk. The VC withdrew under the cover of darkness.

The next morning revealed a scene of devastation, with 245 VC and 17 Australian bodies scattered over two acres of the tree-shattered plantation.

Long Tan

Nui Dat

Suoi Da Bang

Nui Dat East

Xa Long Tan

0   1 km

0   1 mile

Paddy fields

Rubber plantation

N

Thus, when the VC fired mortars and recoilless rifles into Nui Dat early on August 17, killing one member of the ATF and wounding 23, the Australians were caught by surprise. Their response was disjointed. With his two battalions already stretched, Jackson had few reserves available to search for the attackers: the whole of 5RAR and A Company, 6RAR (A/6RAR), were out on patrol, leaving only three companies to guard the base and search the surrounding area. Recalling his patrols in case the

mortar attack had been a prelude to an all-out assault, Jackson sent the under-strength B/6RAR to sweep an area to the east of the base.

They found nothing on August 17 and were ordered to return on the 18th, when D/6RAR would take over. By then, unknown to the Australians, seven VC battalions (over 4,000 men) were closing in on Nui Dat, three swinging north, while the other four advanced from the east, using the Long Tan rubber plantation for cover.

D Company, commanded by Major Harry Smith and made up of 108 men divided into three rifle platoons (Numbers 10, 11, and 12) plus a small headquarters group, was tasked to continue B Company's eastward sweep to the rubber plantation. By 1100 hours on August 18, they had left Nui Dat, spear-headed by Second Lieutenant David Sabben's 12 Platoon. Two hours later, they linked up with B Company and were shown a number of mortar pits discovered earlier that day on the western

The art of ambush

The Australian SAS prided themselves on their ability to spring ambushes on an unsuspecting enemy. A five-man SAS team, operating deep inside Communist-controlled territory, would carefully select a likely ambush spot, usually on a jungle trail showing signs of recent use.

After a period of observation, the ambush would be set up. SAS troopers would position themselves about 50 yards up and down the trail to warn of enemy approaches, while the rest of the team set up U.S.-supplied M18A1 Antipersonnel (Claymore) Mines. These lethal pieces of

hardware each contained 700 steel balls that, once detonated by tripwire or remote control, were sprayed out in a 60-degree fan-shaped pattern effective up to 50 yards. The mines would be camouflaged and placed in overlapping positions to create maximum damage. The SAS team would then wait to see what happened.

Usually an NVA or VC column would be preceded by a forward scout, who was allowed through unharmed. As soon as the main column appeared, the Claymores would be set off and rifle fire poured onto the trail. If the column was large, the team

would then withdraw to a prearranged rallying point; if the enemy was wiped out, the bodies would be searched and documents, weapons, and equipment carried off. In the right circumstances, an ambush could be extremely effective, destroying Communist forces and undermining their morale. U.S. Army Special Forces and Australians worked very close together—even having mixed teams in Vietnam. Tactics were developed and utilized mutually. The Regular U.S. Army showed disdain, however, for the Green Beret arrangements with Australian warfare experts.

Soviet M46/Chinese Type 59 130mm Gun-Howitzer (Towed)

Weight	16,978lb
Rate of fire	5–6rpm
Crew	9 men
Range	27,150yd

U.S. M114A1 155mm Medium Howitzer (Towed)

Weight	12,950lb
Sustained rate of fire	1rpm
Crew	12 men
Range	15,967yd

U.S. M101/M102 105mm Light Howitzer (Towed)

Weight	4,466lb/3,298lb
Sustained rate of fire	3rpm
Crew	8 men
Range	12,325yd/12,576yd

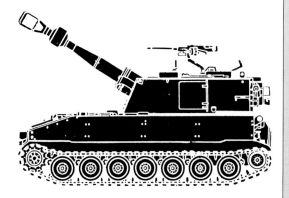

U.S. M109 155mm Howitzer (Self-propelled)

Weight	55,000lb
Rate of fire	1rpm
Crew	6 men
Range	21,872yd

The role of artillery

Without artillery support, U.S. and Allied infantry would have found it virtually impossible to operate in large areas of South Vietnam. When patrols or search and destroy operations were mounted, invariably into inhospitable terrain, the knowledge that substantial weights of accurate and sustained artillery fire could be called down quickly did much to boost troop morale, giving even the smallest unit the chance to survive an NVA/VC ambush or attack. The Australian units at the battle of Long Tan were immeasurably helped by artillery fire from their base at Nui Dat. U.S. artillery, positioned in Fire Support Bases, played an integral part in the military response to the Communist threat. The Communists themselves, however, were capable of hitting back, using Soviet- or Chinese-supplied artillery pieces dragged laboriously down the Ho Chi Minh Trail.

U.S. M107 175mm Gun (Self-propelled)

Weight	57,690lb
Rate of fire	1r per 2m
Crew	13 men
Range	35,760yd

Soldiers of the Royal Australian Regiment enter a village (OPPOSITE PAGE), looking for indications of Communist activity during an operation west of Nui Dat.

An Australian 105mm howitzer (RIGHT) fires from Nui Dat in support of the 1st Battalion, Royal Australian Regiment. During the battle of Long Tan, it was sustained and accurate artillery fire that helped to prevent the VC from overrunning members of D Company, 6RAR.

edge of the plantation, about 2,000 yards from Nui Dat. Smith decided to follow a track going east. After about 300 yards the track split, with a trail on the left skirting the northern edge of the plantation and one on the right going straight on, into the evenly spaced rubber trees. Second Lieutenant Geoff Kendall's 10 Platoon took the northern route, with Second Lieutenant Gordon Sharp's 11 Platoon moving east. Twelve Platoon and the Company HQ group followed Sharp. It was just after 1500 hours.

Forty minutes later, the lead section of 11 Platoon suddenly spotted six VC, described by Private Allen May, the forward scout, as "a bunch of kids sitting around a fire having lunch." The Australians fired, then pursued the group deeper into the plantation, past a rubber-tappers' hut and toward a small clearing. This was, in fact, the eastern edge of the rubber plantation, beyond which an area of jungle growth created a "wall of green."

A patrol from the 1st Battalion, Royal Australian Regiment, makes its way through elephant grass toward a rubber plantation near Ba Ria, southwest of the Australian base at Nui Dat. Aggressive Australian patrolling helped to disrupt the VC infrastructure in Phuoc Tuy province.

At 1608 hours, as Sharp's men entered the clearing, they were met by a hail of fire. According to Private Peter Ainslie, "a million little lights seemed to come out of the rubber, from knee height to above our heads, and a helluva noise." Two Australians died and the rest of the platoon sought cover as best they could. The fire intensified as parties of VC tried to move around the flanks of the beleaguered platoon.

Simultaneously, Smith's HQ group, with 12 Platoon farther behind, was hit by mortar fire and stalled, leaving 11 Platoon in a perilous position. However, once the initial shock of contact had passed, the Australians stayed calm, picking their targets carefully and preventing a quick VC victory. They were helped enormously by 105mm artillery fire from Nui Dat, brought down to the east of 11 Platoon by Captain Morrie Stanley, the

Communist influence in Phuoc Tuy

When the 1st Australian Task Force (ATF) was deployed to Phuoc Tuy in 1966, it entered an area under Communist control. ARVN operations had been carried out, and South Vietnamese civic action groups were present, but their record of success was low; they had also been hit hard in ambushes mounted by locally raised VC with an intimate knowledge of the terrain and firm support from the people.

At the very lowest level, the VC were active in persuading (or intimidating) local villagers to oppose the Saigon regime. Once sympathetic, the people would be organized into groups for propaganda and "education," and trained for more active involvement as laborers or supply carriers for the guerrillas. Small groups existed in most of the villages of Phuoc Tuy, but they were dependent for protection on the

military capabilities of the D445 Regional Battalion—locally raised and known to the Australians as "Phuoc Tuy's Own." In turn, D445, made up of an estimated 550 activists in 1966, depended on the regulars of the 5th VC Division in the May Tao hills to the northeast for any operations beyond the level of guerrilla attack.

In 1966, the 5th Division was made up of two regiments, the 274th and 275th, each of which contained about 2,000 well-equipped, well-trained soldiers. Just as the lower echelons depended on the 5th Division, however, so the 5th Division depended on the guerrillas and more passive supporters to survive. The creation of the ATF base at Nui Dat was designed to drive a wedge between VC military units and their sources of recruits, information, and supplies in the villages.

An infantryman of the Royal Australian Regiment. He wears the ubiquitous jungle "boonie" hat in preference to a steel helmet and is armed with an Owen submachine gun. U.S.-issue water canteens are attached to his belt, and M60 ammunition belts, wrapped inside homemade covers from an inflatable mattress, are worn bandolier-style.

New Zealand Forward Observation Officer attached to Smith's HQ. He continued the bombardment, under fire himself and in appalling weather conditions, for the next two and a half hours. However, he succeeded in coordinating a ceaseless 24-gun barrage that proved crucial to the outcome of the battle. The American 155mms also joined in.

As 11 Platoon fought for survival, surrounded by VC in a nightmare of noise, 10 Platoon moved down from the northern track in an attempt to relieve the pressure. It then began to rain. "And when I say rain," Kendall recalled, "it rained like it rains in Vietnam in the afternoon. It absolutely started to pour monsoonal rain." This cut visibility to about 50 yards and, together with the crash of artillery from Nui Dat, enabled 10 Platoon to approach the VC who were firing into the 11 Platoon position.

Kendall ordered his men to open fire and "we all sort of dropped to our knees and ripped into them . . . I don't think they even knew where the firing was coming from." But the enemy quickly recovered, shifting troops to pin down 10 Platoon, which was only saved by Stanley "walking" artillery fire back and forth in the vicinity. Even so, the attempt to relieve 11 Platoon had failed, and D Company was in deep trouble.

The firefight was being monitored back at Nui Dat by Lieutenant Colonel Colin Townsend, the commanding officer of 6RAR, and he began to put together a relief force. Realizing the need for speed, he decided to send A/6RAR (who had only just returned to base) to the battle area on board M-113s of the 1st APC Squadron. They were alerted at 1640 hours and Lieutenant Adrian Roberts hastily gathered together a total of ten vehicles, many of them "rather old and tired," having been inherited from 1RAR earlier in the year.

Some of the APCs lacked protective armor shields for their 50-cal machine guns; others had no intercom and were directed by the commander pulling strings attached to the driver's shoulder-straps. Even so, A/6RAR boarded the APCs without undue delay and the column left Nui Dat at 1745 hours, heading for a crossing point on the Suoi Da Bang River. Two APCs had been tasked to pick up Townsend, who was to take command at Long Tan, but Roberts was confident that he could effect a relief.

Meanwhile, D Company continued to survive, despite a shortage of ammunition and an abortive attempt by two sections of 12 Platoon to fight through to

11 Platoon from the northwest. At about 1700 hours, Smith ordered his untrapped platoons to pull back onto the HQ group, situated by now in a small hollow slightly to the west. The wounded were brought in and a defensive perimeter was hastily set up. Eleven Platoon, now under Sergeant Bob Buick following Gordon Sharp's death some time before, consisted of only 10 or 12 unwounded men; it was left to fend for itself, at least until the APCs arrived.

Once the bulk of D Company was concentrated, it could be resupplied using two Australian-crewed UH-1 helicopters from Nui Dat. At about 1800 hours, the artillery barrage ceased, allowing the helicopters in, guided by colored smoke. They did not land, but hovered low above Smith's HQ, rolling slightly to allow ammunition boxes, wrapped in blankets, to fall out.

The resupply was only just in time: as the artillery started up again, the VC attempted a "human-wave" assault that was broken up only with difficulty. Buick and the survivors of 11 Platoon had been able to identify the Company perimeter by the arrival of the helicopters and were under marginally less pressure now that the VC had a larger target; they raced through the trees to rejoin the main party.

The VC, despite heavy casualties from the renewed artillery fire, were determined to wipe out D Company, sending men of the D445 Battalion around to the west to complete an encirclement. As they did so, Roberts's M-113s, having crossed the Suoi Da Bang, crashed into them, taking them completely by surprise. At first, neither side reacted, but once the spell had been broken an intense firefight developed as Australian 50-cal gunners and riflemen poured fire down onto the confused guerrillas. Roberts kept his vehicles moving—some of them literally ran over VC in their path—and, although one APC pulled back, its commander

badly wounded, the others fought through to Smith's HQ. As they arrived, at 1840 hours, the battered survivors of D Company raised a heartfelt cheer.

B/6RAR, having approached the battle area on foot, took the opportunity to break through to D Company, and this influx of reinforcements, despite its small size, seemed to knock the spirit out of the VC. As their fire slackened, Townsend took command of the Australian perimeter, ordering the men to pull back to a small clearing to the west, from which the dead and wounded could be evacuated by helicopter.

It was now dark, and, although the rain had ceased, conditions were still poor. The Australians spent a tense night, listening to the sounds of the VC scouring the battlefield for their casualties. However, no further attacks materialized, enabling supplies to be brought forward both to Nui Dat (where artillery had used 2,639 rounds of 105mm ammunition, plus

COIN and "search and destroy"

The Australian aim in Phuoc Tuy province was to conduct a counterinsurgency (COIN) campaign. This meant a mixture of military operations and civic aid ("hearts and minds") that would simultaneously protect the people and give them an interest in preserving the political status quo.

After Long Tan, an extensive civic action program was introduced, designed to improve the health, education, and living standards of the ordinary villagers. Relations between the Australians and the local people were generally good, making it difficult for the VC to maintain or extend their subversive influence. Similar techniques were used by U.S. Special Forces (often with Australian troops in attendance), principally among indigenous tribesmen in the Central Highlands.

U.S. main-force units elsewhere in South Vietnam developed a different response to the Communist threat. Known as "search and destroy," this approach involved large formations of troops, often projected into enemy territory by helicopter and backed by artillery and airstrikes, who would search villages and rural areas, destroying all evidence of Communist activity, even to the extent of removing the population to more secure locations. The aim was to force the enemy to fight or withdraw, while destroying his infrastructure of support among the people.

Neither approach worked on its own. COIN had the advantage of gaining popular support, but could only be successful in small, self-contained areas. Search and destroy did help to curtail NVA/VC military activity, but only at the cost of alienating the very people the government needed on its side. In the end, despite an enormous commitment of men and materiel and an elaborate (but uncoordinated) U.S./South Vietnamese civic action program, the "Free World" forces were just not used properly to fight a campaign combining both techniques.

COIN and search and destroy operations worked on different principles: while Australian soldiers (LEFT) try to win the allegiance of a local farmer, a trooper of the 1st Cavalry Division (FAR LEFT) hears the pleas of a woman whose village has just been set on fire.

Buddhist monks and protesters watch a U.S. Army jeep burn during an angry demonstration against the government in Saigon on June 14, 1966.

THE WAR YEARS

March 9/ 11, 1966	NVA/VC destroy U.S. Special Forces camp in the A Shau valley, ICTZ. Survivors rescued by helicopter.
March 10	Dismissal of Lieutenant General Thi, a leading Buddhist, from the Saigon government and command of I Corps leads to Buddhist demonstrations and anti-government protests in ICTZ.
April 4, 1966	U.S. aircraft hit rail links between China and North Vietnam.
April 12	VC attack on Tan Son Nhut airfield outside Saigon destroys helicopters and aircraft; seven people killed.
April 23	In an air clash over North Vietnam, USAF F-4C Phantoms shoot down two MiG-17s.
May 15, 1966	Prime Minister Ky sends 1,500 loyal troops into Da Nang to reassert government control; this leads to more Buddhist demonstrations.
June 2, 1966	Operation El Paso (Phase Two) begins in IIICTZ (ends July 13).
June 14	Anti-government riots break out in Saigon.
June 29	U.S. air raids near Hanoi/Haiphong destroy an estimated 50 percent of the North's fuel supplies.
Aug. 18, 1966	Battle of Long Tan, Phuoc Tuy province.

155 rounds of 155mm) and the 6RAR perimeter.

Next morning, Townsend ordered his troops, spearheaded by D Company, to reoccupy the battlefield. They advanced into an area of unbelievable devastation—"as big as two or three football fields and several hundred bodies spread all over the place." Two wounded Australians were found and evacuated, but the real shock came when the initial contact point was reached. There, in an arc, still clutching their rifles, lay the dead of 11 Platoon, "as if they were frozen in a drill and it only needed a touch to bring them back to life again." Altogether, the ATF had lost 17 dead at Long Tan, but VC casualties were heavy: 245 bodies were found and buried, with evidence of many more having been dragged away.

The battle of Long Tan gave the initiative to the Australians in Phuoc Tuy. They did not waste it, forcing the VC 5th Division back into the May Tao hills and

gradually extending control over the entire province. Contacts continued to be made: in June, 1969, for example, two companies of 5RAR, with tank support, killed 43 VC in a 24-hour battle at Binh Ba, north of Nui Dat. But the campaign really became one of constant patrols, cordon and search operations, and "hearts and minds," in which the local people were persuaded to give their support to the government rather than to the Communists.

A significant degree of success was achieved, but it did not last. Once the Australians withdrew from Vietnam in late 1971, having suffered a total of 423 men killed and 2,398 wounded, they left a vacuum in Phuoc Tuy which the ARVN proved unable to fill. As a result of this, the VC were able to return to the villages, free at last from the "Australian mercenaries" they had grown to fear.

71

OPERATION ATTLEBORO

September 14–November 24, 1966

ROM THE AMERICAN POINT OF view, 1966 was a crucial year, in which the tools and techniques of fighting in Vietnam had to be forged. After the engagements of 1965—especially in the Ia Drang valley—it was obvious that this was no ordinary war. Although the NVA was a conventional army, it was not fighting according to the rule book, preferring infiltration and ambush to set-piece battles. It was a way of fighting known as "area warfare," in which there were no clearly demarcated front lines or safe rear zones. To U.S. forces trained primarily for an "atomic battlefield" in central Europe, area warfare came as a shock that had to be absorbed and for which effective counter-measures had to be found as quickly as possible.

There was also political pressure on the U.S. commanders to achieve results. On December 31, 1965, therefore, MACV adopted a joint U.S./South Vietnamese Campaign Plan (codenamed AB-141) which called for the maintenance of four "National Priority Areas." They were located around Saigon, the center of the Mekong Delta, and the coastal bases of Qui Nhon and Da Nang. Each was to be secured and NVA/VC forces pushed back, preparatory to major offensives at a later date. On July 1, 1966, Secretary of Defense Robert McNamara went further, predicting that such offensives, scheduled for 1967, would destroy 40 to 50 percent of Communist bases in the South, securing up to 60 percent of the population for the Saigon government. It was a tall order which General Westmoreland would be hard-pressed to put into effect.

He certainly could not do it with the forces available to him at the beginning of the year. On January 1, 1966, he had 116,700 U.S. Army troops and 41,000 Marines "in-country"—a total of 35 battalions. But their duties were heavy: the Marines were confined to ICTZ in the northern provinces, protecting bases at Chu Lai, Phu Bai, and Da Nang; while the Army, despite Australian and South Kor-

"It was fantastic. At times there would be drumfire of enemy bullets spurting in on us."

PFC WILLIAM WALLACE, CO. C, 1/27th INFANTRY, NOVEMBER 4, 1966

ean aid, was hard-pressed to cover trouble spots farther south in II and IIICTZ.

The far south (IVCTZ) was ostensibly the responsibility of the ARVN (with U.S. Special Forces support) as, indeed, were all aspects of the "Village War" against the VC. However, the ten regular divisions of the ARVN were demoralized, poorly led, and riddled with political corruption. In April, 1966, elements of the ARVN in ICTZ effectively mutinied, confronting U.S. forces in their opposition to the Saigon regime. Any intention of using U.S. units solely against the NVA in a "main-force" war was swiftly undermined: until the ARVN could be revitalized, the Americans and their non-Vietnamese allies had to bear the brunt of the war.

In such circumstances, it was hardly surprising that 1966 should see a massive increase in U.S. force levels in Vietnam to 390,000 men. Throughout the year, fresh units poured into the country. In April, the 25th Infantry Division arrived at Cu Chi, west of Saigon; in June, the 1st Marine Division moved to Chu Lai in ICTZ. Two months later, the 196th Infantry Brigade (Light) arrived in Tay Ninh, north of Saigon, while the 11th Armored Cavalry Regiment settled in at Long Binh in September.

In October, the 4th Infantry Division moved to Pleiku in the Central Highlands; two months later the 199th Infantry Brigade (Light) and 9th Infantry Division arrived in Long Binh and the Mekong Delta respectively. By then, MACV had 83 battalions at its disposal, 24 under Marine command in ICTZ, the rest divided between two new Army commands farther south: I Field Force in IICTZ and II Field Force in IIICTZ.

It took time for an infrastructure to be set up to cater for this influx of troops and much of the year had to be spent securing base areas and opening up lines of communication between them. Fortunately for the Americans, the North Vietnamese also had to pause to recover from the 1965 battles, but this did not mean that the

72

Insignia of the 196th Infantry Brigade, a unit which took part in Attleboro.

Wounded by shrapnel and under threat from VC attacks, Major Guy S. Meloy (BELOW, LEFT OF PICTURE), of the 1/27th Infantry, gives orders during Operation Attleboro on November 4, 1966.

A gun crew (BOTTOM) fires a 105mm howitzer in support of men of the 1st Infantry Division during the operation.

An infantryman (RIGHT) of the 25th Division ("Tropic Lightning"), which was first deployed in Vietnam on March 28, 1966. He is armed with grenades and an M-14 assault rifle, and has a spare magazine strapped to his steel helmet. Men of the 1/27th, 25th Division, took part in Attleboro, in which they were attached to the 196th Infantry Brigade.

fighting ceased. As U.S. forces arrived in Vietnam, they entered an active war zone, subject to Communist subversion, infiltration, and attack. They had no choice but to react, even though a strategic counter to area warfare had yet to emerge.

Because of this, operations tended to develop on Communist terms, with the Americans foregoing the initiative, at least until their forces had been built up. In ICTZ, for example, the Marines remained confined to the vicinity of their bases for the first three months of the year, carrying out search operations, such as Double Eagle and Utah, in response to NVA/VC activity.

The situation deteriorated in April, when the ARVN effectively ceased operations. This diverted Marine attention, allowing the NVA to infiltrate forces into the A Shau valley, northwest of Da Nang, and across the DMZ. Elements of the Marines—by now reinforced—moved north in July and, for the rest of the year, guarded the DMZ, trying to bring the enemy to battle in operations such as Hastings and Prairie.

During the latter, three battalions of Marines fought a bitter 12-day battle at Nui Cay Tre—dubbed "Mutter's Ridge" by the survivors. The NVA units were driven off by airstrikes and artillery strikes as well as infantry action, but the Marine strategy was still essentially reactive.

The situation was little different in IICTZ, where army operations concentrated on safeguarding military installations and securing Binh Dinh province around Qui Nhon—one of the "National Priority Areas." In the process, troopers of the 1st Cavalry Division continued to show the merits of airmobility, racing from valley to valley at treetop height in operations such as Masher/White Wing and Davy Crockett, but the Communists were determined not to be caught in another Ia Drang.

At the same time, brigades of the 25th Infantry and 101st Airborne Divisions carried out similar clearing operations, searching villages for VC, protecting Special Forces camps, or securing the rice harvest in operations such as John Paul Jones and Seward. Contacts beyond the level of guerrilla action were rare, although in December, 1966, U.S. forces, caught on LZ Bird, southwest of Bong Son, had to fight hard to survive a Communist assault.

More significant action developed in IIICTZ, and it was here that, as the year progressed, new strategic ideas gradually emerged. Saigon and its approaches were clearly top priority for both sides and, although U.S. forces began the year securing base areas and opening up lines of communications, they did conduct offensive operations into known VC bases, especially in War Zone C to the north of the capital, close to Communist sanctuaries in Cambodia.

It soon became obvious that when the NVA or VC were attacked in their bases, they were far more likely to stand and fight. In such cases, set-piece battles could be fought, in which the American advantages of mobility and firepower would be brought to bear. Colonel George S. Patton (son of the famous World War II general) summed it up in 1968 when commanding the 11th Armored Cavalry: "Find the bastards, then pile on." But the technique had originated in War Zone C two years earlier.

Advantages first became apparent in May and June, 1966, during Operation El Paso, carried out by the 1st Infantry Division (which had been in Vietnam since July, 1965) under its energetic commander Major General William E. DePuy. El Paso was divided into two phases. Phase One, in May, concentrated on an area southeast of Loc Ninh, but few contacts were made, persuading DePuy that a second phase, in the following month, should project his units deeper into War Zone C. He aimed to block the VC 9th Division, which, by now, was

A 500-pound bomb explodes on target as F-100 aircraft of the 308th Tactical Fighter Squadron attack enemy concrete bunker emplacements. The action took place in a heavily wooded area near the U.S. airbase at Bien Hoa at the time of Operation Attleboro in November, 1966.

Rifle power

Infantry firefights in Vietnam frequently occurred at distances considerably less than 330 yards. In such circumstances, weight of fire was more important than range, and this was reflected in the widespread use of assault rifles, capable of being fired on either semi- or fully-automatic settings. Although the Communists were known to use captured rifles, they were often issued with the reliable Soviet Kalashnikov AK-47 (or Chinese copies of it).

However, it took the experience of Vietnam to boost the development of an American assault rifle geared to jungle warfare. This was the Colt M-16, based on a design by Eugene Stoner. Adopted throughout the U.S. Army by 1969, it suffered significant teething troubles—not least a tendency to jam when dirty—but it became a trusted, and often devastating, weapon.

Soviet Kalashnikov AK-47/ Chinese Type 56

Length	34.2in	Weight	10.6lb	Range	437yd
Number of rounds	30 × 7.62mm				

U.S. Colt M-16A1

Length	38.9in	Weight	7.6lb	Range	300yd
Number of rounds	20 or 30 × 5.56mm				

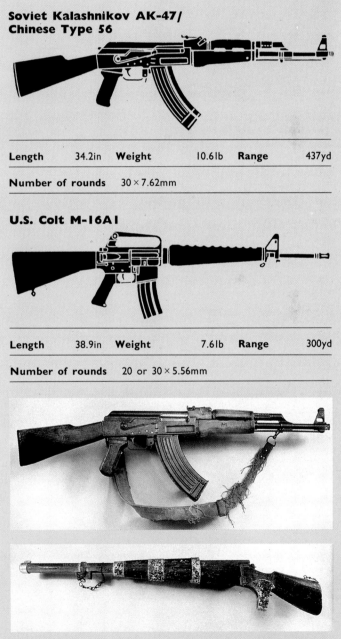

A homemade VC rifle (ABOVE) and an AK-47 Kalashnikov assault rifle (TOP), both captured by U.S. troops, show the variety of firepower the VC had at their disposal.

Counting the bodies

Throughout the period of American involvement in Vietnam, there was constant pressure from Washington to "quantify" the war, providing tangible evidence of the losses inflicted on the enemy. One result was the policy of "body count," based on the seemingly simple process of counting the number of enemy dead after a firefight or battle, as shown by the South Korean Marines (LEFT) counting VC dead in ICTZ in 1966. Statistics would be relayed up the chain of command, enabling the Department of Defense (DOD) to issue figures that would show how effectively the Communists were being worn down.

But body count was more difficult in practise. Quite often it was physically impossible to identify enemy remains, even if the Americans succeeded in occupying the disputed ground. At other times, it was equally impossible to distinguish between combatant and non-combatant dead, leading to an understandable, but unfortunate, tendency to count all black-clad bodies, male or female, as part of the VC infrastructure.

This led to distorted figures—sometimes overstated by at least 30 percent, according to an official DOD report—made worse by double counting, as different units, both ground and air, claimed the tally for themselves. More invidiously, body count became associated with military efficiency in some units. Major General Julian J. Ewell, for example, when commanding the 9th Infantry Division in 1968–69, was widely believed to be obsessed by body count, imposing on his subordinates quotas that had to be satisfied if they were to receive favorable efficiency reports.

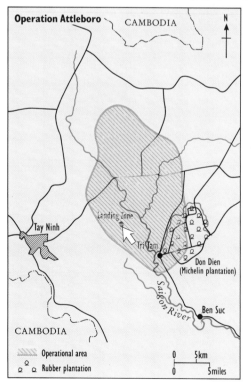

In 1966, the political pressure on General Westmoreland to achieve greater military success against Communist bases in the South resulted in a massive increase of U.S. troops to 390,000 men. Even with these numbers, a sound strategy had to be found to counter the Communists' area warfare infiltration and subversion.

By August, 1966, in IIICTZ, U.S. Special Forces intelligence was convinced that the VC 9th Division, recently battered by the U.S. 1st Infantry Division, was recovering its strength. NVA reinforcements were coming down the Ho Chi Minh Trail, and an offensive against the Special Forces camp at Suoi Da, northeast of Tay Ninh, seemed to be in the offing. As a result, Brigadier General Edward H. DeSaussure's

196th Infantry Brigade, reinforced by a battalion of the 27th Infantry, was ordered to launch Operation Attleboro.

Operation Attleboro — CAMBODIA — N

Tay Ninh
Landing Zone
Tri Tam
Don Dien
(Michelin plantation)
Saigon River
Ben Suc
CAMBODIA

///// Operational area
Ω Rubber plantation

0   5km
0   5miles

During the first phase of Attleboro in early October, 1966, huge enemy supplies were found to the south of the Don Dien Michelin plantation. Phase Two, a search and destroy operation in the same area, began on November 3, when Major Guy S. Meloy's Company B, 1/27th Infantry, landed on an LZ west of the plantation. Then, as all seemed quiet, Company C was ordered to land: at 1029, as the first Huey helicopters (1) came in, heavy VC fire from the treeline (2) swept the LZ.

Under a blazing sun, the men of Company C (4) took cover as best they could in the elephant grass. Meanwhile, Company B (3), which had fanned out after landing, was also pinned down by the intense automatic-weapon fire.

With artillery and air support called up from his command helicopter, Meloy managed to land with Company A. However, little progress against the enemy was made, and the Americans had to suffer in the heat all day. Only at nightfall was Meloy in a position to set up a defensive perimeter.

The next day, two companies of the 2/1st Infantry reinforced Meloy and were promptly sent out to probe to the east of the LZ. Meanwhile, as another battalion, the 4/31st, approached from the south, the 1/27th swept to the northeast, but fell into a VC ambush.

To help the 1/27th, the 2/1st and 4/31st were ordered to move up through dense jungle, which hampered their progress. Then, the 2/27th Infantry, advancing to the action from the east, also fell into an ambush, losing an entire platoon. Only nightfall saved the 1/27th from being wiped out by VC human-wave attacks.

On November 5, Major General William E. DePuy took over command of the operation from DeSaussure. DePuy brought in other units and, with 22,000 Allied troops now committed, the VC 9th fell back across the Cambodian border.

Attleboro ended on November 24. More than 1,000 VC bodies were counted, suggesting that with mobility, superior numbers, and firepower, the Americans could prove equal to the threat of area warfare.

Securing the roads

One of the most important tasks facing U.S. forces in 1965–66 was route security, making sure that lines of ground communication between the major cities and bases in South Vietnam were cleared of the enemy and kept open for the movement of troops and supplies. VC ambushes and the constant threat of mines meant that many roads were virtually unusable.

There were a number of responses available. Infantry patrols could be mounted to counter any ambush parties, but with thousands of miles of road to cover, this was hardly practical. Similarly, airpower could be used to spot and attack the VC, but aircraft had other, more pressing, tasks to carry out and were of limited value at night when the VC were most active. The most efficient option was the use of armor, both M-48 tanks and M-113 APCs, for they could cover large distances quickly and were relatively invulnerable to VC weapons except mines.

As early as 1965, armored vehicles were employed to conduct all-day (or all-night) road marches between key points, laying down machine-gun or cannon fire along the roadsides to trigger potential ambushes or deter the VC from operating. These journeys were known as "Thunder Runs" and, although expensive in terms of ammunition, were successful; so much so that Highway 13 between Phu Cuong and Loc Ninh, north of Saigon, was nicknamed "Thunder Road." Another method was for much larger units to go out on armed route reconnaissance, searching for the enemy as well as clearing the way for supply or reinforcement columns which were, in turn, protected as they moved along.

A column of M-113 APCs protects the Tay Ninh road.

Patrolling: hardships and perils

Throughout the Vietnam War, the key to American tactics was finding the enemy, which meant patrolling. All U.S. infantrymen, whether Marines or Army, spent much of their tour of duty in the countryside, looking for the VC. They may have traveled to and from a firebase or LZ by helicopters, but once on the ground—in mountains, jungle, rubber plantations, or rice paddies—the whole point of their existence was to scout the countryside and destroy the enemy in a shadowy war.

The dangers were many. As U.S. infantry squads, platoons, or companies moved into the countryside, they entered an environment that, regardless of previous training, was alien. Jungle patrolling was undoubtedly the worst, for the heat and high humidity—to say nothing of the drenching rain during the monsoon—sapped both energy and morale. These conditions—plus the mosquitoes, leeches, and poisonous snakes—made the task of hacking through thick, tangled undergrowth seem the least of the soldiers' worries.

Nor was that all: throughout a patrol there was the constant danger of VC booby traps or ambush. Any trail, in whatever sort of terrain, could (and often did) contain myriad traps laid by guerrillas with over 20 years of experience. One of the favorites was the punji-stake trap, in which sharpened bamboo stakes, dipped in human excrement to guarantee gangrene, were planted point upward in a pit covered in seemingly innocuous undergrowth. As one veteran later wrote: "Step on one of those, and your foot would infect, swell up like a balloon and hurt like . . . well, like a sharpened bamboo stake had been punched through your foot." Other traps included grenades or mines attached to tripwires, bridges sawn through and the cuts camouflaged with mud, and the notorious "whiplash" branches festooned with punji-stakes.

known to be building up its strength preparatory to an attack around Saigon in the forthcoming monsoon period. Once committed, DePuy's men soon encountered the enemy.

As early as June 8, elements of Troop A, 1/4th Cavalry, were ambushed at Tau-O; three days later, Company A, 2/28th Infantry, suffered a similar experience northwest of Loc Ninh. On both occasions a stiff firefight developed, and the Americans were able to pour in air and artillery fire. On June 30, Troop B, 1/4th Cavalry, was ambushed near Quan Loi on Route 13 and was saved from annihilation only by heavy air support. DePuy, however, was beginning to get the measure of his enemy. As the cavalry fought for survival, he sent in Companies A and B, 2/18th Infantry, as reinforcements and deployed both 1/2d and 2/28th Infantry in support. After two days of combat, in what was known as the battle of Srok Dong, the VC managed to pull back.

DePuy took the process further on July 9, when he sent two troops of cavalry, with infantry support, down the Minh Thanh road, hoping to trigger an ambush. When this occurred, the surrounding area was saturated with 22,200 rounds of artillery and 99 airstrikes, while four infantry battalions were sent in to cut the enemy off. In the event, the VC withdrew before the ring could be closed around them, but their 9th Division, battered in a succession of encounters with the "Big Red One," fell back into Cambodian sanctuaries to recover.

This was the situation confronting the 196th Infantry Brigade (2/1st, 3/21st, and 4/31st Infantry) when it arrived at Tay Ninh, on the western fringe of War Zone C, in August. Commanded by Brigadier General Edward H. DeSaussure, the 196th was inadequately trained for service in Vietnam, having been raised specifically for peace-keeping duties in the Caribbean before being hastily redirected to Southeast Asia in June. Many of its units lacked experienced officers or senior NCOs, and the men had not had time to adjust mentally to their new task.

Such shortcomings were by no means unique during the period of U.S. build-

Patrolling usually entailed carrying a hefty pack (LEFT). For soldiers on patrol, such as the Marines (BELOW), the hazards included punji-stake traps, shown being made by VC women (FAR LEFT).

When triggered, these swung across the trail at chest or face height.

Finally, there was the sheer physical discomfort of carrying everything that was needed on the back or hung around the body. Personal weapons were essential, but that was only the start. The individual equipment belt and suspenders would be hung with ammunition pouches, field dressings and water canteens; into (or onto) the canvas combat field pack or lightweight rucksack would be placed Claymore mines, grenades, spare ammunition for the machine gun, extra water, trip-flares, C-rations, heat tablets, insect repellent, spare clothing, weapons-cleaning kit, extra field dressings, cigarettes, toilet articles, an entrenching tool, a machete, and anything else of value. Add a steel helmet and a flak jacket, and the soldier often had trouble just moving.

up, but in the case of the 196th, they were exacerbated by the need to maintain the pressure in War Zone C. By August, U.S. Special Forces intelligence was already noting a recovery in the ranks of the VC 9th Division, reinforced by NVA units coming down the Ho Chi Minh Trail. There was also speculation that a new Communist offensive, specifically against the Special Forces camp at Suoi Da, just northeast of Tay Ninh, was imminent. DeSaussure was ordered to investigate in an operation codenamed Attleboro. He was given a battalion of the 27th Infantry ("The Wolfhounds") from the 25th Division to bolster his brigade.

Attleboro, like El Paso, was fought in two distinct phases. The first began on

September 14, when the 2/1st Infantry was lifted into an LZ west of the Don Dien Michelin rubber plantation, an area of gnarled jungle, thick vines, and clearings covered in shoulder-high elephant grass to the east of Route 13. The soldiers made few contacts and, although searches continued in oppressive heat, turning up tunnels, supply caches, and the occasional weapon, the real breakthrough did not come until early October, when the same battalion shifted south to Dau Tieng. There they uncovered vast supply dumps of rice, salt, and ammunition, which persuaded the American high command to authorize a brigade-sized "search and destroy" operation: this was Phase Two of Attleboro.

DeSaussure received his new orders on November 1, by which time Special Forces patrols were painting a more elaborate picture of VC intentions. According to their findings, the 9th Division was moving south through Don Dien to the supply caches at Dau Tieng, preparatory to an assault on Suoi Da from the east, where their reconnaissance elements were already active. It was decided to commit one U.S. battalion to an LZ between Don Dien and Suoi Da, while other battalions moved on foot toward it, flushing out any VC in the area.

Early on November 3, Company B of Major Guy S. Meloy's 1/27th Infantry landed in a rough elephant-grass clearing to the west of the Don Dien plantation.

By 0922 hours, they had reported the area clear, and Meloy, flying above the LZ in a command helicopter, ordered the second lift—Company C—to land.

The Hueys came in at 1029 hours but, as they touched down, a hail of automatic-weapon fire swept the LZ. Men tumbled out of the helicopters, only to be pinned down under a blazing sun, unable to see their enemy—a reconnaissance company of the VC 9th Division who were expertly hidden behind the treeline at the edge of the clearing. Company B, caught between the VC and Company C, suffered just as badly. As Meloy called in airstrikes and artillery strikes, the firing slackened enough to allow him to land, together with Company A, but it was obvious that no one was going very far.

In fact, the men of 1/27th had to suffer all day, for it was not until darkness fell that they were able to pull back into a defensive perimeter. The VC did not press their advantage, however, enabling Meloy to resume operations on the 4th. By then, two companies of the 2/1st Infantry had arrived. They were sent to the east of the LZ, while the 1/27th, with Company C in the lead, moved northeast, searching for the attackers. Another battalion, the 4/31st, was coming up from the south as part of the original plan.

Company C, 1/27th, entered an area tailor-made for ambush—the trail narrowed and visibility was cut to less than 30 feet to left and right. The inevitable happened. In Meloy's own words, "One moment it was as quiet as can be, and the next instant, it was like a Fort Benning Mad Minute." As the lead platoons edged forward, the VC opened up at virtually point-blank range, adding to the confusion by lobbing 60mm mortar shells into the follow-up companies. Company C, its commanding officer dead, took cover, while Meloy, now wounded, tried to coordinate a response over the radio.

The two companies of the 2/1st were

Infantry support from the skies

Whenever American ground forces came under attack, regardless of the terrain, time, or location, they could call in air support and expect to receive it with the minimum delay. As soon as the firefight began, the unit radio operator would call up Tactical Air Control Airborne (TACAIR) and transmit a call for help.

The response would come through a Forward Air Controller (FAC) flying over the area of operations in a light, propeller-driven aircraft. Before 1967, the Cessna 0–1 Bird Dog, a single-engined, two-seater machine with virtually unrestricted all-round vision, was used. But, when the enemy proved capable of downing such aircraft, aiming for the single engine, the twin-engined OV-10 Bronco was preferred. Flying such aircraft was a dangerous job because the Forward Air Controller had to dive down low, often into the teeth of Communist fire, to locate the source of the trouble. Having pinpointed the spot, he would then call in flights of fighter-bombers such as A-1 Skyraiders or A-4 Skyhawks, available in a "cab-rank" system over Vietnam. The Forward Air Controller would mark the enemy position with white phosphorus rockets and guide the fighter-bombers in, liaising all the time with the forces on the ground. As a result of this procedure, napalm, rockets, and bombs could be delivered with great accuracy.

If the firefight began at night, the radio operator could call in an AC-47 gunship, known by the call-sign "Spooky" but nicknamed "Puff the Magic Dragon." Packed with miniguns, up to 24,000 rounds of ammunition, and parachute flares, these reconditioned C-47s (replaced later by AC-119s and AC-130s) could lay down a devastating weight of fire.

An FAC (OPPOSITE PAGE) scans the ground. Observation was made from light aircraft, such as the OV-10 Bronco (BELOW LEFT), before fighter-bombers, such as the A-1 Skyraider (BELOW), were called in.

Maintaining the logistic flow

The American army committed to Vietnam in the 1960s was one of the most sophisticated ever seen, requiring an enormous logistic "tail" to maintain its front-line effectiveness. By 1968, it was estimated that more than 75 percent of the troops in South Vietnam were tied down in the construction or maintenance of base facilities essential to the logistic flow, while the system of supply was so complex that it had to be controlled by primitive large computers.

One of the major difficulties was the fact that everything the Americans needed—from bullets to bootlaces, rations to spare parts—had to come from the United States, a distance of 10,000 miles. Air supply could satisfy some of the needs, but with over 200 million tons of dry cargo and 14 million tons of petroleum being delivered between 1965 and 1968 alone, the only effective answer was to use merchant ships.

This, in turn, caused further problems, as South Vietnamese ports were not geared to accepting such enormous amounts of material. Saigon or Cam Ranh Bay (BELOW), for example, virtually had to be rebuilt to accept the ships, and special supply depots, often covering thousands of square acres, had to be constructed. By 1968, the Americans had spent billions of dollars on new construction projects, deploying 57 construction units and 51,000 civilian contractors to South Vietnam.

The problems did not end there. Once in-country, the supplies had to be sorted and distributed. The bulk of movement was done by truck convoys using the roads. As they were susceptible to ambush, route security became a top priority.

ordered to move up in direct support and the 4/31st was requested to advance quickly toward the sounds of battle. Neither force made much headway, hacking through jungle growth that blunted their machetes. DeSaussure committed the 2/27th Infantry, directing the men to advance from the east. But they, too, fell into a VC ambush, losing an entire platoon and their commanding officer to mine blasts and automatic-weapon fire. The ambush was developing into a battle the Americans were close to losing.

Meanwhile, Meloy's men were suffering, not just from enemy fire, but also from dehydration in the searing heat. As the day wore on and relief efforts stalled, the VC came out in the open, mounting human-wave attacks that were only fought off by the 1/27th with the aid of accurate artillery support.

As one of Meloy's sergeants recalled: "I heard them let out a whole bunch of whooping and hollering and screaming, and then there was about 100 of them coming at us through the undergrowth . . . so close together, they could have held hands with the men on either side of them as they charged us." This action enabled the lead company of the 4/31st to get to within 500 feet of Meloy's position, but it, too, was halted by a VC ambush. Once again, the battered Americans were saved only by the onset of night.

By dawn on November 5, Attleboro had been taken out of DeSaussure's hands (he was, in fact, transferred to another command on November 14, when it was widely felt that the 196th had "cracked" under the pressure of its first combat) and DePuy took over. He moved in elements of his own division and then, as units of the 4th and 25th Divisions plus the 173d Airborne Brigade were added, the operation became a II Field Force responsi-

Lurps: gathering intelligence

Long Range Reconnaissance Patrols—LRRPs, invariably pronounced "Lurps"—were organized in response to the nature of the war in Vietnam. Confronted by an enemy adept at using terrain to mask movement, thereby leaving "friendly" forces blind to their intentions, it was only natural that the Americans should create a capability to monitor and disrupt deep within enemy-held territory. It was dangerous and exacting work, usually carried out by small, close-knit teams of five or six lightly equipped (but well-armed) volunteers, such as those (BELOW), operating beyond artillery support in difficult country. Their tasks—to gather information, mount ambushes, and take the occasional prisoner—were vital if the Communists were to be denied the initiative.

Many combat units in Vietnam formed their own Lurps, but it was the Special Forces who controlled the most effective ones, using their own expertise and that of indigenous tribesmen (who knew the ground) to produce a series of operations known collectively as the "Greek-Letter Projects." They began in May, 1964, with Project Delta, in which units were used throughout South Vietnam to gather intelligence and, as "Roadrunners," to monitor NVA or VC infiltration routes.

In August, 1966, Project Omega was set up at Ban Me Thuot to cover the border in IICTZ; Project Sigma had similar aims in IIICTZ. However, all were consolidated under MACV-SOG (Studies and Observation Group) control in November, 1967. At a more shadowy level was Project Gamma, involving intelligence operations over the border into Cambodia. Long-range reconnaissance continued to be used until the U.S. Special Forces were withdrawn in 1973. Left on their own, the ARVN never achieved this role with the same success.

bility. By then, over 22,000 U.S. and Allied troops had been committed, making it the largest operation so far in the war. The VC 9th Division prudently fell back once more to Cambodia.

Attleboro continued officially until November 24. Its success was difficult to gauge. In physical terms, the VC 9th Division had been given another bloody nose—1,106 VC dead were found on the battlefield and, since September 14, enormous quantities of supplies had been seized. Conversely, the Americans had lost 155 killed and 494 wounded, and one of their formations had been judged not

to have made the grade. On balance, however, the fact that the VC had been flushed out and hit hard suggested that Attleboro, following on from El Paso, contained within it the seeds of an effective response to area warfare. If the Americans could concentrate their forces on known VC base areas, forcing the enemy to fight, a combination of numbers, mobility, and firepower might inflict such attritional damage that the Communists would be deterred from continuing their offensive operations. It was a line of thought that was to be developed further in 1967.

THE WAR YEARS

Sept. 1, 1966	French President de Gaulle condemns U.S. policies in Southeast Asia and calls for withdrawal of U.S. forces from the area.
Sept. 11	Elections to a Constituent Assembly held in South Vietnam; 81 percent of registered voters take part.
Sept. 14	Operation Attleboro (Phase One) begins in War Zone C, IIICTZ.
Sept. 22	Battle of Nui Cay Tre ("Mutter's Ridge") begins in ICTZ (continues until October 4).
Sept. 23	MACV announces that defoliants are being used to destroy jungle cover in Vietnam.
Oct. 24/25, 1966	Manila Conference of Allied leaders (U.S., Australia, New Zealand, South Korea, South Vietnam, Thailand, the Philippines) pledge to continue support until North Vietnam ceases infiltration of the South.
Oct. 25	U.S. Navy shells the coast of North Vietnam after being fired on by coastal guns.
Oct. 26	President Johnson visits troops in South Vietnam.
Nov. 3/5, 1966	Operation Attleboro (Phase Two): 196th Infantry Brigade fights for LZ to west of Don Dien rubber plantation, IIICTZ.
Nov. 12	A *New York Times* report estimates that 40 percent of U.S. aid to South Vietnam is not reaching its destination because of corruption.
Nov. 17	Secretary of Defense McNamara sends secret report to President Johnson suggesting that U.S. troop reinforcements have not led to increased Communist casualties: the report, however, is rejected.
Dec. 2, 1966	U.S. aircraft hit fuel-storage depots and air-defense sites close to Hanoi; eight aircraft lost.
Jan. 2, 1967	Operation Bolo: F-4Cs of the 8th TFW shoot down seven MiG-21s over Hanoi.
Jan. 8/26	Operation Cedar Falls: U.S. and ARVN troops attack the Iron Triangle, north of Saigon.

OPERATION BOLO

January 2, 1967

THE VERY FIRST U.S. AIRSTRIKE against North Vietnam under the codename Rolling Thunder, carried out on March 2, 1965, was not a complete success. Forty F-100 Super Sabres from Da Nang, 40 F-105 Thunderchiefs from bases in Thailand, and 20 B-57 bombers from Tan Son Nhut (outside Saigon) converged on an ammunition store at Xom Bang, 35 miles north of the DMZ. It was chaotic. The intricate timing of the raid soon collapsed as aircraft came in from all directions and, although the target was hit by 120 tons of bombs, six aircraft were lost, making the costs seem far greater than the gains.

President Johnson authorized the bombing with three basic aims in mind. First, it was designed to impede North Vietnamese infiltration of the South, principally by hitting roads, rail links, and supply dumps north of the DMZ close to entry points on the Ho Chi Minh Trail. Second, it was hoped that a display of U.S. airpower would boost the sagging morale of the South Vietnamese and, third, that such a display would also persuade the politburo in Hanoi to stop supporting aggression in the South for fear of irreparable economic damage.

None of this was simple. A release of airpower over North Vietnam—a country actively supported by the Soviet Union and China—carried with it an inherent danger of escalation, possibly to a superpower confrontation. As a result, Rolling Thunder was subject to a wide range of political restrictions.

Throughout the campaign (which went on until November 1, 1968), targets were chosen, not by commanders on the spot, but by civilian politicians—invariably the President himself—who, although advised by the Joint Chiefs of Staff, understood little of the practical problems involved. In addition, for much of the time, certain areas of North Vietnam, such as the population centers of Hanoi and Haiphong as well as a buffer zone close to the Chinese border, were declared off limits.

> "A relatively underdeveloped Asian country with a surplus of men can stand an awful lot of bombing without saying 'uncle'."

PAUL WARNKE, ASSISTANT SECRETARY OF DEFENSE, FEBRUARY, 1968

This caused friction in the American command chain. Military commanders fought constantly for operational control, arguing that they, as the experts, should be able to choose the targets to be hit and the amount of force needed to do so effectively. They were opposed, not just by the President, but also by civilian analysts in the Defense Department, who were apprehensive that unrestricted bombing would cause escalation.

For that would destroy their own preference for a "stick and carrot" approach to the North, using the threat of increased force as an incentive to the politburo to begin negotiations for peace. As the two sides in the argument vied for control, the campaign progressed in fits and starts, allowing the North to absorb a series of jabs instead of a killer blow.

On a more practical level, Rolling Thunder was not easy to put into effect in its initial stages. Since the early 1950s, the United States Air Force (USAF) had concentrated on nuclear warfare and close air support: by 1965, many of the techniques of conventional strategic bombing had been neglected, and suitable aircraft were not available.

If the military "hawks" had prevailed, the B-52 Stratofortress bombers would have been used over the North, but their destructive power and symbolism—guaranteed to provoke both domestic and international condemnation—led Johnson to order them to be confined to hitting tactical targets around the DMZ.

Instead, the commanders of Rolling Thunder had to make do with what were effectively close-support aircraft, such as the F-100 and F-105, designed for a different role and already approaching obsolescence. The Navy was no better off, deploying F-8 Crusaders and A-4 Skyhawks that had similar limitations.

Because of these restrictions and practical problems, Rolling Thunder got off to a poor start. Despite a steady rise in sortie rates, culminating in September, 1965, when over 4,000 sorties were flown by the USAF from Thailand and South

F-4 Phantoms (BELOW and RIGHT) were used by the U.S. 8th Tactical Fighter Wing—the "Wolfpack"— for Operation Bolo on January 2, 1967. The Phantoms, with their superior firepower, downed seven North Vietnamese MiG-21s in an action that lasted less than 15 minutes.

The F-100 Super Sabre (BOTTOM) carried out numerous missions during Operation Rolling Thunder, the bombing campaign against the North which began in March, 1965, and ended in late 1968.

More than 643,000 tons of bombs were dropped during the operation, but the cost to the U.S. was a total of 922 aircraft.

Vietnam, and by the USN from carriers offshore, the strategic effects on the enemy were minimal.

Johnson kept a firm grip on the bombing, limiting it to targets just beyond the DMZ in March and permitting strikes farther north in April, but only if they were restricted to lines of communication associated with infiltration. Bridges such as the Dong Thoung and Thanh Hoa, well south of Hanoi, were hit, along with rail and road choke points, but the impact was weakened by a bombing halt in May. The aim was to give the North a chance to enter into negotiations: the Hanoi government ignored it.

Other problems were by now apparent. Heavy forests and jungle terrain, particularly around the DMZ, made target location difficult, and the annual northeast monsoon curtailed air oper-

Flying under radar control with a B-66 Destroyer aircraft, U.S. Air Force F-105 Thunderchiefs bomb a military target through low clouds over the southern panhandle of North Vietnam. The mission, which took place on July 13, 1966, was one of many conducted against the North during Operation Rolling Thunder.

ations over the North between October and March. At the same time, the North Vietnamese were proving adept at absorbing the attacks, camouflaging key targets, dispersing supply dumps, and switching from rail to road transportation. North Vietnamese defenses also increased in size and effectiveness during 1965. When Rolling Thunder began in March, the North had about 1,000 antiaircraft guns available; by the end of the year, the figure had risen to nearly 5,000.

Moreover, in April, 1965, U.S. air reconnaissance began to report the construction of sites for Soviet-built surface-

to-air missiles (SAMs) around Hanoi. Refused permission to hit these sites for fear of killing Soviet technicians, the U.S. airmen had to wait for the inevitable to happen: on July 24, an F-4 Phantom was shot down by an SA-2. In response to this, a special Iron Hand directive was issued in August, allowing SAM suppression, but only if the site could be seen to be operational. It was not until October 16 that this happened. By then, more than 50 such sites had been plotted.

A further threat emerged from the North Vietnamese Air Force (NVAF), which took to stationing its Soviet- or Chinese-built MiG fighters inside the sanctuary areas around Hanoi/Haiphong or along the Chinese border. By the end of 1965, some 50 U.S. aircraft had been lost over the North to this combination of guns, missiles, and fighters. None of the aims of Rolling Thunder had been

achieved, and what little momentum there was had been dissipated by Johnson's policy of imposing "pauses." The longest of these (37 days) occurred over Christmas and New Year 1965–66, but once again Hanoi refused to enter into negotiations.

Johnson reacted by gradually loosening some of the restrictions. Already, in December, 1965, he had allowed strikes against selected industrial targets closer to Hanoi. But, by spring, 1966, he was being offered a more tempting proposition: a concerted assault on petroleum, oil, and lubricant (POL) storage sites in

the North. According to a USAF report, some 97 percent of the North's POL supplies – essential now that transportation had been switched to the roads – were concentrated in just 13 sites around Hanoi and Haiphong. After much debate, Johnson gave the go-ahead and, on June 29, 1966, the POL campaign began.

Initial results were encouraging, with the Defense Department announcing the destruction of more than 50 percent of the chosen targets; but political disillusionment soon crept in. By September 4, when the POL campaign officially ended, the CIA was predicting strategic failure: far from being dependent on the storage sites, the North Vietnamese had dispersed enormous amounts of fuel in drums along the infiltration routes. As little as seven percent of the North's fuel had been destroyed and that could easily be replaced from Soviet tankers, immune to the bombing in Haiphong harbor.

Once again, the sortie rate peaked in September, just before the monsoon, when a total of 12,000 strikes took place. By now, despite the CIA POL report and Secretary of Defense McNamara's increasing disillusionment with Rolling Thunder, the Americans were beginning to claim a degree of success, listing the destruction of thousands of enemy trucks, hundreds of railcars, bridges, supply dumps, and storage facilities.

In addition, it was estimated that Hanoi had been forced to divert over 300,000 people to repair bomb damage, while U.S. commanders in the South were reporting a discernible reduction in "battalion-sized attacks" by the NVA, implying a fall in the levels of infiltration. Despite some domestic opposition to the bombing, the majority of the U.S. public could be persuaded that the bombing campaign was succeeding.

But this was illusory, not least in terms of the costs to the United States. Another CIA study in early 1967 showed that the financial cost of the air war had nearly tripled, from $460 million in 1965 to $1.2 billion in 1966: it now cost $9.60 to inflict a dollar's worth of damage on the North. More worryingly for the U.S., by the end of 1966, improved SAM defenses and more modern interceptor aircraft had increased U.S. aircraft losses over the North to a total of 455. Also, many of the pilots of the downed planes were now PoWs and potential hostages in future political negotiations.

Real concern was expressed over the NVAF fighters, particularly now that Soviet-built MiG-21s, equipped with air-to-air missiles, had appeared. To a certain

North Vietnamese air defenses

Any thought that the technology of American airpower would make attacks on North Vietnam easy was quickly dispelled. The country may have been seen as an unsophisticated "peasant society" by many Americans, but it was tightly organized and the North Vietnamese were able to get hold of a wide range of Soviet and Chinese air-defense weapons.

When the air war began in 1964–65, most of these were conventional 37mm or 57mm optically sighted weapons, capable of reaching a restricted altitude of about 18,000 feet. U.S. pilots could avoid them simply by flying high, although the need to approach precise targets at low altitude, often "straight and level," inevitably brought the aircraft into the killing zone. As they did so, they came within range of rifles and machine guns in the hands of local peasants, organized into a countrywide militia. It took only a single bullet in a vulnerable spot to be able to down a jet fighter-bomber.

As the campaign intensified, 85mm and 100mm radar-guided antiaircraft artillery (AAA) was added to the inventory, and this proved deadly. Highly mobile and difficult to spot from the air, such weapons had a range of up to 45,000 feet: by 1968, over 80 percent of U.S. air losses had been attributed to AAAs. In addition, in July, 1965, a number of Soviet-supplied surface-to-air missiles (SAMs) had been acquired and, although the kill ratio of the SA-2 or SA-3 was comparatively low, it made flying over the North that much more dangerous.

A North Vietnamese antiaircraft unit (BELOW) mans its gun near a bridge on the Ma River.

Air-defense weapons, such as this one, made bombing the North hazardous for U.S. pilots.

North Vietnamese air defenses ranged from the simple to the sophisticated. Peasant militia (ABOVE RIGHT) were organized countrywide to counter U.S. air attacks with rifles and machine guns. After July, 1965, American pilots also had to contend with Soviet-supplied surface-to-air missiles (SAMs) (RIGHT).

By late 1966, the U.S. Rolling Thunder bombing campaign was in full swing over North Vietnam. By then, however, enemy SAM missiles and NVAF fighter planes were beginning to take their toll of U.S. aircraft. Since North Vietnam's main airfields in the Hanoi–Haiphong area were forbidden targets for American airstrikes, the increasing threat posed by the NVAF MiG-21s could only be met in the air.

In December, 1966, at a meeting at the U.S. Seventh Air Force Headquarters in Saigon, a plan codenamed Operation Bolo was devised to draw North Vietnamese fighter aircraft into battle.

The plan was for a force of F-4C Phantoms from the 8th Tactical Fighter Wing to fly over North Vietnam posing as bomb-laden F-105 Thunderchiefs. NVAF MiGs would be lured into intercepting the "Thuds," only to find themselves amid a superior force of Phantoms.

Operation Bolo was launched on January 2, 1967, after a short delay due to bad weather. The first of the "Wolfpack's" three flights of four aircraft, headed by the charismatic Colonel Robin Olds, entered the Phuc Yen airfield target area near Hanoi at 1500 hours.

The enemy MiGs, true to plan, were lured into combat, their silver fuselages glinting in the sunlight as they rose above the cloud layer.

As the dogfight developed into a melee of Phantoms and MiGs, Colonel Olds skillfully maneuvered his F-4C(1) in a vector roll, enabling him to fire his AIM-9 Sidewinder missiles at a MiG (2) streaking in front of him. The MiG was destroyed and fell, Olds recalled, "twisting, corkscrewing, tumbling lazily toward the top of the clouds."

During the frenetic encounter, SA-2 missiles (4) rose through the clouds, some exploding (3) before reaching their intended targets, creating an added danger to both sets of aircraft.

With their fuel running out, the F-4Cs of the first two flights disengaged, allowing the third flight under Captain John B. Stone to enter the fray. Three more MiGs were downed, bringing the total to seven, against no American losses. Operation Bolo had been a resounding success.

extent, the SAM threat could be contained using electronic countermeasures (ECM) against the missile radars, as well as special "Wild Weasel" suppression aircraft, but the MiGs were a growing menace. During the last four months of 1966, the number of interceptions had risen dramatically, forcing the Americans to pull their F-4s out of the Rolling Thunder strike package to conduct combat air patrols. Ironically, it was out of this that one of the few successes of Rolling Thunder emerged, early in 1967. It resulted from Operation Bolo.

U.S. air commanders in Vietnam had called repeatedly for permission to hit the

MiG bases around Hanoi – at Phuc Yen, Kep, Gia Lam, Kien An, and Cat Bi. President Johnson, however, refused to give his consent. This meant that the only way to counter the threat was to lure the MiGs into an air battle on American terms. In December, 1966, Colonel Robin Olds, the charismatic commander of the 8th Tactical Fighter Wing (TFW)—the "Wolfpack"—stationed at Ubon Royal Thai Air Base, was called to the headquarters of the U.S. Seventh Air Force in Saigon to discuss the problem. The outcome was Bolo, an offensive fighter sweep over the MiG bases that would lure the enemy out.

To achieve surprise, the F-4Cs of the Wolfpack would be disguised to appear on North Vietnamese radars as F-105s engaged in a normal strike mission. This meant they would have to use the same refuelling rendezvous points, fly at the same speed and altitude, use the same radio call-signs, and carry the same ECM jamming pods as the ordinary Thunderchiefs, keeping their true identity secret until the MiGs had been committed to the battle. Once that occurred, the F-4Cs were to use their superior avionics and radar- or heat-seeking missiles to engage the enemy, avoiding if at all possible close-in dogfighting in which the MiGs'

Rescuing the airmen

To U.S. airmen flying over Communist territory in Vietnam, the prospect of being shot down and captured was distinctly alarming. All aviators were equipped, therefore, with a special pocket radio that not only "bleeped" a homing signal, but also allowed a downed airman to talk to his colleagues still in the air. If he had landed safely and evaded capture, a rescue mission would be organized to snatch him out, even if he was deep inside North Vietnam.

Such a mission was an elaborate affair, often involving literally hundreds of men and dozens of aircraft, for it was not just a case of sending in a rescue helicopter. That helicopter had to reach the downed airman, and so needed in-flight refueling from KC-135 tankers; then, as it approached the rescue point, a "safe" zone had to be created, usually by aged, but airworthy,

A-1 Skyraiders—favored because of their ability to carry a variety of weapons— which would aim to prevent the enemy from closing in on the airman.

The Skyraiders, too, needed protection, so F-105 "Wild Weasel" SAM suppression and even F-4 combat air patrols would be provided. Even then, the rescue helicopter—usually an HH-3E Jolly Green Giant (ABOVE) or HH-53C Super Jolly— often had to provide its own suppressive minigun or machine-gun fire to keep the enemy at bay, while para-rescue specialists—Para-Jumpers (PJs)—descended to pick up the airman. Missions such as this could be expensive and highly dangerous, but the boost to the morale of the airmen flying over enemy territory, knowing that a rescue would be attempted in every possible circumstance, was essential.

Floating airbases

Aircraft belonging to the United States Navy (USN) were always involved in the air campaign against North Vietnam, from the Pierce Arrow retaliatory strikes of 1964, through Operation Rolling Thunder (1965–68), to the Linebacker raids of 1972. They flew from aircraft carriers stationed off the coast of Vietnam, following special "Route Packages" over the North to avoid interference with USAF missions from Thailand or the South. A-4 Skyhawks, A-7 Corsair IIs, A-6 Intruders, F-4 Phantoms, F-8 Crusaders, and A-3 Skywarriors flown by USN crews contributed significantly to the campaign.

Carriers had always been available as part of the U.S. Seventh Fleet in the Pacific, but it was not until early 1965 that two (later increased to five) were stationed on a rotational basis off the coast, specifically for operations in Vietnam. The carriers sailed independently, with destroyer escorts, until July, 1965, when they were deployed to an area of ocean, known as Yankee Station, some 87 miles off North Vietnam.

Each carrier, equipped with up to 70 attack aircraft, would normally carry out a five-month tour of duty, during which it would be on call for 12 hours before replenishing and refueling for a further 12. In this way, at least two carriers were constantly available, day or night. For a short time in 1965–66, a sixth carrier was stationed off the coast of South Vietnam, at Dixie Station, but this deployment ceased as soon as new airbases for USAF aircraft became available in the South. However, when President Nixon authorized renewed bombing of the North in 1972, seven carriers were available, all on Yankee Station.

U.S. Navy aircraft, such as the A-4 Skyhawk (RIGHT and ABOVE RIGHT) played a key role in the bombing of North Vietnam.

Nicknamed "The Scooter," the Skyhawk was an attack bomber which flew at a maximum speed of 675mph.

superior maneuverability could be brought to bear.

It took time for Bolo to be arranged, but by early January, 1967, Olds was ready. The MiGs were to be tempted into the air by "West Force," provided by the Wolfpack, which would fly over Phuc Yen as if on an F-105 mission. Meanwhile, F-4Cs of the 366th TFW would approach from the east ("East Force") to cover Kep and Cat Bi, cutting off the enemy from sanctuaries in China. The F-4 flights (of which there were to be 14, each consisting of four aircraft) were timed to appear in the battle area at five-minute intervals, giving the MiGs no respite.

Twenty-four F-105Fs would carry out Iron Hand SAM suppression, and the usual array of KC-135A refueling tankers, EB-66 ECM and RC-121 radar-warning aircraft would be on hand.

Bolo was delayed by poor weather on January 2, and, when Olds led his force out of Thailand, he was aware that the skies would be overcast above Hanoi. This meant that the MiGs would not be vulnerable as they took off or landed and could escape into the cloud as the fight developed. Nevertheless, surprise was achieved: as Olds led his flight over Phuc Yen at about 1500 hours, the North Vietnamese were slow to react. He had to make two sweeps before a radar contact was confirmed, although in the event this particular enemy aircraft did not venture out of the cloud cover. It was not until a third sweep was underway that the battle began. By this time, a second Wolfpack flight, led by Colonel Daniel "Chappie" James, had arrived on the scene.

The first Olds knew of the enemy was when James shouted a warning over the radio: "Olds, you have MiGs at your six o'clock!" Breaking left, Olds allowed his third and fourth flight crews to deal with the problem, while he pursued a second MiG that had popped out of the cloud at his 11 o'clock position, only to see it disappear back under cover, chased by two air-to-air missiles. By then, a third MiG had appeared at Olds's 10 o'clock position, about a mile and a half away. Engaging his afterburner for extra power, Olds pulled his Phantom's nose up and rolled right, aiming to "cut the circle" in a vector roll that would put him below and behind his quarry.

The ploy worked, and the MiG was caught by one of the F-4's AIM-9 Sidewinder heat-seeking missiles. As Olds recalled: "Suddenly, the MiG-21 erupted in a brilliant flash of orange flame. A complete wing separated and flew back in the airstream, together with a mass of smaller debris."

Meanwhile, Olds's 02, piloted by First Lieutenant Ralph Wetterhahn, had destroyed a second MiG; and 03, piloted by Captain Walter S. Radeker III, had dispatched a third. All this happened more or less simultaneously and coincided with James's flight being engaged. Although James failed to achieve a "kill," his wingman, Captain Everett T. Raspberry, Jr., downed a MiG with a Sidewinder. The sky was now filled with fast-moving jets, exploding MiGs, and—as an extra menace to both sides—SA-2s.

Olds and James, running short of fuel, now disengaged, leaving the battle to a third flight, commanded by Captain John B. Stone. Arriving over Phuc Yen at about 1510 hours, Stone's four Phantoms managed to shoot down a further three enemy aircraft before turning for home. In less than 15 minutes, seven MiG-21s—nearly half of North Vietnam's inventory of such aircraft—had been destroyed, with no American loss. It was a remarkable outcome, made more so by the fact that the remaining 11 flights of the Bolo force had not made it through the poor weather to Hanoi.

But victories such as this were rare, and, as the bombing continued in 1967, a solid body of opposition began to emerge in the U.S. American newspapers questioned the wisdom of their national

The "Thud" and "Fresco"

At the beginning of the air war over North Vietnam in 1965, both sides fielded aircraft that were, theoretically, obsolete. The U.S. Republic F-105, the biggest single-seat, single-engine combat aircraft ever built, had been designed initially in the early 1950s. Although it turned out to be an extremely useful machine, chiefly because of its large weapon-carrying capacity, it had to be constantly updated to survive. The Mikoyan/Gurevich MiG-17, designed in the Soviet Union before 1950, was even more aged, in particular lacking the speed to intercept enemy aircraft, except when it performed "power dives" out of the sun. Both aircraft were reinforced (although not replaced) by more modern designs as the war progressed.

Republic F-105D Thunderchief ("The Thud")

Weight	52,546lb	Max speed	1,480mph (Mach 2.25)
Armament	One 20mm M-61 gun in the left side of the fuselage; internal bomb load of 8,000lb plus wing pylons for another 6,000lb	Range	230 miles

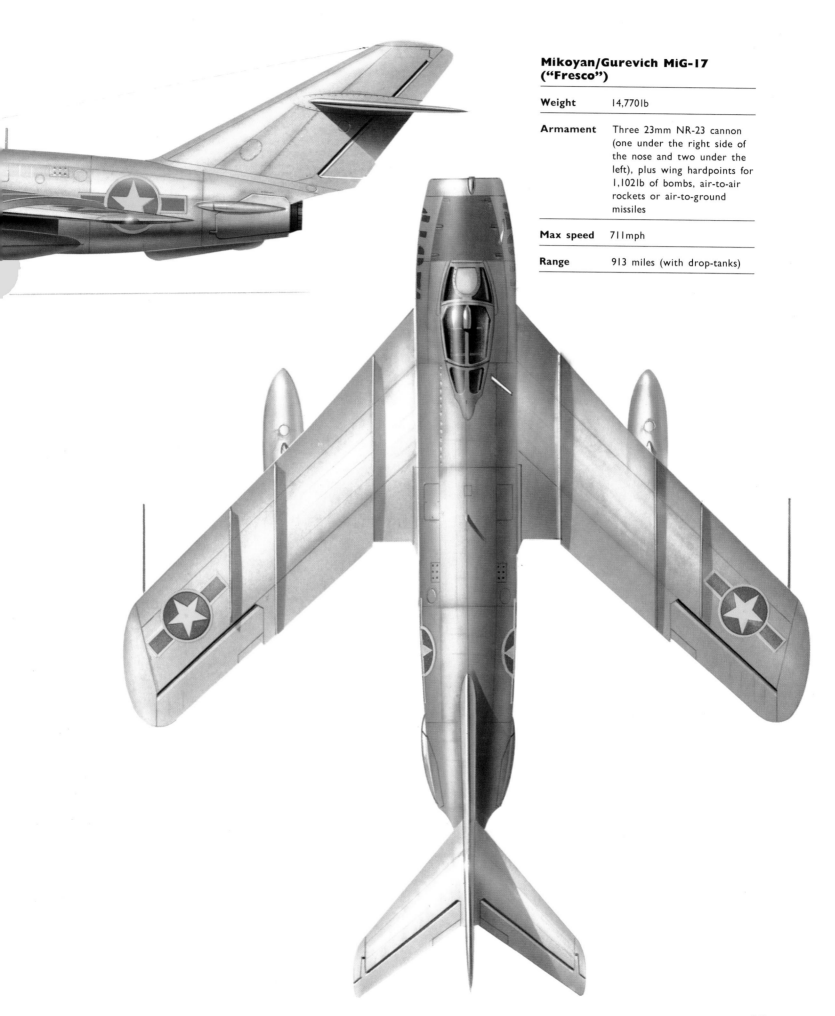

Mikoyan/Gurevich MiG-17 ("Fresco")

Weight	14,770lb
Armament	Three 23mm NR-23 cannon (one under the right side of the nose and two under the left), plus wing hardpoints for 1,102lb of bombs, air-to-air rockets or air-to-ground missiles
Max speed	711mph
Range	913 miles (with drop-tanks)

PoWs in the North

In February and March, 1973, following the Paris Peace Accords, 591 Americans (26 of them civilians) were released by the Communist authorities. All had been held as prisoners of war (PoWs), principally in North Vietnam, and the vast majority were USAF or USN airmen shot down during operations Rolling Thunder (1965–68) and Linebacker (1972). Some had been held in confinement under inhumane conditions for up to eight years: one of them, USN Lieutenant Everett Alvarez, had been shot down during a Pierce Arrow retaliatory strike on Hon Gai in August, 1964.

Any U.S. airman who ejected over the North faced immediate problems. In many cases, the process of ejection led to physical injury. This, coupled with the trauma of suddenly being shot out of the sky and the fact that, as a pale-skinned American, he could not hide among the local people, made evasion extremely difficult. Although air rescue was possible and did occur, most airmen were quickly picked up by the Communist authorities—in many instances not before being beaten by irate civilians.

The usual procedure was for the captive airman to be paraded before the people (and the propaganda cameras) as a "capitalist hired gun" or "imperialist air pirate" before being transferred to the old French colonial prison of Hoa Lo in the center of Hanoi. Here he would be stripped, searched, and—usually after a period of solitary confinement to increase disorientation—interrogated in "New Guy Village," part of the Hoa Lo compound reserved for new arrivals. At this stage, he would be aware that he was in the "Hanoi Hilton" and that escape was impossible. He would be allowed no contact with fellow prisoners.

This isolation would continue in other compounds—nicknamed "Las Vegas" and "Heartbreak Hotel"—where he would be subjected to more questioning and, more often than not, brutal torture. The latter was in violation of the Geneva Conventions governing the treatment of PoWs, but the Communists' view was that because war had not been officially declared, the Americans were acting illegally and so deserved no protection.

There was even talk of war-crimes trials of U.S. airmen being held, although this idea was dropped after intense diplomatic pressure on Hanoi. Under torture—which included tying the prisoners so tightly that joints were dislocated and breathing was restricted—many Americans wrote "confessions," couched in such ridiculous language that no one took them seriously outside the Communist bloc. One PoW, brought before the press in Hanoi, even winked the word "torture" in Morse code to alert the U.S. government.

The personal effects (RIGHT) brought home from North Vietnam by an American PoW include locally produced cigarettes, matches, and toothpaste.

Lieutenant Colonel James Lindberg-Hughes, shot down over the North in 1967, is marched into custody in Hanoi by his captors.

Such bravery was indicative of the resolve of the majority of the PoWs, who maintained their dignity and discipline throughout their ordeal. Contact between them was established by means of a simple code, transmitted by tapping pipes, winking, or coughing; and, after the unsuccessful U.S. Son Tay raid in November, 1970, most of the men were brought together in the Hanoi Hilton from outlying compounds such as the "Briarpatch" (35 miles northwest of Hanoi) and the "Zoo" (in Cu Loc). A more communal life was then possible. The prisoners were eventually returned by the Hanoi government to the United States in early 1973—an event that was highly emotional for both the men and their long-suffering friends and families.

leaders in undertaking a sustained bombing offensive, especially when it appeared that, regardless of Johnson's imposed restrictions, about 1,000 North Vietnamese civilians were being killed every week. The President reacted initially with another bombing halt in February, but with no response from Hanoi, he allowed the bombers to go for targets closer to the population centers.

In March, the huge Thai Nguyen industrial complex, only 35 miles north of Hanoi, was hit, and two months later electrical power plants actually inside the city were targeted. All the time, U.S. losses mounted—by August, 1967, 649 aircraft had been destroyed over the North—which fueled domestic criticism. When McNamara resigned as Secretary of Defense in November, convinced that Rolling Thunder had failed to achieve any of its objectives, Johnson was left with little support.

His isolation became even more obvious at the time of the Tet Offensive in early 1968, for the size of the NVA/VC attacks throughout South Vietnam destroyed the credibility of Johnson's claims that infiltration had been curtailed. On March 31, the President drew back the bombers to below the 20th parallel and announced that he would not stand for reelection. Three days later, Hanoi responded by announcing a willingness to engage in peace talks in Paris. When the details had been worked out, Johnson halted all bombing north of the DMZ on November 1, 1968.

Rolling Thunder was over. Enormous damage had been inflicted on North Vietnam: over 643,000 tons of bombs were dropped, causing an estimated $600 million worth of damage. But it was not integrated with the land campaign and did not halt NVA infiltration or force a negotiated settlement. Also, it cost the Americans a staggering total of 922 aircraft.

The Son Tay Raid

At 0218 hours on November 21, 1970, an American HH-3 helicopter, carrying 14 heavily armed Special Forces soldiers, crashed into the compound at Son Tay prison camp, about 30 miles west of Hanoi. As Major Richard J. Meadows used a loudspeaker to announce "We're Americans. Keep your heads down," his colleagues rushed to open up the cellblocks and front gate. Guard towers were taken out and, three minutes later, a hole was blown in the south wall as U.S. reinforcements rushed in.

The attack had its origins in May, 1970, when U.S. air reconnaissance first identified Son Tay. Immediately, the idea of a rescue mission was put to the Joint Chiefs of Staff, who passed it on to Brigadier General Donald Blackburn's Office of the Special Assistant for Counter-Insurgency and Special Activities (SACSA). Blackburn turned to Colonel Arthur "Bull" Simons, who recruited a force of about 50 Special Forces experts and put them through an intense period of training at Elgin Air Force Base, Florida. On November 18, President Nixon gave his approval for the raid, and, two days later, Simons's force left Udorn in Thailand to fly by helicopter across Laos toward Son Tay. Unfortunately, despite the skill of the rescuers, no PoWs were found: unknown to the Americans, they had been moved out four months earlier.

The layout of the Son Tay prison camp is shown in this aerial view. The U.S. raid on the camp on November 21, 1970, to liberate American PoWs was well executed but fruitless: the PoWs had previously been moved to another location.

THE WAR YEARS

Feb. 22, 1967	Operation Junction City begins: over 25,000 U.S. and ARVN troops invade War Zone C, north of Saigon (ends May 14).
March 10/ 11, 1967	U.S. planes bomb the Thai Nguyen industrial complex, north of Hanoi—the first major raid on an industrial target in the North.
March 20/21	Conference of U.S. and South Vietnamese leaders at Guam to discuss the war.
April 2, 1967	Local village elections held throughout South Vietnam.
April 7	Secretary of Defense McNamara announces the intention to construct a fortified barrier along part of the DMZ to monitor and stop infiltration by the NVA.
April 15	Massive antiwar demonstrations in New York and San Francisco.
May 2/10, 1967	An "International Tribunal," created by antiwar activists in Stockholm, accuses the U.S. of war crimes in Vietnam.
May 18	U.S. Marines and ARVN troops invade the southeastern sector of the DMZ "purely as a defensive measure."
May 19	Secretary of Defense McNamara sends President Johnson a memorandum in which he recommends a cutback in the bombing of the North.
June 30, 1967	Nguyen Van Thieu is put forward as the Armed Forces Council presidential candidate in the forthcoming elections in South Vietnam, with Nguyen Cao Ky as his running mate.
July 2/14, 1967	U.S. Marines encounter the NVA 90th Regiment at Con Thien, close to the DMZ: 159 U.S. and 1,301 NVA are killed.
July 7/12	Secretary of Defense McNamara visits Saigon; agrees to a 55,000-man troop increase in Vietnam.
July 29	Fire sweeps the U.S. carrier *Forrestal* off the Vietnam coast: 134 crewmen and 21 aircraft lost.
Aug. 11/14, 1967	Bombing of North Vietnam stepped up, with U.S. attacks close to Hanoi and Haiphong.

OPERATION JUNCTION CITY

February 22–May 14, 1967

As EARLY AS NOVEMBER, 1966, Lieutenant General Jonathan O. Seaman, commander of II Field Force, was ordered by MACV to "think big" in terms of an offensive in IIICTZ in 1967. He latched onto the ambitious idea of projecting U.S. and ARVN forces into War Zone C, the VC-dominated area north of Saigon, close to the Cambodian border.

Planning for what would eventually be called Operation Junction City went ahead. At the same time, however, MACV intelligence presented a rather worrying picture—compiled through a correlation process known as "pattern activity analysis"—of VC strength in the so-called Iron Triangle, an area between Saigon and War Zone C. Seaman was quickly persuaded that this area would have to be cleared first and, in mid-December, the assault into War Zone C was postponed while a preliminary operation, codenamed Cedar Falls, hit the Iron Triangle.

Cedar Falls was a "hammer and anvil" operation, designed to clear an area of dense forest and wet, open rice lands, the southern portion of which was only 12 miles from the outskirts of Saigon. The U.S. 25th Division, fielding an organic and an attached brigade (the 196th), was to secure and search the western arm of the Triangle, from the Thanh Dien Forest, through the Ho Bo Woods to the Filhol Plantation. The U.S. 1st Division, meanwhile, fielding two organic brigades and the 173d Airborne Brigade, would hold the eastern arm, from the village of Ben Suc (which was to be air assaulted and destroyed) down to the confluence of the Saigon and Thi Tinh rivers.

With the 25th Division staying in place as the anvil, the 1st would then act as the hammer, sweeping west and south. The aim was to clear the Iron Triangle of all aspects of Communist support. This would entail seizing villages, forcibly removing the population, and destroying everything of value, from jungle cover

and crops to houses, tunnel complexes, and military installations. It was hoped that a by-product would be the destruction of the headquarters of the VC Military Region IV, responsible for co-ordinating operations around Saigon.

The operation began at 0800 hours on January 8, 1967, when 60 helicopters containing 420 men of Lieutenant Colonel Alexander M. Haig's 1/26th Infantry swooped down on Ben Suc, catching the 6,000 inhabitants totally unawares. Once the village had been secured, ARVN interrogators screened the population and ordered them to prepare for movement to special relocation camps close to Saigon. When this process was completed in mid-January, the village was razed to the ground and the ruins were blown up using a 10,000-pound charge of explosives. Only light contact was made with the VC.

A similar pattern emerged as the 11th Armored Cavalry Regiment "swung the hammer" through the Triangle from January 9. VC cadres evaded the Americans, using their superior knowledge of the terrain to avoid U.S. blocking forces. Although enormous tunnel complexes were uncovered (including one, on January 18, that was thought to have been the Military Region IV HQ), no large-scale firefights developed.

Cedar Falls was officially terminated on January 26, by which time the VC had lost 750 confirmed dead to U.S. casualties of 72 killed and 337 wounded. The preliminary operation was brought to an end chiefly because the forces involved were needed for Junction City—the assault on War Zone C. The lack of long-term impact was shown by the fact that renewed VC activity was monitored in the Triangle less than 48 hours later.

War Zone C was a relatively flat area of about 1,500 square miles, bounded on the west and north by Cambodia, on the east by Route 13, and on the south by a line running roughly from Tay Ninh City to Ben Cat. Bisected by two large rivers—

CHINA
NORTH VIETNAM
Hanoi
GULF OF TONKIN
LAOS
Vientiâne
Mekong River
DMZ
Hue
THAILAND
CAMBODIA
Mekong River
SOUTH VIETNAM
Phnom Penh
Operation Junction City
Saigon
Mekong Delta

"They are swarming all over my track. Dust me with canister."

ANONYMOUS U.S. ACAV COMMANDER, AP BAU BANG, MARCH 20, 1967

Shoulder sleeve insignia of the 173d Airborne Brigade. The unit made the only major combat parachute jump of the war during Operation Junction City in February, 1967.

Men of the 32d Artillery (LEFT) load a round into a 175mm howitzer at Tay Ninh during Junction City.

A U.S. "tunnel rat" is lowered into a VC tunnel complex by his colleagues in April, 1967.

Underground complexes, such as those found in War Zone C during Junction City, provided excellent hiding places and munition stores for VC forces.

the Vam Co Dong in the west and the Saigon in the east—it offered reasonably good going for armored or mechanized units, with plenty of clear areas for the construction of Fire Support Bases and landing zones. The area had been under VC influence for at least 20 years, and the aim of Junction City was to wrest that control away, convincing the Communists that one of their major sanctuaries inside South Vietnam was no longer safe. In the process, it was hoped that the Central Office for South Vietnam (COSVN)—the major Communist headquarters, responsible for coordinating operations throughout the South—would be located and destroyed.

Junction City was not unlike Cedar Falls in basic concept—War Zone C was to be secured and then searched in detail—but the sheer size of the area necessitated a more complex plan. As MACV intelligence, using information

gathered in the Iron Triangle, reckoned that the bulk of enemy forces, belonging to the 9th VC Division and 101st NVA Regiment, were in the western portion of the zone, Seaman directed his units there.

Preliminary operations, codenamed Gadsden and Tucson, were to position U.S. brigades on the western and eastern edges of the operational area. Then, in Phase One of Junction City, scheduled for February 22, 1967, these blocking troops would be extended across the north, close to the Cambodian border.

This would create an inverted horseshoe of U.S. units, covering the west, north, and east. Another brigade, backed by armor, would then attack into the open horseshoe from the south, trapping NVA/VC forces and allowing searches to take place. To guarantee that the area would be open to future U.S. operations, Special Forces/CIDG camps were to be built at Prek Klok and Katum, on Route 4

north of Tay Ninh City. Each would have an airstrip capable of taking C-130s laden with supplies or reinforcements.

This phase was to continue for almost a month, after which the bulk of II Field Force would shift its attention to the eastern part of the zone. There they would bridge the Saigon River west of An Loc and build a third Special Forces camp to open up access and sever the Communist link between War Zones C and D. More searches would then take place, and FSBs/LZs would be built both as bases for these operations and for future use. In the event, when Phase Two ended on April 15, U.S. commanders were so pleased with the results that a third phase, lasting until May 14, was added. It involved only a single brigade, which searched the area between Tay Ninh City and Suoi Da. It was a complex plan, eventually involving more than 25,000 U.S. and ARVN troops.

Tunnels and "tunnel rats"

The Communist guerrillas were avid tunnel builders. Faced with enemies who employed mobile forces and aircraft, they had gone underground for safety during the war against the French. By the time that U.S. combat units arrived in South Vietnam in 1965, large areas, notably to the north of Saigon, were riddled with hundreds of miles of underground passages leading to dormitories, hospitals, schools, and supply dumps. Entrances were carefully concealed, sometimes below the water level of a river or stream, and passages were booby-trapped or sealed off with hidden trapdoors to avoid penetration. Life inside the tunnels was never pleasant—the air was constantly stale, food rotted quickly in the humid atmosphere, and disease was rife—but they made excellent guerrilla hideouts and centers for revolutionary work.

U.S. forces were not aware of the tunnels at first. Indeed, when elements of the 25th Infantry Division arrived at Cu Chi in 1966, they constructed a base on top of one of the more elaborate complexes. However, it did not take long to discover the tunnels. At first, the response was to fill them with CS gas to flush the VC out, then to blow them up. But the intelligence value of materials inside the complexes soon persuaded U.S. commanders to send soldiers into them to recover bodies or documents and take on the VC face to face. These soldiers, known as "tunnel rats," needed a special kind of courage: to enter a dark, narrow, foul-smelling and claustrophobic passage, not knowing where the enemy was or what he would do, was something only a few men could even contemplate.

A "tunnel rat" (LEFT) is lowered into a well used by the VC.

A GI (BELOW) hands a detonator cord to a tunnel rat as he goes down to blow up a VC tunnel.

U.S. military intelligence

In any war, information about the enemy, his organization, capabilities, and intentions is of paramount importance, particularly if it can be collected, collated, and turned into usable military intelligence. Vietnam was no different: indeed, it could be argued that in a conflict where the enemy hides among the people and uses terrain as his cover, such intelligence is the key to eventual victory.

In Vietnam, the Americans certainly suffered no shortage of information, coming as it did from agents, defectors, prisoners of war, military patrols, captured documents, signal intercepts, aerial reconnaissance, sensors, and electronic devices. But this in itself created an enormous problem. By 1967–68, MACV's Assistant Chief of Staff for Intelligence in Saigon was literally being swamped with data. The Combined Intelli-

A U.S. trooper presses his M-16 rifle against the head of a peasant woman in order to extract information about local VC activities.

gence Center was receiving an average of three million pages of enemy documents a month, and the same sort of overload was being experienced by other components of the same command, such as the Combined Military Interrogation Center and the Combined Material Exploitation Center.

Just collating the material was a daunting task—in the event, less than ten percent of the documents were even translated—and the process of converting all this into intelligence of value to the "grunt on the ground" proved largely impossible. With the Combined Intelligence Center alone producing half a ton of reports a day, no one had the time to read them all or to extract the information he needed. It was an ironic case of technology and military efficiency in the field producing too much for the system to absorb.

U.S. engineers from the 65th Engineer Battalion clear jungle vegetation from around the river village of Phu Hoa Dong with a D-7 bulldozer during Operation Cedar Falls. The village was known by the Americans to be under the control of the VC.

Operation Junction City (Ap Bau Bang II)

N

Combat Outpost 3

(Not to scale)

VC diversionary attack

Fire
Support
Base 20

VC main attack

Route 13

Abandoned railroad

Ap Bau Bang

Jungle

Rubber plantation

Phase One of Operation Junction City ended successfully in the middle of March, 1967. Over 830 VC soldiers had been killed by U.S. units operating deep in War Zone C. This was a 1,500-square-mile area north of Saigon, contained by a U.S. blocking force forming an inverted horseshoe to the east, north, and west of the zone.

Phase Two began on March 18, with a shift of focus to the east of the zone. U.S. troops began to make their presence felt, building FSBs and taking measures to safeguard truck convoys on Route 13 against likely VC attacks.

At 1150 hours on March 19, Captain Raoul H. Alcala, commanding A Troop, 3d Squadron, 5th Cavalry, established Fire Support Base 20 about a mile north of the village of Bau Bang and just west of Route 13. Aware of the possibility of a VC attack, Alcala ordered his 129-man troop, equipped with six M-48 tanks, twenty M-113

ACAVs, and an assortment of trucks, to draw up into a defensive "wagon train" perimeter.

The battle of Ap Bau Bang II, as it later became known, was heralded at 2250 on the 19th by a VC probe to the northeast of the FSB. Then, at 0030 on March 20, all hell broke loose as the base was pounded by heavy mortar shells, rifle grenades, rockets, and recoilless-rifle fire.

Shortly after the barrage, black pyjama-clad VC (**1** and **4**) of the 273d Regiment came swarming out of the woods and rubber plantation southwest and, especially, southeast of Fire Support Base 20.

The ACAVs (**2**) and M-48s (**3**) directed their spotlights and heavy fire toward the enemy, and maneuvered backward and forward, churning up deep tracks.

Despite torching a couple of ACAVs and, later, swarming over others, the VC were unable to penetrate the outer perimeter line into the heart of the base (**5**).

Lieutenant Colonel Sidney S. Haszard, Alcala's squadron commander, responded to the situation

promptly, sending in reinforcements: 1st Platoon, B Troop, came in from the north and 3d Platoon, C Troop, from the south. Also, Alcala's own 2d Platoon returned from its ambush position north of the base. These units stormed into battle, filling in the gaps in the perimeter and bringing much-needed relief to Alcala's men. The VC attack, for the time being, had been stalled.

At 0500 hours, however, the VC renewed their attack. The Americans responded with blanket tank and ACAV fire, supported by artillery located at Lai Khe, south of Ap Bau Bang. Aircraft created even more havoc with a variety of napalm, cluster and 500-pound bombs. By dawn on the 20th, the VC assault had been broken. The Americans had lost only 3 men, with 63 wounded, against 227 enemy killed.

The 173d Airborne paradrop

Although American regular combat airborne units were deployed in Vietnam as early as 1965, there was only one occasion, except for Special Forces jumps, during the war when any of them used their parachutes to enter combat: on February 22, 1967, during the opening phase of Operation Junction City. On that day, 845 paratroops of Lieutenant Colonel Robert H. Sigholtz's 2/503d Infantry, 173d Airborne Brigade, with A Battery, 3/319th Artillery, in attendance, jumped out of 16 C-130s a couple of miles from Katum, deep in War Zone C. They were led by Brigadier General John R. Deane, Jr., the commander of the 173d Airborne Brigade, and their task was to seize the drop zone (DZ) before moving out to link up with other units, which were arriving elsewhere by helicopter.

As an operation of war, it ran smoothly. The paras boarded their aircraft at Bien Hoa, arriving over the DZ at 0900 hours. General Deane jumped first, followed by the rest of the force. By 0920 hours, command posts had been established on the ground and, five minutes later, heavy equipment began to arrive. There were only 11 minor injuries, all caused by the jump itself, and no contact with the enemy.

In its aftermath, some people criticized the jump as a publicity stunt and, certainly, there was no particular need to use paras for something that other elements of the same brigade achieved just as easily by helicopter. But paras are elite, specially trained troops, whose existence is often attacked as being wasteful of resources: by showing that the paras still had a role to play, even in a high-technology war, the paradrop was a boost to the 173d's morale.

Agent Orange

As early as November, 1961, President Kennedy approved the use of American herbicides in Vietnam, principally for defoliation—the destruction of vegetation (particularly jungle cover) that was being used to hide VC activity. In January, 1962, USAF aircraft—normally C-123 Providers equipped with spray tanks—began Operation Ranch Hand from Tan Son Nhut. By 1971, when the operation ended, 18 million gallons of chemicals had been dropped, affecting 5.5 million acres of South Vietnam as well as undisclosed portions of the Ho Chi Minh Trail in Laos and Cambodia.

A variety of herbicides, developed as weedkillers in the United States, were used. The most notorious was Agent Orange (named for the color of the drums it came in), which contained a growth hormone. Dropped onto trees, it accelerated their development, forcing them to shed their leaves prematurely, thus exposing trails or VC bases beneath to aerial view. Ranch Hand missions, preceded by leaflet drops to warn local peasants, usually involved two C-123s flying side by side to cover an area 250 yards either side of the target area.

At first, the U.S. government believed that Agent Orange was relatively harmless to human or animal life, and teams even went from village to village eating bread dipped in the chemical to show that it was not dangerous. But, in 1969, the U.S. National Cancer Institute discovered that one of its ingredients, dioxin, could cause cancer and possible birth defects. The effects are still being felt in Vietnam and also among those U.S. servicemen who came into contact with the chemical.

Operations Gadsden and Tucson went ahead without a hitch. In the west, along the Cambodian border, the 3d Brigade, U.S. 4th Infantry Division, and 196th Infantry Brigade (both under the operational command of the 25th Division) set up LZs and FSBs before seizing the villages of Lo Go and Xom Giua, almost on the border. Some VC were engaged and tunnel complexes found, but there was no real fighting. Meanwhile, in the east, the 1st and 3d Brigades, U.S. 1st Division, penetrated a triangular area to the south of Minh Thanh. Again, only light opposition was encountered.

These successes allowed Phase One of Junction City to begin on schedule. The operation started in spectacular style, with nine infantry battalions (drawn from the 1st and 3d Brigades, 1st Division, and 173d Airborne Brigade) air assaulting into a series of preselected LZs across the northern arm of the horseshoe, linking forces in Lo Go to those in Minh Thanh. Eight of the assaults were by helicopter into LZs that proved to be undefended by VC; the ninth assault constituted the only major combat parachute landing of the Vietnam War.

At 0900 hours on February 22, a total of 845 men of the 2/503d Infantry and 3/319th Artillery jumped from 16 C-130s onto a dropping zone less than two miles from Katum. Sustaining only 11 minor injuries, all caused by the jump, the paratroopers quickly consolidated; by 1500 hours, mechanized infantry belonging to the 3d Brigade, 1st Division, had linked up, driving north along Route 4 from newly established artillery bases around Prek Klok. The Communists reacted with little more than sniper fire.

As soon as the assault battalions were in place across the north, the 2d Brigade, 25th Division, and 11th Armored Cavalry Regiment advanced into the open horseshoe. They, too, encountered few of the enemy, enabling Seaman to order a "thorough search" of the operational area, beginning on February 25. At the same time, the Special Forces camps at Prek Klok and Katum were carved out and the airstrips built. This proved enough to trigger a response, and U.S. forces were attacked around Prek Klok on two separate occasions.

On February 28, Company B, 1/16th Infantry, encountered a company of the NVA 2/101st Regiment about four miles south of the new base, but were saved from annihilation by air and artillery support. The NVA left 167 bodies on the battlefield, whereas U.S. casualties numbered 25 dead and 28 wounded.

Ten days later, Prek Klok itself came under attack from two battalions of the

U.S. aircraft
(ABOVE and BELOW
LEFT) spray
defoliant chemicals
on Vietnam's
jungle. The
devastating effect
of the herbicides
can be seen (LEFT)
on what was once a
mangrove forest.

VC 272d Regiment. Protected by elements of the U.S. 2/2d Infantry, 2/33d Artillery, and 168th Engineers, the base held out while, once again, airstrikes and artillery strikes rained down. On this occasion, the VC lost 197 confirmed dead to a relatively minor U.S. casualty list of 3 killed and 38 wounded.

To all intents and purposes, Phase One of Junction City had been a success, with the Americans imposing a strong presence on a hitherto secure Communist area. In addition, some highly significant discoveries were being made by the units involved. On February 28, for example, elements of the 173d Airborne, searching to the northeast of Katum, found what was believed to be the "public information office" of COSVN, packed full of propaganda leaflets and crucially important documents. COSVN itself was not flushed out, but the infrastructure around

R and R for the troops

Sometime during his 12-month tour in Vietnam, a U.S. serviceman could take a week's R and R (Rest and Recreation) outside the country. He could travel to a variety of destinations, ranging from Bangkok to Sydney, although most married men preferred Hawaii, where they could be joined more easily by their wives. Wherever they ended up, the aims were for them to escape from the pressures of the war zone, to recharge emotional batteries, and to go back refreshed to finish their tours. It did not always work—some men found that the sudden transition to a peaceful setting, then back to the horrors of war, was somewhat disturbing.

At other times during their tour, the servicemen could enjoy R and R in Vietnam itself, usually for two or three days. Some might go to Saigon—by 1967–68 a center for entertainment of every description—but most went to special camps on the coast. Places such as Vung Tau, Cam Ranh, and Da Nang were chosen for their beaches and idyllic settings, offering men the chance to surf, swim, sunbathe, eat, and drink in relative safety, although it did not take long for other "benefits"—notably drugs and prostitution—to appear.

Finally, both at the R and R camps and elsewhere, official entertainment was often provided. The standard varied. Some shows were highly professional—every Christmas between 1966 and 1970, for example, the Bob Hope Show traveled to Vietnam—whereas others were little more than second rate. But the aim was always the same: to take men's minds off the war, even if it was only for an hour or so, and in this respect they worked.

Entertainment for GIs could take the form of a Saigon bar, or a visit from a celebrity, such as Sammy Davis, Jr. (BELOW).

it was clearly taking a hammering.

Phase Two of Junction City began officially on March 18, although by then, elements of the 1st Brigade, 1st Division, had already moved east to open up the route from An Loc, protecting the engineers who spanned the Saigon River in an impressive four days. Construction of a Special Forces camp and airstrip began immediately and, as more U.S. forces moved over from the west, Route 246, connecting the bridge to Katum, was gradually cleared.

FSBs were set up along the road, but the operation could not exist in a vacuum. To make sure that construction convoys for the new bases could travel freely from Saigon to An Loc, then west to the Saigon River crossing, further FSBs needed to be established along Route 13, from Lai Khe (just north of Ben Cat) to Quan Loi (east of An Loc). It was in this area that the VC struck.

At 1150 hours on March 19, Captain Raoul H. Alcala, commanding A Troop, 3d Squadron, 5th Cavalry (part of the 1st Brigade, U.S. 9th Infantry Division, attached to the 1st Division), set up FSB 20 about 1,650 yards north of the village of Bau Bang, a few miles beyond Lai Khe on Route 13. He ordered his Troop—129 men equipped with six M-48 tanks, 20 M-113 ACAVs, and three 4.2in mortar carriers—to form a "wagon train" perimeter around the trucks and 105mm guns of B Battery, 7/9th Artillery, the proposed inhabitants of the FSB.

Aware that he was in VC country, Alcala detached his 2d Platoon under First Lieutenant Harlan E. Short and sent them in six of the ACAVs to occupy an ambush point about 400 yards to the north, along what appeared to be a well-used trail. This left the 1st Platoon under First Lieutenant Roger A. Festa to guard the western side of the perimeter and the 3d Platoon under Second Lieutenant Hiram M. Wolfe IV to protect the east.

The clearing seemed a natural place for an FSB. In relatively flat country, with Route 13 and an abandoned rail line skirting its eastern edge, there were woods to the north and west and a rubber plantation to the south. It had been fought over already by U.S. troops in November, 1965, so what followed on March 19/20, 1967 became known as Ap Bau Bang II.

The first signs of trouble occurred at 2250 hours on the 19th, when the VC moved across Route 13 behind a herd of belled cattle, then opened fire on the northeastern sector of the U.S. perimeter using a wheeled 50-cal machine gun. This

was dealt with by the tanks and ACAVs, using their turret-mounted searchlights for illumination. But it was obvious that this was just a prelude: at 0030 hours on March 20, the FSB was hit by a deluge of mortar, rifle-grenade, rocket, and recoilless-rifle fire, chiefly from the west. Lieutenant Festa's ACAV was hit,

The 173d Airborne Brigade, shown (ABOVE) in the Iron Triangle, between Saigon and War Zone C, took part in operations Cedar Falls and Junction City.

A captain (BELOW) from the 27th Infantry Regiment burns VC supplies and equipment in Tay Ninh province during Operation Junction City in March, 1967.

RACH BA RAI RIVER

September 15, 1967

B Y EARLY IN THE YEAR 1966, U.S. commanders in Vietnam were seriously concerned about the security of the Mekong Delta— 150,000 square miles of rich, alluvial soil to the south and west of Saigon, containing nearly half the population of South Vietnam. Except for Special Forces, U.S. combat troops had not been committed to the region in 1965; it had been left to the ARVN, with U.S. advisers and Special Forces attached, to control. This they were unable to do: according to MACV intelligence, by mid-1966, some 82,000 guerrillas and their supporters were controlling 24.6 percent of the Delta population and, with it, access to a significant proportion of the annual rice crop. U.S. main-force commitment seemed the only answer.

But the Delta was not an easy area to dominate. Bordered by the South China Sea to the south, the Gulf of Thailand to the west, and Cambodia to the north, it contained not only the Mekong River and its tributaries, but also a myriad waterways, canals, and streams. The population tended to hug the waterways, making offensive military operations difficult, while VC bases—in the Rung Sat Special Zone, Cam Son Secret Zone, Plain of Reeds, and U Minh Forest— were notoriously inaccessible. Although conventional forces could operate in the northern and eastern sectors, much of the Delta was waterlogged, and there were few dry-land bases for combat troops.

The American response was to exploit the very nature of the region by creating a joint Army-Navy riverine force, located on a floating base that could be moved easily from one trouble spot to another using the rivers. By March, 1966, General Westmoreland had accepted the idea; four months later, the recently activated U.S. 9th Infantry Division was earmarked for Delta deployment. As part of the division, Colonel William B. Fulton's 2d Brigade, made up of three infantry battalions and support units, was given the riverine task.

"Enemy access to Delta resources must be terminated without delay."

GENERAL WILLIAM C. WESTMORELAND, MAY 11, 1966

The plan was for the American force to be stationed aboard U.S. Navy barracks ships at a specially constructed base at Dong Tam (meaning, literally, "united in hearts and minds"), five miles west of My Tho on the Mekong. The U.S. force was to be carried into combat on river assault boats—armored landing craft (Armored Troop Carriers, or ATCs) backed by monitors equipped with 40mm or 20mm guns and 81mm mortars. The USN element was to be known as Task Force 117, and the whole outfit was to be called the Mobile Riverine Force (MRF). At full strength, it would be made up of more than 5,000 men.

The MRF began to come together in early 1967, when the 2d Brigade carried out "shakedown" operations in the Rung Sat Special Zone—a tangle of mangrove swamps to the west of Phuoc Tuy province, from which VC sappers had been mining the approaches to Saigon harbor. Little contact with the enemy was made, but, in April, the brigade moved to Dong Tam, conducting cordon and search operations in conjunction with the USN's first river assault division, which had 18 ATCs, two monitors and a Command and Control Boat (CCB). For the first time, a true riverine capability emerged.

Basic techniques were quickly worked out. On May 15, 1967, for example, the MRF entered the Cam Son Secret Zone between the Rach Ba Rai and Rach Tra Tan rivers west of Dong Tam in a "hammer and anvil" operation. Between 0815 and 0830 hours, the 3/47th Infantry and two companies of the 4/47th landed from ATCs to the south, while at noon the third company of the 4/47th helicoptered in to the north as a blocking force. Again, VC opposition was slight, but the speed and surprise of the assault, especially into an area which was hitherto regarded as a Communist sanctuary, was impressive.

This pattern of mobility, maneuver, and surprise became the hallmark of the MRF as it conducted a series of operations under the common codename

The crew of a U.S. monitor (ABOVE) takes time off to talk to local villagers in the Mekong Delta. Monitors played a key role in the Mobile Riverine Force, which began operating in early 1967 to counter the VC threat in the Delta region.

Men of the 9th Infantry Division, whose insignia is shown (LEFT), troop ashore in the Mekong Delta. The division's 2d Brigade arrived in Vietnam in 1967 and formed part of the Mobile Riverine Force.

Coronado between June, 1967, and March, 1968. All were conducted in provinces north of the Mekong, with the aim of clearing that region before progressing south. In the process, however, the Americans projected their forces quickly and effectively from the Rung Sat in the east to Cam Son in the west. On one particular occasion, the MRF moved its floating base 60 miles in just over 48 hours and was ready to conduct operations within 30 minutes of its arrival. The VC, used to virtually a free hand in the Delta, began to lose the initiative.

In early September, 1967, Colonel Bert A. David, who had taken over the 2d Brigade from Fulton on the latter's promotion, received reliable information that the VC 263d Battalion was concentrated in the Ban Long area close to Dong Tam. Moving two battalions in by helicopter, elements of the 3/60th Infantry clashed with Communist forces on September 12, losing 9 men killed and 33 wounded, but counting 134 enemy dead in the aftermath.

From information gathered in this engagement, the precise location of the VC battalion was pinpointed—a salient of land jutting westward on the Rach Ba Rai River, about six miles north of its confluence with the Mekong. On September 14, David pulled the 3/60th back to its floating base—the barracks ship USS *Colleton*—and prepared to mount a major assault.

His plan was to send the 3/60th in an ATC convoy past the salient to land to the north on White Beaches, while the 3/47th, in a similar convoy, went ashore to the south on Red Beaches. The two battalions would then close in as the 5/60th (a mechanized unit) moved overland from the east in M-113s to complete the cordon. Airstrikes and artillery strikes would inflict casualties on the trapped VC, after which the infantry would move in to mop up.

The men of the 3/60th, still tired from their recent action, boarded their assault boats early on September 15. Each of the three companies (A and B of the 3/60th, with Company C, 5/60th, attached) occupied three ATCs, protected by a monitor. The convoy was preceded by two empty ATCs acting as minesweepers. A medical aid boat and a CCB were interspersed in the convoy, and Lieutenant Colonel Mercer M. Doty, the commander of the 3/60th, flew overhead in a command helicopter. As the convoy, under the command of Lieutenant Commander F.E. "Dusty" Rhodes, Jr., USN, moved out into the Mekong at 0415 hours, navy

Patrolling the rivers

During the war in the Mekong Delta, the U.S. Navy provided a wide variety of boats, not just to the Mobile Riverine Force (MRF), but also to their own River Patrol Force (RPF), designated Task Force 116 ("Game Warden").

The MRF depended on converted LCM-6 landing craft, normally used to carry troops or equipment ashore in an amphibious landing. ATCs (Armored Troop Carriers) were merely LCMs with extra armor plate and armament added, although, as the campaign progressed, many had helicopter landing decks welded on. Monitors were more elaborate, entailing removal of the bow-loading ramp and the addition of 40mm or 20mm gun mountings and 81mm mortars as well as armor plate and machine-gun pintles. Deletion of the mortar and the addition of radios transformed a monitor into a CCB (Command and Control Boat). The only new MRF design was the Assault Support Patrol Boat (ASPB), equipped with guns, mortars, and machine guns, yet larger than an ordinary monitor.

For RPF duties, the Navy had to turn to the commercial market because of a shortage of procurement time, and in November, 1965, a contract was awarded to the United Boat Builders of Bellingham, Washington, to produce special PBRs (Patrol Boats, River). With glass-fiber hulls and water-jet propulsion, they were capable of 25 knots in most of the waterways of the Delta. On a less successful level, hovercraft—PACVs (Patrol Air Cushion Vehicles)—were tried, but they proved noisy and difficult to maintain.

A solitary U.S. monitor (ABOVE) patrols a tributary of the Mekong River in July, 1967. Protected by armor plate and equipped with 40mm or 20mm gun mountings, 81mm mortars, and machine guns, this formidable craft played a key role in the Mobile Riverine Force.

U.S. patrol boats (PBRs) (RIGHT) advance between the jungle-covered banks of a river channel. PBRs were fast, maneuverable vessels powered by water-jet propulsion. Although lightly armored, the PBRs' 50-caliber machine guns and 40mm grenade launchers gave them a useful offensive capability.

Hovercraft known as Patrol Air Cushion Vehicles (PACVs) (ABOVE) were included in the Americans' riverine force. These impressive-looking craft could reach speeds of up to 60 knots and were armed with 0.5in, 0.3in, and 40mm cannon. They could also traverse paddy fields and swamps which were too shallow for other riverine craft. However, they were not easy to maintain and made enough noise to signal their presence for miles around.

In June, 1967, the U.S. Mobile Riverine Force (MRF) began a series of operations, under the codename Coronado, to counter the VC threat in the Mekong Delta. In early September, a plan was hatched to trap the VC 263d Battalion on the Rach Ba Rai River near its confluence with the Mekong. Two U.S. units, the 3/60th and 3/47th Infantry, were to land by boat to the north and south, respectively, of the VC positions, while the 5/60th approached from the east. The VC, it was hoped, would be surrounded and destroyed.

At dawn on September 15, the first of two columns of ATCs and monitors, preceded by two minesweepers, carried the men of the 3/60th along the Rach Ba Rai River, bordered by mist-enshrouded jungle. About a mile behind, a second, similar column carried the 3/47th.

Suddenly, at 0730, when the force was about a mile past a bend known as Snoopy's Nose, both river banks erupted with VC rocket and smallarms fire which raked the two minesweepers (**1** and **2**). Soon the lead monitor (**3**) and the first troop-carrying ATCs (**4**) frantically began to maneuver and return fire with machine guns, grenade launchers, and M-16 rifles.

Only one ATC, containing Captain Wilbert Davis and a platoon of soldiers, made it through to the White Beaches area—the designated landing point. With both minesweepers out of action, the column was ordered to withdraw, and Davis had to return through the ambush zone—and was fortunate enough to survive.

The convoy regrouped at Red Beaches, the original landing point for the 3/47th, about a mile north of Snoopy's Nose. A new attack was launched at 1000 hours, preceded by airstrikes with helicopter support. VC fire was again heavy, but the Americans broke through, dropping off the 3/60th at White Beaches.

Meanwhile, south of the ambush zone, the 3/47th landed at Red Beaches, and the two battalions were ordered to advance.

The VC, however, pinned down both battalions for the rest of the day before melting away during the night of the 15th, leaving behind 79 bodies. This pattern of stubborn VC resistance eventually succumbing to superior U.S. firepower and mobility would be repeated until the end of the Coronado operations in early 1968.

Rach Ba Rai River
↑ Cai Lay 2 miles
N

0 ——— 1000m
0 ——— 1000yd

Rach Ba Rai River

Snoopy's Nose

Riverine Base Camp
(Dong Tam), 10 miles →

Mekong River

Paddy fields

crew members manned the guns while the soldiers slept.

At 0700 hours, shrouded in early morning mist, the convoy entered the Rach Ba Rai, and, 50 feet apart, the boats nosed their way north along a narrow channel with closely packed scrub jungle on both sides. They rounded a salient known to the Americans as Snoopy's Nose without incident and approached the area earmarked as Red Beaches on David's plan. Suddenly, at 0730 hours, an RPG2 antitank rocket, closely followed by a second, slammed into the starboard bow of the lead minesweeper. The convoy was caught completely unawares and, as a hail of automatic-weapon fire beat against the hulls of the ATCs, no one was quite sure what was happening. Cries of "I'm hit. I hit a mine," mingled with the crash of navy guns as the Americans reacted. More boats moved into the ambush zone, which was soon covered in a thick fog as the smoke of battle mixed with the morning mist.

The convoy rapidly lost both cohesion and forward momentum. Some boats slowed down, others speeded up; some careered across the channel as their coxswains were hit, others tried to weave through to more open water beyond. As they did so, VC fire—principally from camouflaged bunkers less than two feet from the waterline—was answered by the infantry in the ATCs, pouring round after round from M79 grenade launchers, M60 machine guns, and M-16 rifles into the jungle cover. To add to the noise, Doty called in artillery fire, although its effect was limited by the small nature of the targets, spread out along a 1,650-yard stretch of river bank.

Out of the maelstrom, a single ATC, containing Captain Wilbert Davis and a platoon of Company B, suddenly emerged to reach the White Beaches area. David reported, "I have one element ashore now, waiting for the rest," but there was nothing more available. With both minesweepers out of action and casualties mounting, Commander Rhodes ordered the convoy to turn back. Davis had to reembark his men under fire and return through the ambush zone: he was fortunate to survive.

As the convoy reassembled at Red Beaches, Rhodes called up replacement minesweepers from the 3/47th convoy and, at 1000 hours, went in again, preceded by airstrikes, and with attack helicopters in attendance. Once again, VC fire was heavy—both replacement minesweepers were hit and the ATCs raked from stem to stern—but the column made it through, depositing the 3/60th on White Beaches while the 3/47th came up to land on Red Beaches, south of the ambush zone.

Both battalions were ordered to close in, but it proved difficult to negotiate the scrub jungle. Even when the 3/60th finally broke out into more open ground, the VC kept them pinned down. As dusk approached, David ordered his troops into night defensive positions rather than risk a battle in the dark, but he need not have worried. When the Americans resumed their advance on September 16, the enemy had gone, leaving 79 bodies behind. By comparison, the MRF had lost 7 men killed and 133 wounded.

The Coronado operations continued until early 1968, when the MRF found itself involved in fighting for the Delta

---

"Market Time": stopping the supply line

The movement of Communist supplies from North Vietnam into the South was never an easy operation. Although supply movement was associated primarily with the Ho Chi Minh Trail, running from north of the DMZ through Laos and Cambodia to exit points in the Central Highlands and north of Saigon, the trail did not become fully operational until 1967–68 and was lengthy and dangerous. Before that time, the Communists had depended on the sea, transporting supplies through the South China Sea to any isolated bay between the DMZ and the Mekong Delta, and even going beyond to the port of Sihanoukville in Cambodia, and from there overland to the Vietnam border.

Such a route, covering 1,200 miles of coastline, was difficult to monitor, let alone block. Although some bulk supplies were carried by ship—on February 16, 1965, for example, a trawler was discovered (and destroyed) offloading crates of weapons and ammunition in Vung Ro Bay, between Qui Nhon and Tuy Hoa—the majority were moved in small packages by sampan or fishing junk. At any one time, up to 50,000 such vessels could be on the seas around South Vietnam, so any plan to stop the flow of supplies had to be elaborate.

Before 1965, responsibility for monitoring and searching offshore traffic was firmly in the hands of the South Vietnamese Navy. It was not very effective, for although its statistics were impressive—136,000 vessels and 390,000 people searched in 1963, 212,000 vessels and 880,000 people searched in 1964—it was just not preventing the movement of supplies. This was due partly to inadequate equipment and shortage of manpower, and partly to the enormity of the task, but there was also evidence that the South Vietnamese were more keen on exhorting bribes from innocent fishermen than in searching suspicious sampans.

As in so many other cases, the Americans felt they had to step in. On August 1, 1965, MACV was given responsibility, and a genuine effort to interrupt supply lines began under the naval designation Task Force 115 ("Market Time"). Surveillance bases were established at Vung Tau, Qui Nhon, Da Nang, An Thoi, and Nha Trang, and the entire coast, from the DMZ to the Gulf of Thailand, was divided into coastal patrol areas. Within each of these, a DER (Destroyer Escort Radar) monitored all ship movement, supported by surveillance aircraft from the Philippines (Lockheed P3A Orions) or South Vietnam (Lockheed P2V Neptunes or Martin P5M Marlins).

The DER could be used to stop and search larger vessels out at sea, but intercepting the smaller inshore sampans and junks was the responsibility of U.S. Coast Guard vessels or USN Swift boats, capable of operating in shallow waters. Once stopped, a sampan would be physically searched and the fishermen screened. Although the job was tedious and often dangerous, by the beginning of 1967, some success was being achieved. Indeed, the blockade of the coast was arguably one of the reasons behind a greater Communist dependence on the Ho Chi Minh Trail.

A fisherman is stopped and his papers are checked by a member of the South Vietnamese Navy in 1966.

towns during the Tet Offensive. Once that was over, American policy began to change to one of Vietnamization, preparing South Vietnamese forces to take over the conduct of the war. The MRF continued to conduct search operations—in August, 1968, it even moved far west in the Delta to penetrate the U Minh Forest—but contacts were rare and set-piece battles virtually unknown.

By early 1969, the USN, in conjunction with South Vietnamese forces, was conducting a more elaborate blocking strategy along the waterway, known as SEA LORDS (Southeast Asia Lake, Ocean, River, Delta Strategy), and the need for U.S. combat units was declining. In July, the 2d Brigade became the first major U.S. formation to leave Vietnam, having conducted a unique and generally effective riverine campaign for more than two years. In the process, the VC in the Delta were disrupted, their bases disturbed, and their supplies interdicted, but it was up to the South Vietnamese to exploit the situation. The Communists, for their part, could afford to wait.

Crewmen of a U.S. Navy river patrol search a sampan which is suspected of carrying a cache of VC supplies and equipment. The **search took place during an operation codenamed Slingshot in February, 1969.**

The M60 machine gun

The 7.62mm M60 Machine Gun—nicknamed "The Pig" by its handlers in Vietnam—was (and still is) a robust and reliable weapon. The M60 is gas-operated: as the first round travels down the chromium-plated barrel, it pushes gas into a special cylinder which forces a piston down the chamber to bring the next round into place. Although susceptible to getting dirty under combat conditions in Vietnam, leading to jamming or uncontrolled firing, the M60 could be carried easily into battle. Its sustained fire, either on its own in-built bipod or a special M122 tripod, was often crucial to the fortunes of American units.

Length	43.3in
Weight	23lb (with bipod); 39.6lb (with tripod)
Rate of fire	550rpm (cyclic); 200rpm (automatic)
Range	984yd (bipod); 1,968yd (tripod)

THE WAR YEARS

Jan. 21, 1968	An NVA rocket attack on the U.S. Marine base at Khe Sanh, close to the DMZ and Laotian border in ICTZ, initiates a siege that is to last for 77 days.
Jan. 30	The Tet Offensive begins: NVA/VC units attack cities, towns, and provincial centers throughout South Vietnam.
Feb. 10, 1968	After heavy fighting, most of the Communist units in the Tet Offensive are destroyed—but a battle still rages in Hue.
Feb. 24	Allied forces retake the Imperial Palace in Hue, seized by the NVA in the Tet Offensive.
March 16, 1968	The My Lai Massacre: men of the 1/20th Infantry kill more than 300 civilians.
March 25/26	Secretary of Defense Clifford reports to the President that, in his opinion, the Vietnam War is "a real loser."
March 31	In a TV speech, President Johnson announces an end to the bombing of North Vietnam beyond the 20th parallel and adds that he will not be seeking nomination for the forthcoming presidential elections.

KHE SANH

January 21–April 7, 1968

SINCE OPERATION STARLITE IN August, 1965, U.S. Marines in I Corps Tactical Zone (ICTZ), south of the DMZ, had gradually extended their control to cover some 1,600 square miles, chiefly along the coastal fringe. But it was not enough. If the northern area of South Vietnam, particularly Quang Tri bordering the DMZ, was to be secured, NVA infiltration toward Route 9 from Laos had to be blocked.

The key ground was around Khe Sanh, an area of mist-enshrouded, jungle-covered hills close to the Laotian border. It had been monitored as early as 1962, when U.S. Special Forces advisers began to form Civilian Irregular Defense Group companies (CIDGs) among the local Montagnard tribes. Four years later, in response to an NVA buildup, Marine units were deployed, supported by Army-manned 175mm guns in two firebases, known as Camp J.J. Carroll and the Rockpile, to the east. As the Marines moved in, they partially took over the Special Forces base to the northeast of Khe Sanh village, displacing the CIDGs to Lang Vei, farther west along Route 9.

Khe Sanh Combat Base, built on a low plateau around an airstrip, was quickly seen by both sides as a crucial position. To the NVA, the seizure of the base would not only be a major propaganda victory, but would also open up Route 9 to the coast. To the Marines, it was a rock in the path of Communist expansion, essential if U.S. gains so far were to be protected. It was also a top-secret launch site for vital Special Forces raiding parties across the border into Laos and North Vietnam. There was a feeling among the U.S. commanders, not always explicitly stated, that if the NVA could be drawn into a set-piece battle on ground of American choosing, they could be destroyed in a storm of artillery and aerial firepower.

If this were to work, however, the Marines had to occupy more than just the Khe Sanh plateau—they had to take hold of a series of hills to the west and north of

"This crushing defeat . . . cost the Communists untold casualties . . . and frustrated their dream of a second Dien Bien Phu."

GENERAL WILLIAM C. WESTMORELAND, MACV

---

the combat base. The most important of these were Hills 881 North, 881 South, and 861 (their names denote their height in meters), within sight of the plateau and overlooking the Rao Quan River, a likely NVA attack route from the northwest. If the NVA occupied these hills, they would be ideally placed to bombard Khe Sanh, thus making aerial reinforcement and supply impossible. Between April 28 and May 5, 1967, in a series of hard-fought engagements known as the "Hill Fights," two Marine battalions managed to wrest all three features from already encroaching Communist troops. Khe Sanh seemed safe.

Needing forces for operations elsewhere, the Americans scaled down their presence around the Khe Sanh area, abandoning 881 North and leaving only small, company-sized garrisons on 881 South and 861. Little enemy activity was reported during the rest of the year, although the Marines did take the opportunity to prepare their defenses. Bunkers and trenches were constructed, artillery positions improved, and the airstrip at Khe Sanh upgraded to take C-130 transports.

This was just as well, for, by early December, 1967, it was obvious that trouble was brewing. Special Forces and Marine reconnaissance patrols reported NVA troops crossing the Laotian border but not moving through toward the coast, implying that a buildup around Khe Sanh was taking place. In response, the base was reinforced—by January, 1968, all three battalions of Colonel David Lownds' 26th Marines were deployed to garrison Khe Sanh and the outlying hills—and patrolling activity was increased. Extra outposts were established on Hills 558 and 861A, to the east and northwest of 861, respectively, to block the Rao Quan valley, and the Marines prepared for action.

They did not have long to wait. On January 17, a patrol from Captain William Dabney's Company I, 3/26th Marines, responsible for the defense of 881 South,

Situated near the border with Laos, Khe Sanh Combat Base (BELOW) was built on a low plateau surrounded by hills. Clearly visible is the airstrip, which was crucial during the "siege" for the resupply of the Marines.

The bunker existence (BOTTOM) that the Marines had to endure at Khe Sanh was claustrophobic but afforded good protection against the enemy missiles that hit the base— at an average of 2,500 per week.

Wearing flak jackets and with their M-16 rifles close to hand, Marines (RIGHT) contemplate their predicament during a lull in the hill fighting.

Khe Sanh

Hill 881 North
Hill 950
Hill 861
Dong Tri Mountain
Hill 558
Hill 881 South
Hill 861 A
Rao Quan River
Khe Sanh Combat Base
Airstrip
Route 9
Special Forces Camp
Lang Vei
Khe Sanh

N

0   2km
0   1 mile

Situated near Route 9 just south of the DMZ, the U.S. combat base of Khe Sanh was well placed to block NVA troops and supplies infiltrating from Laos. In December, 1967, U.S. Marine patrols reported an increase in NVA activity around the base. A month later, Colonel David Lownds's 26th Marines, garrisoned at Khe Sanh and on the outlying hills of 881 South and 861, were braced for an all-out enemy assault.

At 0530 on January 21, 1968, with a dawn mist hugging the surrounding hills, the NVA began a massive bombardment of Khe Sanh. Rockets snaked their way up from the southern slopes of NVA-held Hill 881 North (1), lighting up the sky over Hill 861 (2).

One of the first NVA rockets launched hit the base's main ammunition dump, detonating 1,500 tons of bombs, bullets, and other explosives, and producing a great glowing ball of fire (3).

The spectacular and alarming attack on the base was witnessed by Captain William Dabney's Company I, 3/26th Marines, defending Hill 881 South (4). As the first NVA missiles hit their target, Dabney's men rushed to serve their weapons.

Despite the ferocity of their initial attack, the NVA did not gain tangible results from it. The "siege" that followed lasted a nerve-wracking 77 days, with the Marines officially relieved on April 8.

121

consolidated their gains, the siege of Khe Sanh began. It was to last a nerve-stretching 77 days.

In the early stages, the NVA seemed intent on isolating the combat base by capturing outlying American positions. On February 5, exploiting the fact that attention had been diverted away from Khe Sanh by the nationwide Tet Offensive, the Communists renewed their attacks, this time against Hill 861A.

At 0305 a mortar bombardment heralded wave after wave of NVA riflemen, who quickly gained a foothold on the northern edge of the American perimeter. The defenders—men of Captain Earle Breeding's Company E, 2/26th Marines—counterattacked through fog and fought hand-to-hand with the enemy for half an hour in what was described as "a bloody waterfront barroom brawl." According to Breeding, "Charlie didn't know how to cope with it . . . we walked all over them."

The NVA pulled back, only to try again at 0610. This time, they were caught in a hail of American support fire which included mortars, artillery, and even radar-guided airstrikes. Dabney's men on 881 South, for example, fired nearly 1,000 rounds of 81mm mortar ammunition onto the neighboring hill, causing the mortar tubes to glow in the mist-covered dawn. Marines lined up to urinate on the weapons to cool them down and keep them in action. By the end of the battle, Breeding had lost seven Marines killed but could count 109 NVA bodies on 861A.

One of the crucial differences between the U.S. Marines' position at Khe Sanh and that of the French at Dien Bien Phu was that the Americans held most of the high ground around their combat base (1). Two Marine battalions gained control of Hills 881 North (5), 881 South (4), and 861 (7) during the "Hill Fights" between April 28 and May 5, 1967. Hill 881 North was later abandoned, but the other two were occupied by company-sized garrisons.

In the early hours of January 21, 1968, an NVA bombardment from positions northwest of Khe Sanh heralded the start of the battle proper. The NVA forces opposing the Americans were made up of the 325thC Division (6) and the crack 304th Division (3) which had fought at Dien Bien Phu.

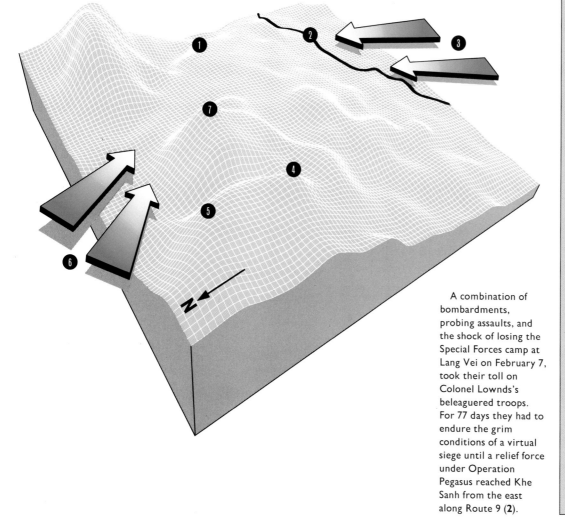

A combination of bombardments, probing assaults, and the shock of losing the Special Forces camp at Lang Vei on February 7, took their toll on Colonel Lownds's beleaguered troops. For 77 days they had to endure the grim conditions of a virtual siege until a relief force under Operation Pegasus reached Khe Sanh from the east along Route 9 (2).

A C-130 Hercules cargo aircraft (LEFT) airdrops supplies to Marines at Khe Sanh on April 8, 1968. In the foreground, members of Company B, 5/7th Cavalry, take over an outlying hill during the operation to relieve the base.

A CH-46D Sea Knight (ABOVE) heads for Khe Sanh on March 7, 1968, on a Super Gaggle mission.

A U.S. Air Force C-130 (BELOW) delivers cargo at Thien Ngon via the Low Altitude Parachute Extraction System.

Three days later, it was the turn of the combat base itself to come under attack, when elements of the 325thC NVA Division carried out a daylight assault on U.S. positions on the southwestern edge of the perimeter. A platoon of Company A, 1/9th Marines was surrounded and isolated on a low mound known as Hill 64, surviving only by virtue of heavy support fire from within the combat base. Reinforcements from the rest of Company A were rushed to the spot, arriving at 0900 to mount an immediate counterattack, which drove the NVA out.

As the Communists withdrew, they were caught in an artillery barrage, losing at least 150 men, but the Americans had not escaped lightly. With 21 Marines killed and 26 wounded, Hill 64 had proved costly; it was abandoned and the perimeter made tighter. Only 24 hours earlier, the NVA had overrun the Special Forces camp at Lang Vei, sending a shiver of apprehension through the defenders of Khe Sanh. The siege was beginning to bite.

But "siege" is perhaps a misnomer, for U.S. Forces never quite lost the ability to reinforce the base and always held the vital hill positions to west and north. In addition, patrols beyond the perimeter were conducted on a regular basis, reflecting the fact that for most of the 77 days the enemy was content to bombard Khe Sanh, firing 122mm rockets from the vicinity of 881 North, 82mm and 120mm mortars from positions in an arc about 2,200 to 3,300 yards north and west of the base, and long-range 130mm and 152mm artillery from concealed positions across the border in Laos. The results should have been devastating—an average of 2,500 rounds a week landed in an area little more than 1,750 yards long and 875 yards wide, with a record 1,307 rounds on February 23 alone—but the 6,680 Marine and ARVN defenders (plus an unspecified number of U.S. Special Forces) were relatively safe as long as they stayed in their bunkers or trenches.

Indeed, as the monsoon weather closed in, a routine emerged: defenses would be repaired and supplies distributed under cover of darkness and morning fog, with the Marines going underground as soon as the latter cleared in late morning, to re-emerge as daylight waned. It was far from an ideal lifestyle—the NVA bombardment was enough to affect anyone's nerves—but it was survivable.

This immediately calls into question the strategy behind the NVA attacks, for, with an estimated 20,000 men in the surrounding hills, the reluctance to

A U.S. Marine at the time of Khe Sanh. He wears a flak jacket and is holding an M-16 assault rifle and a smoke grenade. His equipment includes a water canteen, ammunition pouches, sturdy jungle boots, and a steel helmet onto which more personal items are strapped. On his back he wears a lightweight rucksack— although the Marines often preferred the smaller canvas combat field pack.

mount continuous direct assaults on the combat base seems strange. The Americans were certainly expecting such assaults, particularly after the events of February 5–8, but it was in their response that the key to their survival lay.

From the beginning of the siege, President Johnson displayed a keen interest in events at Khe Sanh—he had a model of the base constructed in the White House and would pore over it for hours, discussing the details with military advisers who had been made to promise that the position would not fall to the Communists. And, although there was some controversy about whether Khe Sanh was a diversion for the Tet Offensive, or vice versa, American resolve was never in doubt. Parallels with what Johnson insisted on calling "Din Bin Phoo" were easy to draw, and the President had no intention of suffering the military and political ramifications of defeat that the French had experienced in 1954. Perhaps without intending to do so, the Communists made Khe Sanh a symbol of America's determination "to hold the line in Southeast Asia."

Such determination was manifested in two ways, both of which were crucial to the survival of Khe Sanh. The first was the decision to keep the combat base supplied, almost regardless of cost. The garrison had been augmented in late January with the commitment of 1/9th Marines and the 37th ARVN Ranger Battalion, increasing the numbers of defenders (including those in the outlying hills) to more than 6,680.

Resupply in terms of ammunition, food, water, and fuel—to say nothing of the need to evacuate casualties and send in replacements—was the responsibility of USAF C-130 and C-123 transport aircraft, together with Marine CH-46, Army CH-53 and UH-1E helicopters. Their task was by no means easy, partly because of the monsoon weather (which remained appallingly bad for most of February, with constant rain and low clouds) and partly because of NVA fire, preset to land on the airstrip whenever aircraft were heard approaching. Under such conditions, pilots had to be prepared to land, unload their cargoes, and take off again in less than three minutes.

Casualties were inevitable and when, on February 10, a C-130 carrying fuel was caught in an NVA barrage and exploded on the airstrip, landings by such aircraft had to be suspended. Instead, the C-130 crews used parachute drops of supplies or new techniques of delivery at low altitude. C-123s and helicopters continued to

124

use the airstrip throughout the siege, but only the latter could be deployed to resupply the outposts. This proved to be particularly hazardous, requiring a turn-around time of only 19 seconds if NVA mortar fire was to be avoided. On Hill 881 South, for example, at least five helicopters were lost carrying out this essential duty.

As casualties mounted, new techniques evolved, the most impressive of which was the "Super Gaggle," in which helicopters approached Khe Sanh under the close protection of strike aircraft and gunships. First introduced on February 24, it proved remarkably effective.

The use of aircraft in this way is indicative of the second key factor in the siege: that the Americans could call on an enormous weight of aerial fire support to prevent an all-out NVA attack. As early as January 22, Johnson authorized an operation codenamed Niagara: its mission was "to destroy enemy forces in the (Khe Sanh) area, interdict enemy supply lines and base areas . . . and provide maximum tactical air support of friendly forces." Using Tactical Air Controllers, flying 0-1E Bird Dog light aircraft, wave after wave of USAF and Marine fighter-bombers could be called down onto NVA positions, firing rockets or dropping napalm and bombs to devastating effect in poor weather.

If the target could not be seen, ground-based radars (known as TPQs) in Khe Sanh could be used to guide the aircraft

The deadly use of napalm

Napalm is a deadly weapon whose name derives from naphthenic and palmitic acids, the salts of which are used in its manufacture. It is, in simplified terms, jellified gasoline. Designed initially as fuel for flame-throwers and then for bombs, it was used extensively in World War II and the Korean War, where it proved particularly effective against enemy trenches and concealed positions. To be caught in a napalm attack is a horrible way to die.

When U.S. aircraft were first deployed in Vietnam in the early 1960s, the main napalm bomb was the BLU-1 (Bomb Live Unit). By the early 1970s, this type had been superseded by the BLU-27, but the basic principles of operation remained the same. On each end of a 200-gallon napalm container was an igniter filled with white phosphorus, which burned as soon as it was exposed to the air. When the bomb hit the ground and broke up, spraying napalm over a wide area, fuses exploded the ignitors, exposing the white phosphorus, which, in turn, ignited the napalm. All this happened in a split second, so there was no escape for those in the immediate vicinity.

The searing burst of flame of a napalm attack became a familiar image of the Vietnam War and triggered protests in the United States about its use. The famous photograph (BELOW) of a young Vietnamese girl, badly burned in a napalm strike (by South Vietnamese aircraft), running naked and screaming toward the camera, continues to shock even today.

Marines take cover during a heavy enemy bombardment of Khe Sanh base. During the siege, 205 Marines lost their lives. Against this, 1,600 enemy bodies were counted on the battlefield around the base, a figure that does not include the estimated thousands of NVA killed by U.S. airstrikes and artillery strikes.

A U.S. A-1 Skyraider heads off after dropping its bombs on an NVA artillery position in the low-lying hills near

Khe Sanh base. The devastating aerial firepower, which the Marines could rely on, played a crucial part in the base's survival.

in; and a similar technique was employed for the B-52s, each carrying 54,000 pounds of high explosives, which arrived over Khe Sanh every 90 minutes. When their efforts were added to those of the artillery, both within the base and at Camp Carroll and the Rockpile, the

effects could be awesome. Altogether, over 100,000 tons of bombs and 150,000 artillery rounds were delivered onto suspected or actual NVA positions between January 22 and March 31.

Such a massive display of force undoubtedly prevented the long-awaited Communist assault on Khe Sanh in late February. On the 29th, reports came in that NVA units were on the move, aiming for the eastern perimeter; however, the attack fizzled out under a tremendous artillery and air bombardment, and once the weather began to clear in early March, the threat of attack gradually subsided. Marine and ARVN patrols pushed out from the base and, although clashes continued to occur, it soon became obvious that the enemy had withdrawn his major units across the Laotian border.

Attempts were already being made to link up with the Marines on the ground, using the helicopter assets of the 1st Cavalry Division (Airmobile) to create a series of landing zones along Route 9 from Ca Lu. Codenamed Pegasus, the operation began in late March with construction of LZ Stud between Ca Lu and the Rockpile, enabling U.S. engineers to start repairing Route 9, and the helicopters of 1st Squadron, 9th Cavalry, to reconnoiter the ground ahead.

On April 1, the advance toward Khe Sanh began, encountering only sporadic resistance. New landing zones were carved out, and, as Marines and ARVN Rangers pushed out from the combat base, a linkup was effected at 1350 on April 6. At 0800 on April 8, the 3d Brigade of the 1st Cavalry Division officially relieved Khe Sanh, although six days later, on Easter Sunday, the 3/26th Marines rounded off the battle by seizing Hill 881 North. It was a fitting finale.

The siege had cost the Americans at least 205 men killed and 852 wounded. They counted over 1,600 enemy dead on the battlefield, but this took no account of the casualties caused by the airstrikes and artillery strikes, which may have been as high as 10,000. The 304th and 325thC NVA Divisions had suffered badly, and the U.S. claimed a major victory.

By April, 1968, however, the nature of the war had changed, chiefly in response to the Tet Offensive in early 1968: political considerations now took precedence over military ones, making the outcome of individual battles virtually irrelevant. The evacuation of the Khe Sanh plateau in June, 1968, less than three months after it had been the center of American attention and hopes, summed up the incongruity of the war.

Operation Niagara

Even before the siege began at Khe Sanh, American forces were taking action against the NVA in the area. As early as January 5, 1968, General Westmoreland convened a high-level meeting to discuss the growing threat to the base, out of which emerged Operation Niagara. Divided into two parts, Niagara I (put into effect immediately) concentrated on identifying targets; Niagara II—full-scale artillery and air res-

ponse—came into play once the NVA had opened their attack.

Niagara II was a devastating display of U.S. power. Between January 21 and March 31, a total of 24,000 tactical airstrikes were flown by USAF and Marine fighter-bombers, supplemented by 2,700 "Arc Light" strikes by B-52 Stratofortress bombers. In addition, artillery from Khe Sanh, Camp Carroll, and the Rockpile joined in, creating a storm of fire throughout the Khe Sanh area.

Fire Support Coordinators at Khe Sanh demonstrated the effect of this power in an operation known as "Mini Arc Light." This strike involved plotting a 550-yard by 1,100-yard block around a reported NVA position. Then, two A-6 Intruders, each carrying 28 500-pound bombs, would be called in; 30 seconds before they arrived, the 175mm guns from Camp Carroll or the Rockpile would hit one half of the block, firing about 60 rounds. The A-6s would then go for the middle of the block, while 155mm and 105mm guns, plus 4.2-inch mortars from Khe Sanh, would saturate the other half. All the rounds would be timed to strike simultaneously.

B-52 bombers made 2,700 "Arc Light" strikes on the Khe Sanh area between January 21 and March 31, 1968.

The loss of Lang Vei

Just after midnight on February 6/7, 1968, the Special Forces camp at Lang Vei, five miles southeast of Khe Sanh, was overwhelmed by NVA forces, spearheaded by 11 Soviet-built PT-76 tanks. It was the first time the NVA had used armor and, as the defenders—comprising 22 U.S. advisers and about 400 CIDG native troops—struggled to cope, their commander, Captain Frank C. Willoughby, radioed for support. He did not have much luck. Although artillery fire from Khe Sanh, Camp Carroll, and the Rockpile arrived within 15 minutes, requests for overland relief from Khe Sanh were refused for "fear of ambush." In the air, a "Spooky" gunship and a flareship offered some support, but fighter-bombers could not be committed until dawn.

By then, the base had been lost. The defenders managed to destroy five of the tanks but could not prevent the rest from advancing, chiefly because their light anti-tank weapons (LAWs) proved faulty. Willoughby and a small command group, besieged in the central bunker, called down

An NVA tank lies abandoned at Lang Vei Special Forces camp in a picture taken after the U.S. defeat there.

artillery and airstrikes on top of their position. Then, in the lull that followed, they succeeded in breaking out to the east. When they were picked up by rescue helicopters that afternoon, half the original garrison were unaccounted for. More significantly, as news of the disaster filtered out,

the fact that the enemy was now using tanks affected U.S. morale throughout Vietnam. Mike Herr, in his book *Dispatches*, summed up the crisis of confidence: "Jesus, they had tanks. Tanks! . . . after Lang Vei, how could you look out of your perimeter at night without hearing the treads coming?"

THE WAR YEARS

April 3, 1968   North Vietnam indicates a willingness to establish contact with the U.S. to "talk about talks."

April 8   Operation Pegasus forges a ground link with the U.S. Marine base at Khe Sanh, lifting the siege.

A U.S. 1st Cavalry convoy heads west along Route 9 during Operation Pegasus.

April 11   Secretary of Defense Clifford calls up 24,500 military reservists and states a new U.S. troop-ceiling in Vietnam of 549,500.

April 19/ May 17, 1968   U.S./ARVN offensive in the A Shau valley in ICTZ: Operation Delaware/Lam Son 216.

May 5/ June 4, 1968   "Mini-Tet": NVA/VC forces attack cities, towns, and military installations throughout South Vietnam.

May 11, 1968   Formal negotiations begin in Paris between U.S. and North Vietnamese representatives.

June 5, 1968   Senator Robert Kennedy, Democratic presidential hopeful, is shot; he fails to recover and dies the next day.

June 10   General William C. Westmoreland hands over MACV command to General Creighton W. Abrams.

June 19   President Thieu signs a general mobilization bill, by which all South Vietnamese men between 16 and 50 will be liable for military service.

THE TET OFFENSIVE

January 30–February 24, 1968

I N JULY, 1967, THE NORTH VIET-namese government convened a high-level conference to consider the war in the South. It was not going as well as the Communists had hoped, chiefly because of an American military commitment which, in two years, had blunted NVA infiltration and imposed heavy casualties on them. But, on closer analysis, two areas of potential enemy weakness emerged: on the one hand, there was no disguising the continued ineffectiveness of large portions of the ARVN, shielded by U.S. firepower; on the other, U.S. public opinion was not wholeheartedly in favor of the war.

These two factors were enough to persuade the North to plan a major attack, designed to shatter the ARVN, trigger an internal uprising in the South, and deal such a blow to U.S. prestige that popular support for the war would crumble. Although the North Vietnamese were looking for a military victory in what became known as the Tet Offensive, there is little doubt that their aims were primarily political. They intended to destroy the people's will to support the Saigon regime and create a climate in which a Communist seizure of power would be possible.

Preparations for the attack began immediately. NVA troops and supplies were fed down the Ho Chi Minh Trail and VC units in the South were alerted. At the same time, deception operations were put into effect, diverting U.S. and South Vietnamese attention from the cities and towns—the main targets—by threatening remote outposts, such as Khe Sanh and Loc Ninh. Diplomatic channels were used to hoodwink the Americans into believing that the North was interested in peace negotiations. Finally, the choice of Tet (the Vietnamese New Year, in late January) was deliberate: not only would the time be marked by a ceasefire, as in previous years, but ARVN soldiers would be on leave, away from their units. Surprise would be complete.

"You must dig the rats from their holes."

LIEUTENANT COLONEL ERNEST C. CHEATHAM, OC 2/5TH MARINES, HUE, FEBRUARY 3, 1968

In the event, it was, despite a VC mix-up that led to attacks on towns such as Ban Me Thuot, Kontum, and Pleiku, on January 30, 1968, a day too soon. Indeed, this probably led to increased complacency among the Allied troops, for information had been received that a Communist offensive was imminent: the events of January 30 and the relative ease with which the attacks were contained, persuaded many that they constituted the sum total of the threat. General Westmoreland put U.S. forces on alert and advised President Thieu to do the same with the ARVN, but few people expected the widespread assaults of Tet proper, delivered throughout the South in the early hours of January 31.

The Communists used the Tet celebrations as a cover for the operation. Disguised as peasants, they mingled with the holiday crowds, taking advantage of lax security to smuggle weapons into the towns and cities, or linking up with local VC units and opening up secret caches of supplies. The Allies were overwhelmed by the scale and audacity of the subsequent attacks: by February 1, Saigon had been hit, along with 36 of the 44 provincial capitals, 5 of the 6 autonomous cities, and 64 of the 242 district capitals of the South. Altogether, the Communists were fielding 84,000 troops—a mixture of NVA regulars and VC guerrillas—spread out to inflict maximum damage before the overstretched Allied forces could react.

In Saigon, VC sappers from the locally raised C-10 City Battalion attacked the ARVN Joint General Staff Command building, the Presidential Palace, the National Broadcasting Station, and, most audacious of all, the U.S. embassy in Thong Nhat Boulevard—the very symbol of the American presence in Vietnam. The embassy assault was easily countered, but not before the press had had a field day. Pictures of U.S. civilian staff helping to dislodge enemy guerrillas, followed by photographs of those same guerrillas lying dead on the well-kept

The blood-stained bodies of VC guerrillas (TOP and ABOVE) lie outside the American embassy after the unsuccessful attempt to storm the building on January 31, 1968.
The countrywide attacks that took place during the Tet—New Year—celebrations caught the Allies by surprise. Although, in the end, the Communists failed to gain any ground, they inlicted severe political damage on the Americans.

ARVN Rangers (LEFT) take cover behind a fence as fires blaze in Saigon during the Tet Offensive.

The impact of the media

The U.S. involvement in Vietnam was the most reported conflict in history. From the beginning, selected journalists traveled to the war zone in search of dramatic stories, and as U.S. force commitment increased in the mid-to-late 1960s, so did that of the press and media. Photographers, newspaper reporters, and, most significant of all, TV cameramen flocked to Saigon. Some progressed no farther than the nearest hotel, gaining all they needed from the daily MACV briefings (known to the more cynical among them as the "Five o'clock Follies"), but a few went as close to the fighting as was possible. Their reports, often flashed to news desks or TV stations while the action was still going on, provided the American public with some of the most shocking images of the war.

Such instantaneous and intimate reporting undoubtedly had an impact on public opinion, particularly during the Tet Offensive in early 1968. First reports of the Communist attack on the U.S. embassy in Saigon, which included the sights and sounds of furious gun battles on what was effectively American soil, made many viewers doubt the truth of General Westmoreland's recent claims that the enemy was close to defeat; and the public execution of a VC suspect (RIGHT), shot in the head by Saigon police chief Nguyen Van Ngoc Loan without a trial, left many Americans stunned. Westmoreland may have condemned the media for painting a "lurid and distorted" picture of the war, but these were images that could hardly be disguised.

The real impact of the media was felt on February 27, 1968, when CBS anchorman Walter Cronkite—whose hitherto even-handed approach to the war had done little to undermine President Johnson's policies—gave his personal assessment of events. Cronkite, shown (BOTTOM) holding a microphone, visited Saigon to see the situation for himself. Afterward, his broadcast was eagerly awaited. "It seems now more certain than ever that the bloody experience of Vietnam is to end in a stalemate," he claimed, adding that there was only one way for America to escape the morass—by negotiating with Hanoi. The judgment came as a hammer-blow to those who heard it: Johnson reportedly turned to his press secretary and said, "If I've lost Walter, I've lost Mr Average Citizen."

In the aftermath of Vietnam, some commentators criticized the press and media for molding public opinion to fit a preconceived

antiwar sentiment. But it would be wrong to claim that the media "lost the war" for America. In most cases, journalists merely reflected what they saw, and although it might be argued that they did so with a freedom unsuited to the chaos of war, that was hardly their fault.

lawns of the embassy building, came as a shock to the American public.

Any belief in Westmoreland's recent claim that the war was being won rapidly faded as people began to ask an obvious question: "If we are winning, how come the Communists are still active in downtown Saigon?" President Johnson had no ready answer and, as even more shocking pictures emerged—such as that of a VC suspect being summarily executed in the street or of U.S. helicopters pouring rockets into residential sectors of the city—the "credibility gap" between the administration and the people widened. Somehow, the war had gone sour.

In reality, the military response to Tet was both swift and effective. Saigon was back in government hands by February 5, having been cleared of infiltrators by a combined U.S./ARVN effort, and this pattern was repeated almost everywhere else on much the same time-scale. The only exception was Hue, South Vietnam's third-largest city, situated about 100 miles south of the DMZ in ICTZ. There the fighting was extremely hard, continuing until the end of February, but, as elsewhere, it ended in an Allied victory.

The NVA/VC attack on Hue—a city hitherto spared the worst of the war because of its cultural significance as the old imperial capital of Annam—began at 0340 hours on January 31. Rockets fell on the city from mountains to the west, while Communist infantry moved swiftly across the Huong Giang (Perfume River) to enter the Citadel, a three-square-mile section surrounded by a wall up to 20 feet high and between 50 and 200 feet thick, containing the Imperial Palace. Buildings south of the river, in a newer residential area known as the South Side or New City, were seized, severing Route 1—the main highway north to the DMZ—and catching the Allies unawares.

Hue was the headquarters for the 1st ARVN Division under Brigadier General Ngo Quang Truong—the HQ building was in the northeastern corner of the Citadel, with a MACV compound for attached advisers south of the river. Truong, however, had deployed the bulk of his forces outside the city. The nearest U.S. combat base was at Phu Bai, eight miles south along Route 1, but its Task Force X-Ray, under Marine Brigadier General Foster C. Lahue, was weak: although it was made up of two Marine regiments (the 1st and 5th, each consisting of three battalions with full supporting arms), much of its strength had been diverted elsewhere in order to protect more rural areas.

A medic and two aides (LEFT) rush across an exposed area toward a wounded Marine during the fighting at Hue on February 16, 1968. The battle for the old imperial city was the fiercest of the Tet Offensive.

Alert and holding his pistol at the ready, a Marine officer (BELOW) takes shelter during the battle of Hue. Unused to urban fighting in Vietnam, the Marines had to fight hard to clear the NVA out of the city's rubble-strewn streets.

The Tet Offensive (Hue)

ARVN Compound
Gia Hoi District
Tay Loc airfield
The Citadel
Imperial Palace
MACV Compound
Perfume River
Route 1

0   1000m
0   1000yd

N

By January 31, 1968, NVA/VC forces had seized most of Hue, the old imperial capital of Vietnam. U.S. Marine units were sent to regain control of the city. However, confronted by urban fighting—a scenario they had not yet encountered in Vietnam—the Americans found the going tough.

Slow but steady progress was made in flushing out the enemy street by street. But, by mid-February, U.S. and ARVN troops still had to dislodge the Communists from the Imperial Palace area of the Citadel, the Old City of Hue.

At about midday on February 19, amid smoke and drizzle, fierce house-to-house fighting continued in the Citadel. In what was typical of the action, men of the 1/5th Marines (**1**) advanced down a narrow street behind an M-48 tank.

While a Marine Ontos (**3**) maneuvered to fire its recoilless rifles, infantry, armed with M-16 assault rifles and M60 machine guns (**4**), took cover in the rubble, pinned down by enemy snipers (**2**).

After five more days of hard fighting, the VC flag flying over the southern wall of the Citadel was finally torn down on February 24. With only small pockets of enemy resistance to be mopped up, the battle was effectively over.

133

By dawn on January 31, the Communists had seized all of Hue except the ARVN HQ and MACV compound, and their red and gold flag was flying provocatively above the southern wall of the Citadel. From the U.S point of view, the immediate need was to relieve the MACV advisers, so, at 0830 hours, Lahue dispatched Company A, 1/1st Marines, to move up Route 1 toward the New City.

It made little progress, being pinned down between the river and the Phu Cam Canal, short of the MACV building. Two hours later, Lieutenant Colonel Marcus J. Gravel, commanding officer of the 1st Marines, left Phu Bai with a hastily created relief force structured around Company G, 2/5th Marines. These troops linked up with A/1/1st and, as four M-48s of the 3d Marine Tank Battalion outflanked the Communist ambush force, Gravel fought through to the MACV compound by 1500 hours, much to the relief of the embattled advisers.

As the Marines consolidated, creating a valuable enclave in an otherwise enemy-controlled area, they seized the southern edge of the Nguyen Hoang bridge leading into the Citadel, along with a stretch of riverbank that included a park (rapidly transformed into a helicopter LZ) and a pier used by the Navy to offload landing craft. Colonel Gravel was ordered to push G/2/5th across the bridge and, despite his reservations, the company succeeded in breaching the outer wall of the Citadel. They entered a warren of narrow streets and close-packed houses, all containing Communist troops. Pinned down and taking heavy casualties, they were lucky to get out. When the NVA destroyed the Nguyen Hoang bridge that night, the Marines were extremely relieved to see it go.

But the Marines' nightmare was only just beginning. Used to jungle fighting, nothing in their Vietnam experience had prepared them for war in an urban setting. Yet, to guarantee the security of the MACV compound, they had to tighten their grip on the surrounding streets.

On February 3, Lieutenant Colonel

A trooper of the 101st Airborne Division guides in a helicopter so that a wounded comrade can be evacuated. The incident happened during a patrol to the west of Hue on April 30, soon after the battle.

Ernest C. Cheatham, commanding officer of the 2/5th Marines, arrived to take command of three line companies—F, G, and H—of his battalion, under orders to clear the New City. His plan sounded simple: as the 2/5th moved west along the river from the MACV compound, Gravel's 1/1st would shield their left flank as far as the Phu Cam Canal. But the reality was far more complex. From the MACV compound to the confluence of the Perfume River and Phu Cam Canal was about 11 blocks, each transformed by the Communists into a fortress which would have to be cleared building by building, room by room.

The Marine attack began with an advance toward the Treasury and Post Office, but tactics were, at this stage, poor. As Cheatham's men tried to push

LBJ bows out

President Johnson's broadcast on March 31, 1968, in which he restricted U.S. airstrikes to an area of North Vietnam below the 20th parallel and announced his decision not to seek nomination for another term in the White House, was a turning-point in America's conduct of the Vietnam War.

Chief coordinator of the change in Johnson's attitude was Clark Clifford, his Secretary of Defense, once a supporter of the war, but whose investigations into U.S. aims and strategies had radically altered his opinion. He realized that others felt the same and, on March 25, gathered together the so-called "wise men"—respected elder statesmen and soldiers whose opinions Johnson valued. The "wise men" met Johnson for lunch on the 26th. The President,

caricatured (BELOW LEFT) and shown writing his TV speech (BELOW), was stunned by their change of heart and thus proved susceptible to the idea of curtailing the bombing of the North to induce peace negotiations. However, the decision not to seek reelection was Johnson's alone. He realized that his policies were losing public backing and was worried about his health.

Opposing the war

There was always a degree of public opposition to the U.S. involvement in Vietnam. As early as March, 1965, 25,000 antiwar demonstrators took to the streets of Washington in protest at the Marine commitment to Da Nang, and, as the year progressed, they were joined by a variety of like-minded groups, from traditional pacifists to left-wing radicals. They had little immediate effect: opinion polls in the summer of 1965 indicated that more than two-thirds of the American people supported President Johnson's Vietnam policies.

But as U.S. force levels (and casualties) increased, so did the number of protesters. Some merely demanded a ceasefire, blaming both sides for the violence; but others saw the war as symbolic of the administration's lack of care about more pressing social and political issues, mixing their opposition to the Vietnam conflict with their demonstrations against racism, poverty, and the influence of the military-industrial complex. Others joined as part of the youth rebellion of the 1960s, following the call of the influential guru-figure Timothy Leary to "turn on, tune in, and drop out." Vietnam was the catalyst. By October, 1967, crowds of up to 50,000 protesters were not uncommon; by the time of the incursions into Cambodia in 1971, every college campus across the nation had its share of vociferous antiwar demonstrators.

The impact of such protest is difficult to gauge, for it is impossible to say with certainty whether it molded or reflected public opinion. What cannot be denied, however, was its effect on the soldiers in Vietnam. Aware of widespread dissension at home, many questioned why they had to fight at all.

Two more casualties of Viet Nam.

Is it worth it?

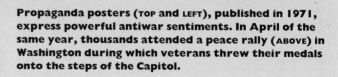

Propaganda posters (TOP and LEFT), published in 1971, express powerful antiwar sentiments. In April of the same year, thousands attended a peace rally (ABOVE) in Washington during which veterans threw their medals onto the steps of the Capitol.

down the main street, even with M-48 tank support, they were hit by a withering hail of mortar, rocket, and machine-gun fire which poured out from expertly hidden Communist positions.

It took 24 hours of tough fighting to seize the Treasury, which they eventually approached from the rear through court-yards blasted open by the M-48s; even then, the building fell only after it had been plastered with 90mm tank fire, 106mm recoilless rifles, 81mm mortars, and, finally, CS gas. Poor weather—Hue was affected by the monsoon, with over-cast skies and constant, drizzly rain—prevented air or artillery support. Also, the Americans were deliberately curtail-ing their firepower to minimize damage to the city for political reasons: the Marines were on their own.

This pattern of urban fighting—small groups of Marines moving doggedly from house to house, assaulting enemy positions under whatever ground-sup-port fire was available, then clearing each building with grenades and M-16s—continued without respite day after day. The 1/1st Marines attacked and seized the Joan of Arc school and church, while the 2/5th took the Cercle Sportif, Hue University library, and the City Hospital. Progress was slow, bitter, and costly, but it was being made. On February 5, in a particularly bloody encounter, H/2/5th took the Thua Thien province capitol building and the Communists began, almost imperceptibly, to weaken.

Cheatham regarded this action as decisive: "When we took the province headquarters, we broke their back. That was the tough one." But the fighting in the New City was by no means over. Despite the Marines' rapid adaptation to street fighting, using M-48s and tracked, tank-busting Ontos to blast a way for-ward for Marines to go in with grenades and rifles, it was not until February 11 that the 2/5th reached the confluence of the river and the canal. Two days later, they crossed into the western suburbs of Hue, aiming to link up with troopers of the 1st Cavalry and 101st Airborne Divisions, moving in toward the city. By February 14, most of the New City was in American hands, although mopping-up operations were to take another 12 days.

Meanwhile, the center of the fighting had shifted firmly to the Citadel. Although Truong had maintained control of the HQ complex and had been reinforced by units of his division battling through from the north to link up on February 3, the ARVN had not succeeded in dislodging the enemy. After a week's

The My Lai massacre

Early on March 16, 1968, Company C, 1/20th Infantry, commanded by Captain Ernest Medina, landed by helicopter to the west of the hamlet of My Lai (4) (marked as "Pink-ville" on American maps) in Quang Ngai province, ICTZ. Lieutenant William L. Cal-ley's 1st Platoon landed first, fanning out to cross dried-out paddies before entering the southern half of the hamlet. They were joined by 2d Platoon, which swept through the northern half before diverting to the neighboring hamlet of Binh Tay. Company C was searching for the 48th VC Battalion.

My Lai—a reputed VC village—was quiet; yet in the next four hours more than 300 old men, women, and children were killed, livestock destroyed, and houses burned. No American casualties were sus-tained, either here or in Binh Tay, where similar warcrimes took place.

The events of March 16 were officially covered up for over a year until Ronald Ridenhour, a soldier who had heard about the massacre from its perpetrators, sent copies of evidence he had compiled to 30 prominent politicians. As news of the atro-city leaked out, the Army ordered an official investigation, the result of which was that a number of officers and men were charged with unlawful killing. Only Calley stood trial, raising criticisms that he was being used as a scapegoat and that the real culprits—his superior officers who were stressing the need for aggression and a large body count—escaped. In March, 1971, Cal-ley was convicted by a jury of six senior officers of the first-degree murder of 22 unarmed civilians. He was given life impri-sonment, reduced to ten years on appeal. He was released on parole in 1974.

Lieutenant William Calley (BELOW) was charged with war crimes that shocked the American public.

One of the victims (RIGHT) of the massacre waits for her imminent death.

heavy fighting, ARVN airborne troops had effectively stalled among the houses, alleys, and narrow streets adjacent to the Citadel wall in the northwest and southwest, leaving the Communists still in possession of the Imperial Palace and most of its surrounding area. Truong had no choice but to request U.S. aid. He was given Major Robert H. Thompson's 1/5th Marines, fresh from operations in Phu Loc, just north of Hai Van Pass.

On February 11, two platoons of Company B were lifted by helicopter into the ARVN HQ complex (the third platoon was forced to turn back when their pilot was wounded by ground fire); 24 hours later, Companies A and C, plus the missing platoon from Company B, made the journey by landing craft from the MACV compound in the New City along the moat to the east of the Citadel and through a breach in the northeast wall. They were under Communist fire the whole way.

Their task was to relieve the ARVN airborne troops and revitalize the advance down the east wall toward the river, with the Imperial Palace on their right. At 0815 hours on February 13, Company A moved out, following the wall toward a distinctive tower. As they neared their objective, the Communists opened fire from concealed positions in the tower, wall, and surrounding houses. The

Crowds of South Vietnamese people, some carrying their bicycles, pour across a bridge over the Perfume River in a bid to escape the fighting in Hue. The battle created at least 116,000 refugees.

ARVN airborne had gone (they were withdrawn to Saigon as soon as the Marines arrived in the Citadel), leaving the Americans, with no experience of city fighting, to suffer alone. Within minutes, two Marines were dead and 30 wounded. Thompson pulled them back, sending Company C to replace them, with Company B to their right among the buildings, but no progress was made.

The same happened on the 14th, even though by then all restrictions on fire support had been lifted: despite airstrikes and artillery strikes, Companies B and C managed an advance of less than 100 yards. It was not until February 15—by which time Captain Myron C. Harrington's Company D, 1/5th Marines, had been brought into the Citadel by Swift boat and committed to the fray—that the wall tower was finally taken.

The bitter hand-to-hand fighting went on relentlessly, with Company D bearing the brunt of it. They were operating in a defender's paradise—row after row of single-story, thick-walled houses jammed together close to a solid wall riddled with spiderholes. M-48s and Ontos were available, but these vehicles found it extremely difficult to maneuver in the narrow streets, leaving the Marines to extract the enemy one by one.

By February 17, 1/5th had almost run out of ammunition and, as the attack toward the Imperial Palace continued after a pause to resupply, morale began to suffer. On the 19th, the 1/5th edged a little farther along the wall, but it was not secured until the 21st. By then, the Marines had been brought virtually to a standstill.

Thus the final attack, on the Imperial Palace itself, was left to a fresh unit, Captain John D. Niotis's Company L, 3/5th Marines. They faced a tough job, pushing parallel to the wall before breaching the outer perimeter of the palace on February 22. Once inside, however, they encountered entrenched opposition, forcing Niotis to pull back preparatory to a more concerted effort on the 24th.

Much to the relief of the Marines, at the last moment it was considered politically expedient for the Palace to be liberated by the ARVN, whose "Black Panther" Company advanced under support fire. The Communists, by now cut off from their supply centers to the west by the link-up between 1st Cavalry and 2/5th Marines, melted away. Late on February 24, the VC flag atop the southern wall of the Citadel was torn down.

Small pockets of enemy troops remained—mopping up in and around

the Citadel was to take some time—but the battle for Hue was effectively over. The city had been badly damaged—about 10,000 homes had been destroyed or damaged, 116,000 (out of a pre-Tet population of 140,000) were officially classed as "refugees," and up to 5,000 civilians had been murdered by the Communists. Also, the battle had been costly to both sides. According to figures compiled later, the Communists lost 5,113 confirmed dead to the ARVN's 384. U.S. casualties were 147 killed and 857 wounded.

The Marines had fought magnificently, achieving a military victory in appalling conditions. But, politically, Tet was an American defeat. U.S. public support, affected by the press coverage of the action, began to shift away from the government and, on March 31, 1968, the full impact was evidenced by President Johnson's TV broadcast, in which he halted all bombing of the North beyond the 20th parallel and gave notice that he would not be seeking reelection to the White House. In this respect, one of the Communist aims had been achieved, although in the process their forces had been temporarily shattered: they lost an estimated 30,000 fighters in the offensive. The South had survived, but the war would never be the same.

Was the U.S. close to winning?

By early 1968, before the shock of the Tet Offensive, General Westmoreland was convinced that the Americans and their allies were within sight of military victory in Vietnam. Since 1965, U.S. forces had not lost a major battle and had forced the Communists to abandon many of their border enclaves with enormous casualties. With extra troops and fewer politically imposed restrictions on the conduct of the war, Westmoreland believed that he could seal the borders of the South, destroy NVA capabilities by mounting attacks into Laos, Cambodia, and the southern provinces of North Vietnam, and then concentrate on rooting out the VC as well as remaining NVA forces in the South.

But it was a plan that no U.S. president could sanction. Increased force levels would mean extending the draft and mobilizing the reserves. Similarly, any idea of invading states around South Vietnam was unthinkable for fear of escalating the war into a possible superpower confrontation. The Communists recognized this: their strategy was to impose such a drain on U.S. forces that the American people would grow to oppose the war. The war was about people's attitudes, not about the outcome of battles. In that sense, military victory was irrelevant.

THE WAR YEARS

Oct. 9/14, 1968	Hanoi hints that it will no longer object to South Vietnamese participation in peace talks if the U.S. stops bombing the North.
Oct. 31	President Johnson announces that Operation Rolling Thunder will end officially at 0800 hours (Washington time), November 1.
Nov. 5, 1968	Richard M. Nixon elected President of the U.S.
Jan. 22/ March 18, 1969	Operation Dewey Canyon: 9th Marine Regiment attacks the Da Krong valley.
Jan. 25	First plenary session of the Paris peace talks begins.
Feb. 22, 1969	Communist forces attack Saigon and a number of other targets in the "Post-Tet" Offensive.
March 18, 1969	B-52 bombers hit Communist sanctuaries in eastern Cambodia: the beginning of the "Menu" secret bombings.
March 19	U.S. Secretary of Defense Melvin Laird asks Congress for $156 million for "Vietnamization."

Electing a new president

The race for the White House in 1968 took place against a background of growing public unease about the U.S. role in Vietnam, forcing the war to the forefront of election issues. Lyndon Johnson's dramatic decision not to seek the Democratic Party's nomination, coupled with the events of Tet and the prospect of peace talks, meant that both presidential candidates—Hubert Humphrey for the Democrats and Richard Nixon for the Republicans—had to put forward credible proposals on Vietnam. In the event, Nixon's promise to "end the war and win the peace" won him the election.

Nixon believed that if the Soviet Union and even China could be persuaded to back the idea of peace negotiations in exchange for U.S. technology and arms control, then the Vietnamese would have no choice but to comply. If that failed, he was prepared to use the threat of overwhelming force to put pressure on Hanoi. He called it his "Madman Theory": "We'll just slip the word to [the North Vietnamese] that, 'for God's sake, you know Nixon is obsessed about Communists. We can't restrain him when he's angry—and he has his hand on the nuclear button'—and Ho Chi Minh himself will be in Paris in two days begging for peace."

Richard Nixon was elected President on November 5, 1968.

HAMBURGER HILL

May 11–20, 1969

IN THE AFTERMATH OF THE TET Offensive in early 1968, the Americans and their allies in South Vietnam enjoyed a distinct military advantage. Despite the failure of the Communists to trigger a countrywide revolt, by the end of February the Communists had suffered grievous manpower losses and had been forced back to their border bases. With half a million troops in-country, the Americans could contemplate offensive operations into such bases, inflicting yet more casualties while impressing upon the North—about to engage in peace negotiations in Paris—that the costs of continued aggression would be crippling.

General Westmoreland, in his last weeks as MACV commander, looked particularly toward the A Shau valley on the far western edge of Thua Thien province in ICTZ. About 28 miles long and up to 2 miles wide, this "slash in the mountains," close to the Laotian border, had long been a natural route for NVA troops and supplies entering South Vietnam. Surrounded by towering, jungle-covered mountains, the valley was isolated and exceptionally difficult to penetrate, especially during the monsoon with its torrential rain and thick fog.

U.S. and South Vietnamese Special Forces had established camps at A Loui, Ta Bat, and A Shau village, but the first two were abandoned in December, 1965, and the third was overrun by the NVA in a bruising battle the following March. Since then, the A Shau valley had been abandoned to the Communists, something that Westmoreland found deeply frustrating. In April, 1968, he ordered the 1st Cavalry Division to mount an offensive—codenamed Delaware—to reassert Allied control.

U.S. aero-rifle teams entered the valley on April 14, intending to seize the former Special Forces camp at A Loui in the northern sector. They encountered a wall of antiaircraft fire which 200 B-52 and 300 fighter-bomber sorties failed to quell;

and, although battalions of the 7th Cavalry did take A Loui, conditions were appalling. Low cloud and rain effectively negated the advantages of airmobility; Delaware was called off on May 11.

This pattern was repeated in August, when the 101st Airborne Division entered the valley in Operation Somerset Plain. The only answer seemed to be the construction of a road from the coast into the A Shau, reducing the dependence on helicopter resupply. By the end of 1968, this had been pushed to the eastern edge of the valley, but if it was to go further, operations would have to be carried out to clear the way.

These began in January, 1969, with Operation Dewey Canyon—a Marine assault south through the Da Krong valley into NVA Base Area 611 astride the Laotian border. It enjoyed a degree of success, persuading the new MACV commander, General Creighton Abrams, to order a follow-up offensive.

In March, the 2d Brigade, 101st Airborne, air assaulted the central sector of the valley in Operation Massachusetts Striker. It culminated in a three-day battle at Dong A Tay ("Bloody Ridge"), in which the 1/502d Infantry lost 35 men killed and over 100 wounded. The NVA were clearly prepared to fight.

Massachusetts Striker forced the NVA back toward the northwestern sector of the valley, around a mountain (Dong) known as Ap Bia, but marked on U.S. maps as Hill 937. Situated close to the Laotian border, 937 and its neighboring ridges—Hills 900 and 800 to the south and Hill 916 to the southwest—were covered in thick jungle, tangled vines, and impenetrable bamboo. In residence since 1964, the NVA had fortified the area, building log-covered bunkers and camouflaged spiderholes to protect all avenues of approach. By May, 1969, when the A Shau valley was chosen as an objective of the 101st in Operation Apache Snow, Ap Bia was being held by over 1,200 men of the crack NVA 29th Regiment.

A paratrooper from the 101st Airborne Division, whose insignia is shown (RIGHT), gazes across the A Shau valley from the top of Dong Ap Bia—dubbed "Hamburger Hill" by the Americans—six days after the battle.

While a wounded trooper of the 101st Airborne (LEFT) is rushed to a medevac helicopter, another GI (ABOVE) grimaces with pain as he waits to be evacuated from the U.S. base camp at Hamburger Hill. Seventy Americans were killed in the battle.

The end of the nightmare for the men of the 101st Airborne Division, engaged in the battle for Hill 937 (Hamburger Hill), came on May 20, 1969. At 1000, after nine days of savage fighting, the Americans were ready for a multi-battalion assault on the NVA bunkers.

On the northeast side of Hill 937 (**10**), the 2/501st (**9**) started up the steep slope. Later, near the summit, they would link up with the 2/3d ARVN Battalion (**15**), advancing from the east.

On the southern side of the mountain, the 1/506th moved out: Companies A (**14**) and C (**13**) pushed forward from the south, with Company B (**11**), to their left, advancing from the southwest.

Meanwhile, over to the northwest, Colonel Honeycutt ordered his battle-scarred troops into the fray. Companies A (**6**) and C (**7**), 3/187th, moved off together and formed a skirmish line, with Company A, 2/506th (**8**), on their left.

By noon, Company C, 3/187th, had fought its way to the top of Hill 937, precipitating numbers of NVA soldiers (**1**) to flee down a draw to the southwest between Hills 916 (**2**) and 900 (**12**). Here, however, a force from Company B, 1/506th, was dispatched to engage the enemy and prevent them from escaping.

At about 1500, with the other battalions in blocking positions around the hill, Honeycutt's men began a final sweep of the summit of 937, flushing out pockets of resistance. As more NVA (**3** and **5**) began to run for their lives down through draws leading to the Laotian border (**4**), U.S. artillery was brought to bear on them.

By 1700, the battle was drawing to a close, leaving the NVA with an estimated 633 killed, the Americans with 70 killed and 372 wounded. The agony of the fight for Hill 937 was over; but the controversy over what became known simply as Hamburger Hill, had only just begun.

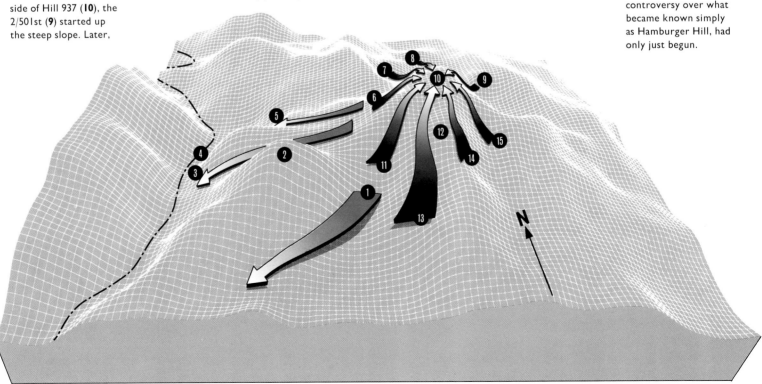

Apache Snow began on May 10 with helicopter assaults by five Allied battalions (three from the 101st Airborne Division and two from the 1st ARVN) into the northern A Shau. At LZ2, about 2,000 yards northwest of Hill 937, Lieutenant Colonel Weldon Honeycutt's 3/187th Infantry landed without incident and began to conduct RIF (reconnaissance-in-force) operations toward the mountain and Laotian border. A more permanent LZ and battalion command post was set up closer to 937 and, with no reaction from the NVA, Company B was ordered to seize the summit.

Starting out at 1640 hours, the paratroopers followed a trail to the southeast of the new LZ which took them into thick jungle, enclosed by tall trees, matted vines, and bamboo. Moving forward over fallen trees, the lead scouts trod warily while their comrades, sweating in the dank, humid air, plodded behind. As they crossed a low saddle, the NVA struck, firing RPGs (rocket-propelled grenades) and AK-47s into the American column. Airstrikes were called in, and, as dusk was gathering, the company pulled back into an NDP (night defensive position).

With only three men wounded, the skirmish was hardly significant, but when another ambush was sprung in the same area the following morning, killing three Americans, it was obvious that the enemy had been found. This suited Honeycutt, who immediately revised his plan. Recalling Company C from its RIF along the Trung Pham River, he ordered it to attack, parallel to Company B, along a ridge that ended between Hills 900 and 937, while Company D worked around the northern edge of the mountain. The aim was to have all three companies in position to assault the summit by first light on May 13. It did not work.

The companies moved out at 0830 hours on May 12, after intense air and artillery "prepping" fire. They entered a nightmare of close-quarter fighting that was to continue with little respite for eight days. During that time, the 3/187th was to be shattered, both mentally and physically, as enemy resistance hardened and conditions deteriorated. On Company B's line of advance, the NVA drew the Americans closer to the mountain, into a clearing that sheltered line after line of bunkers, each of which seemed impervious to airstrikes or artillery strikes.

Day after day, the company moved up, attacking the bunkers with grenades, recoilless rifles and machine guns, only to be forced to pull back, dragging their

Nixon and Abrams: a new team

Born in California in 1913, Richard Milhous Nixon (FAR RIGHT) was elected to the White House in 1968. He faced the daunting task, as President, of effecting a U.S. troop withdrawal from Vietnam while continuing to protect the South. He did so by a tough diplomacy of détente with China and the Soviet Union, while responding to attacks on the South by the NVA. In 1972, after the North's Easter Offensive, he authorized renewed bombing beyond the DMZ, forcing Hanoi to seek a peace agreement, signed in Paris in early 1973. Nixon offered continued aid to Saigon but, with his resignation in 1974, he was unable to carry out his promise.

General Creighton Williams Abrams, Jr. was appointed to command MACV in Saigon in 1968 when General Westmoreland was promoted to the post of Chief of Staff of the U.S. Army. Born in Massachusetts in 1914, Abrams graduated from West Point in 1936. After various divisional and corps commands in the early 1960s, he moved to the Pentagon and, in 1967, was appointed Westmoreland's deputy in Vietnam. During his time as MACV commander (1968–72), he supervised Vietnamization and U.S. troop withdrawals. In 1972, he replaced Westmoreland as Chief of Staff but died in office two years later.

The decline in morale

No one wanted to be the last GI to die in Vietnam. Against a background of peace negotiations in Paris, increased antiwar sentiment in the United States, the first troop withdrawals from South Vietnam, and the introduction of Vietnamization, many U.S. servicemen began to question the need for aggressive combat operations.

Such an attitude inevitably affected morale. Before 1969, U.S. morale had been very good, but once the war changed, it diminished. There were a host of indicators. Desertion rates in U.S. services reached unprecedented heights, peaking in 1971 when 73.5 desertions per 1,000 men were recorded. Drug abuse flourished to the extent that in the same year, a Department of Defense report estimated that over half the army personnel in Vietnam had used marijuana, as shown (BELOW); just under a third had taken psychedelic drugs; and over a quarter had experimented with hard drugs such as heroin and opium.

At the same time, military discipline faltered. A number of unpopular officers and NCOs were murdered, and there were 788 incidents of "fragging" (murder, usually with fragmentation grenades) recorded between 1969 and 1972, many of them related to drug disputes. Also, "combat refusals" occurred (in the 1st Cavalry Division, 35 "individual refusals" were logged in 1970 alone) and standards of dress and respect for rank diminished.

From May 10, 1969, for nine days, the crack NVA 29th Regiment had stubbornly held their strongly fortified positions on Hill 937—Hamburger Hill—in the A Shau valley against determined assaults by the U.S. 101st Division.

With mounting casualties and their morale faltering, General Melvin Zais, commander of the "Screaming Eagles," ordered fresh troops to reinforce the battle-weary 3/187th for an all-out assault on May 20.

U.S. fighter-bombers, including A-1 Skyraiders, began "prepping" the mountain at 0630, before the infantry assault. By this time, Hill 937 (**2**) was a wasteland of charred and burning trees, splintered logs, collapsed bunkers, and mud. While supply helicopters (**1**) continued to shuttle to and from the Battalion HQ, the men of the 3/187th grimly began the final push up the northwestern face of Hill 937.

Meanwhile, on the eastern and northeastern sides of 937, a blocking force, made up of the 2/501st and 2/3d ARVN, advanced to near the top and, by 1500, had taken up their positions (**3** and **4**, respectively). To the south, three companies (**5**) of the 1/506th had edged their way from Hill 900 (**6**) to the bunker-ridden slopes of 937.

144

Hamburger Hill

Battalion HQ
3/187th ●

Laos

Hamburger
Hill
(Hill 937)

Hill
900

Hill 916

Hill
800

N

The determination of the NVA during the battle was encapsulated by what the Americans found by a clump of trees near the center of 937: eight dead NVA soldiers, four of them tied or chained to the trees, all of them wearing shirt patches with the words "Kill Americans."

Although Hill 937 was eventually taken after ten days of bitter fighting, the victory turned into a political defeat for the Americans. U.S. public opinion was incensed by what was commonly perceived to be a waste of the lives of young GIs who had died to secure a hill that was abandoned less than three weeks later. The resulting political controversy accelerated the U.S. policy of preparing the ARVN to fight the war alone.

Toward late afternoon, the men of the 3/187th advanced across the summit of 937, causing pockets of NVA to run for their lives down draws leading to Laos. Despite being sheltered by the green jungle canopy, the fleeing Communists were hit by shell bursts (**7** and **8**) from U.S. artillery.

145

wounded to safety. By May 15, Company B was exhausted and had to be replaced by Company D, itself less than strong after terrible experiences farther north. On May 12, the company had found its way blocked by a steep-sided ravine. On reaching the bottom 24 hours later, they had been ambushed and forced to reverse their journey, in the dark and under torrential rain, manhandling seven of their wounded (including the pilot of a downed medevac helicopter) up a virtually sheer slope. They had then returned to recover seven dead, killed in the initial ambush.

Horrific as all this was, it did not match the experiences of Company C as it pushed along its designated ridge. Once again, the NVA drew the Americans closer to the mountain before springing a carefully prepared ambush on May 13. The company lost 2 dead and 35 wounded in a matter of minutes: Honeycutt had no choice but to withdraw the survivors to his command post, sending Company A to take their place. It fared no better,

Medics act quickly to attend to a wounded trooper of the 101st Airborne Division. He has been hit in the face by an enemy hand grenade during an advance up the NVA-held slopes of Dong Ap Bia.

The underground press

U.S. servicemen in Vietnam were always desperate for news from the outside world. They also wanted diversions so that, for a moment at least, they could forget the horrors of war. Official radio stations and service newspapers such as *Stars and Stripes* could satisfy the need to a certain extent, but they were never critical of government or policy; various antiwar newssheets also found their way to the front line, but were seen as alien and insulting.

It is not surprising, therefore, that the servicemen produced their own underground tabloids. It has been estimated that between 1967 and 1972 more than 240 unofficial newspapers existed, although in a vast majority of cases their circulation was low and their print run small. Some were highly critical of the war—in 1969, one paper offered $10,000 to anyone who killed Lieutenant Colonel Honeycutt of the 3/187th Infantry, held responsible in many soldiers' eyes for the losses on Hamburger Hill—while others were nothing more than organs of amusement. The most successful was *Grunt* (images from which are shown here), founded by Air Force combat historian Ken Sams, which began life in February, 1968, as a "glossy" based on the *Playboy* format of stories, poems, cartoons, and nudes. With an eventual circulation of 30,000, it changed its name to *Grunt Free Press* in 1969 and survived until 1971.

stalling in front of a line of bunkers which defied all efforts at destruction. Meanwhile, the 1/506th, ordered to move from the south toward Hills 916 and 900, made little progress amid a maelstrom of enemy fire and violent thunderstorms.

By May 16, all attacks had ground to a halt, and soldiers were beginning to react to the appalling strain of the situation. Honeycutt, with his repeated demands for action, became the focus of the men's discontent: "If that sonofabitch wants to take this . . . mountain so bad, why don't he do it himself?"

But the fighting did not end. On May 17, the 1/506th edged closer to Hill 900 and, 24 hours later, the weary assault companies of the 3/187th made enough progress to suggest that one final effort would take the summit of 937. They were blocked, not by the enemy, but by one of the most spectacular thunderstorms yet experienced. As visibility declined to zero, the rain turned the slopes of 937—by now devoid of vegetation—into a sea of sticky mud. The attack was called off.

During the night of May 18/19, Major General Melvin Zais, commanding the 101st, ordered three fresh battalions—the 2/501st, 2/506th, and 2/3d ARVN— to join the battle. They landed without incident on the 19th, taking up blocking

positions to the southeast and northeast of Ap Bia. On May 20, all five battalions attacked, surrounding the NVA and cutting them off from their bases in Laos.

As the 2/501st and 2/3d ARVN climbed the precipitous northeastern and eastern faces of 937, respectively, the 1/506th put in a three-company assault across Hill 900 and into a deep draw—the major NVA escape route—to the southwest. At the same time, Honeycutt's men continued their attacks over familiar ground, gradually clearing the bunker lines and reaching desperately for the summit.

Enemy fire did not slacken, even when small groups of Company C scrambled onto the western edge to set up a defensive perimeter. But once they were joined by squads from Company A, the paratroopers were able slowly to clear the mountaintop. By 1655 hours, the fighting was dying down.

In any other war, the Battle of Dong Ap Bia—soon to be dubbed Hamburger Hill by the 3/187th, "because they say this mountain turns men into hamburgers"— would have been hailed as a great victory. Despite heavy casualties—the Americans lost 70 killed and 372 wounded in the 10 days of fighting—over 630 enemy bodies were found, and a well-defended base had

been taken. But Vietnam was different and, as news of the battle filtered out, controversy began.

Publicly condemned by Senator Edward Kennedy as "senseless and irresponsible," the action fueled the antiwar lobby, particularly when, on June 5, the 101st abandoned Ap Bia and allowed the enemy to return. Military arguments that the strategy was to impose casualties, not occupy real estate, cut little ice, especially when, on June 27, *Life* magazine ran a misleading feature on "The Faces of the Dead in Vietnam. One Week's Total."

Many readers imagined that the 241 photographs shown were all of men killed at Ap Bia. Under considerable political and public pressure, President Nixon ordered Abrams to cease offensive operations in NVA-controlled territory, accelerating the process of Vietnamization to allow U.S. troops to be withdrawn. U.S. involvement in Vietnam was drawing to a close.

THE WAR YEARS

May 20, 1969	Senator Edward Kennedy accuses the military in Vietnam of "senseless and irresponsible" tactics at Dong Ap Bia.
June 8, 1969	Presidents Nixon and Thieu meet at Midway; Nixon announces that 25,000 U.S. troops are to be withdrawn from South Vietnam by the end of August.
July 7, 1969	A battalion of the U.S. 9th Infantry Division is the first U.S. unit to be withdrawn from South Vietnam.
Aug. 4, 1969	Dr Kissinger has private talks with Hanoi representative Xuan Tuy in Paris, in an effort to boost the peace negotiations.
Sept. 3, 1969	President Ho Chi Minh dies in Hanoi. He is replaced by "collective leadership."
Sept. 16	President Nixon announces a second round of U.S. force withdrawals from South Vietnam (35,000 men).
Sept. 30	It is announced that 6,000 U.S. troops will be withdrawn from Thailand by July 10, 1970.
Dec. 15, 1969	President Nixon announces a third round of U.S. force withdrawals from South Vietnam (50,000 men by April 1970).

Blacks, Hispanics, and others

Throughout America's involvement in Vietnam, soldiers of various ethnic backgrounds fought alongside whites in military units that were fully integrated. The old policy of strict segregation, exemplified by "Negro"

units (under white officers) supporting all-white combat formations in World War II, had disappeared during the Korean War. In Vietnam, the army gave blacks, such as the off-duty GI (LEFT), and other minorities a chance to advance their careers and raise their social standing. Many senior NCOs were black and numerous Special Forces sergeants were Hispanic. Other ethnic groups also rose relatively high in the ranks.

Although distinctions of color disappeared under enemy fire, the soldiers tended to stick with their own race when off-duty. Each, for example, had its own bars and brothels in Saigon—Khanh Hoi ("Soulsville") for the blacks, Tu Do for the whites—and this reinforced the division. It was made worse as news of the racial tension in the United States came through—culminating in the assassination of Martin Luther King in April, 1968—and blacks arrived who had grown up in riot-torn ghettos or under the influence of fringe groups, such as the Black Panthers. To cap it all, when casualty figures were analyzed, it seemed as if the blacks particularly were bearing an unfair burden of the violence in Vietnam: 23 percent of men killed in combat were black.

147

OPERATION LAM SON 719

February 8–April 6, 1971

ALTHOUGH THE U.S. ANNOUNCED in 1969 its intention to withdraw forces from Vietnam, it could not merely pack its bags and leave. The security of the South was still important, necessitating policies to help guarantee that the Saigon government would survive against both internal and external pressure. While American troop levels decreased, NVA manpower increased within South Vietnam and largely replaced the weakened VC.

The American response was to emphasize the twin policies of pacification and Vietnamization. This meant concentrating resources to extend government control over rural areas while making sure that South Vietnamese armed forces were strong enough to take over the war against the NVA as U.S. units returned home. Pacification had always been a South Vietnamese responsibility, backed by U.S. Special Forces and a host of civilian agencies that had been brought together in May, 1967, in CORDS (Civil Operations and Revolutionary Development Support).

In November, 1968, however, an Accelerated Pacification Campaign began. By early 1970, more than 15,000 Communist suspects had been arrested or killed (chiefly by means of the *Phuong Hoang*, or Phoenix, program), democracy had been introduced at village level through elected councils, and land reform had been initiated. It was estimated that, by 1971, only five percent of the South Vietnamese population was still under Communist control.

Vietnamization was less easy to quantify. The first priority was to increase the size of the South Vietnamese armed forces, both to protect the pacified villages and to face the NVA. In June, 1968, President Thieu promulgated a general mobilization law, making military service of some description obligatory for all able-bodied South Vietnamese males between the ages of 16 and 50, and this coincided with an expansion of the

---

"There's a big op coming down.

ARVN's jumping the border into

Laos to kick some ass and take

names."

ANONYMOUS GI's REACTION TO LAM SON 719, JANUARY, 1971

Regional and Popular Forces (RF/PF or "Ruff-Puffs") to guard the rural areas.

As a result, South Vietnamese armed strength (ARVN and Ruff-Puffs together) rose from 643,000 in 1968 to more than a million in 1971. At the same time, American equipment, including helicopters, tanks, and M-16 rifles, was poured in to provide a continuance of mobility and firepower. In the event, the ARVN remained a force riddled with corruption and subject to staggering desertion rates, but the Americans were doing all they could to duplicate their own, proven, capabilities.

It was not enough. For, until the ARVN had proved itself in battle, preferably before the bulk of U.S. ground forces had been withdrawn, it would lack self-confidence and deterrent value. Evidence suggested that the NVA realized this: according to U.S. intelligence in early 1970, Communist formations were gathering in bases in eastern Cambodia, ready to advance on Saigon as soon as the Americans left. It seemed an ideal opportunity: if a joint U.S./ARVN incursion into Cambodia could be mounted, not only would the NVA be disrupted, but the ARVN would be psychologically boosted at a critical time.

There was a problem, however: Cambodia, like Laos to the north, was officially neutral and the border inviolable. This had certainly been President Johnson's attitude, but by 1970, things had changed. The ruler of Cambodia, Prince Norodom Sihanouk—a wily politician who shifted allegiance to suit his own perception of his country's needs—had turned to the Americans in early 1969 when his previous policy of appeasing the Communists had come unglued. President Nixon had responded by authorizing secret B-52 strikes on NVA sanctuaries in eastern Cambodia; but this put Sihanouk under pressure as the Communists sought shelter deeper in his country.

By March, 1970, Sihanouk was beginning to lose control: when he left Cambo-

South Vietnamese airborne troops and U.S. armor (ABOVE) gather near South Vietnam's border with Laos. Because the ARVN operation in Laos, codenamed Lam Son 719, was intended to be an acid test of Vietnamization, no U.S. troops or advisers were allowed to move across the border.

With a crudely made peace flag fluttering in the wind (LEFT), U.S. artillerymen relax at a firebase on the border of Laos and South Vietnam. The gunners are providing covering support for ARVN units during their incursion into Laos—Operation Lam Son 719.

dia to travel abroad, he was ousted in a coup (widely believed to be CIA-backed) led by his prime minister, Marshal Lon Nol. He requested even more American support, giving Nixon the "excuse" he needed to allow cross-border operations.

These operations, carried out principally in May/June 1970 in areas known as the "Parrot's Beak" and "Fish Hook" to the north of Saigon, were, in military terms, disappointing and, for the Americans, politically embarrassing. When 12,000 ARVN moved into the Parrot's Beak on April 29, backed by U.S. airstrikes and artillery strikes, the NVA pulled back, preferring not to offer battle.

The same happened in the Fish Hook, assaulted by a joint U.S./ARVN force on

May 1. In both cases, searches uncovered vast quantities of supplies—around the small town of Snoul in the Fish Hook, for example, the caches were so enormous that they were dubbed "The City" by delighted GIs. Nixon had made it clear, however, that, for U.S. forces at least, the incursions would end by June 30. Before then, other operations were mounted, but the results were the same.

U.S. units pulled back on schedule, aware that their actions (plus reports about the U.S. "secret bombing" of Cambodia) had produced a crisis in Washington. As soon as the incursions were announced, nationwide antiwar demonstrations broke out, especially on college campuses; on May 4, four students were

shot dead by National Guardsmen at Kent State, Ohio, raising the level of protest to new heights. Congress reacted by repealing the 1964 Gulf of Tonkin Resolution, curtailing Nixon's power to commit U.S. forces without Congressional backing. The President tried to cool things down by promising to accelerate the withdrawal of U.S. forces from Vietnam.

Cambodia, therefore, proved little in terms of ARVN combat capabilities, but it forced the pace of Vietnamization. This was made more urgent by reports that NVA forces were building up in Laos, opposite ICTZ (to be known from July, 1970, as Military Region, or MR, I). Nixon was again under pressure to auth-

The Pathet Lao and Khmer Rouge

Both Laos and Cambodia had indigenous Communist groups, owing their origins, like the Viet Minh/VC, to the growth of nationalist opposition to French colonial rule in the 1930s. Despite this, however, they developed in different ways and, although both groups seized political power in 1975, they did so in different ways.

In Laos, the *Neo Lao Hak Sat* (Lao Liberation Front, or Pathet Lao) opposed the post-colonial monarchy from 1954. Indeed, by 1961, they posed such a threat that an international conference was convened in Geneva to declare Laotian neutrality under a coalition government. It did not work, chiefly because it coincided with North Vietnamese infiltration of eastern Laos to set up the Ho Chi Minh Trail. This incursion diverted attention away from the Pathet Lao, who increased their pressure on the Royal Lao government. In April, 1975, a new coalition between the Communists and monarchists was formed, but four months later the Pathet Lao took over.

The Khmer (Cambodian) Liberation Army, dubbed the Khmer Rouge by Prince Sihanouk, had to fight a much more sustained guerrilla campaign to take over in Phnom Penh. Rivals to, rather than allies of, the NVA, the Khmer Rouge had little success as long as Sihanouk adopted a conciliatory policy toward the North Vietnamese; but once he had veered toward the Americans in 1969, their power began to grow. After the 1970 coup in Cambodia, the Khmer initiated a guerrilla campaign which gradually destroyed the Cambodian Army, despite U.S. air support. By 1975, Phnom Penh was at the mercy of Khmer Rouge forces: they took over in April.

Communist guerrillas (ABOVE RIGHT and FAR RIGHT) of the Laotian Pathet Lao move into battle. In Cambodia, the indigenous Communist group was known as the Khmer Rouge (RIGHT).

orize a cross-border operation, yet in no position to sanction U.S. involvement beyond South Vietnam. In the event, he agreed that U.S. units would clear the Khe Sanh plateau up to the border, provide artillery support from firebases just inside MRI, and give air backing to a South Vietnamese attack along Route 9 toward the Laotian town of Tchepone.

However, no U.S. ground troops—not even advisers—were to cross the border: the South Vietnamese were to go it alone in an acid test of Vietnamization. If it failed, at least U.S. units would still be available to protect MRI in case the NVA counterattacked.

The Americans began their part of the plan—Operation Dewey Canyon II—on January 30, 1971, sending the 1st Brigade, 5th Infantry Division (Mechanized), with engineer support, to clear Route 9 up to the border and reopen Khe Sanh as a helicopter base. Four battalions of the U.S. 108th Artillery Group set up firebases along the border, while elements of the 101st Airborne Division put in a feint attack toward the A Shau valley to distract NVA attention. It was all they were permitted to do.

Meanwhile, Lieutenant General Hoang Xuan Lam, commander of the ARVN I Corps, had gathered an impressive array of South Vietnamese forces to carry out Operation Lam Son 719 (named after a Vietnamese victory over the Chinese in the 15th century). His plan was to send his 1st Armor Brigade straight down Route 9 to Tchepone, protecting its flanks by committing the ARVN 1st Infantry Division to a series of LZs and firebases along an escarpment to the south, and the ARVN 1st Airborne Division and 1st Ranger Group to similar locations in mountains to the north. The Vietnamese Marine Corps Division was in reserve. Once Tchepone had been seized (something Lam imagined would take about three days), the next move depended on NVA reactions: if they melted away as they had done in Cambodia, the advance would continue toward the Ho Chi Minh Trail; if the fighting was hard, Lam would inflict maximum damage, then withdraw.

OPERATION LAM SON 719/3

Early in 1971, the ARVN were given a chance to prove their combat capability in the first major test of Vietnamization. An operation codenamed Lam Son 719 was planned in which an ARVN force, unaided by U.S. advisers or ground troops, would conduct a preemptive strike across the border with Laos to counter the growing presence of NVA troops there.

The incursion began on February 8, 1971, with the 1st Armor Brigade advancing west along Route 9. Men of the ARVN 1st Infantry and Airborne Divisions and the 1st Ranger Group, carried by U.S. helicopters, created LZs north and south of Route 9, thereby protecting the Armor Brigade's flanks.

After a promising start by the ARVN, the NVA mounted a determined counterattack, threatening all ARVN positions. Despite taking the town of Tchepone, Lieutenant General Hoang Xuan Lam, the officer in charge of the operation, decided to call a retreat before the NVA could exploit his stretched-out and vulnerable position.

Operation Lam Son 719

- Laos
- Ranger North
- Ranger South
- South Vietnam
- Hope
- 31
- 30
- Tchepone
- Route 9
- Aloui
- Khe Sanh
- Sophia
- Liz
- Alpha
- Lolo
- Moon
- Xe Pon River
- Hotel
- Route 914
- Delta
- Route 92

N

- ■ Fire Support Base
- ■ Landing Zone
- ▨ Elevations above 300 meters

0 — 5 miles
0 — 5 km

Early on March 19, the 1st Armor Brigade began their retreat back down Route 9, hampered by 17 damaged tanks and APCs which they had on tow. Then, at 0800, the convoy was ambushed as it crossed a stream east of the town of Aloui. The retreat turned into a rout as NVA rocket fire (**2**) slammed into the ARVN vehicles (**1**).

Thrown into chaos, ARVN troops returned fire—some using the machine guns from M-41s (**3**), which had been abandoned by their crews. Others began to maneuver their APCs (**4**) to drag out the tanks from the stream. It took three hours to move the tanks, thus allowing the stricken column to advance again. The 17 vehicles under tow were left behind and later destroyed by U.S. Cobra gunships.

The 1st Armor Brigade finally reached the border. But here the presence of NVA forces along Route 9 remained a threat and precipitated the abandonment of U.S. firebases in the area.

Operation Lam Son 719 ended officially on April 6. It had proved expensive, with 1,529 ARVN killed and 5,483 wounded. More than 100 U.S. helicopters were lost with a further 618 damaged. Although the NVA had suffered nearly 20,000 killed, serious deficiencies in the ARVN had been highlighted. It was clear that Vietnamization had a long way to go.

South Vietnamese M-113 APCs trundle toward the Cambodian border. In April, 1970, 12,000 ARVN troops advanced into an area of Cambodia known as the "Parrot's Beak," northwest of Saigon; and, later in the same month, a U.S. and ARVN force moved farther north into an area known as the "Fish Hook." Both incursions, however, failed to inflict much damage on the NVA or their Cambodian sanctuaries.

The Kent State shootings

When, on April 30, 1970, President Nixon announced his intention to send U.S. troops into Cambodia, the reaction in the United States, especially among college students, was predictable. On May 1, history graduate students at Kent State, Ohio, organized a rally in the middle of the campus. About 500 people attended and then dispersed. That night, however, riots broke out in the town. The Mayor, Leroy Statrum, declared a state of emergency and alerted the Ohio National Guard.

On May 2 and 3, the students again organized demonstrations, one of which had to be cleared by the National Guardsmen, but the trouble was contained. On the 4th, however, between 1,500 and 3,000 people gathered, calling for the release of students already arrested and for the right to present their antiwar case to the mayor. The National Guard took over responsibility for the campus and, after their calls for the crowds to disperse had been ignored, the troopers used tear gas. When this failed, at 1225 hours they fired 61 live rounds, killing four students and wounding a further ten. An FBI investigation subsequently concluded that "the shootings were not necessary and not in order," but those responsible were acquitted when they were brought to trial.

A young woman cries with anguish over the body of one of the students shot by National Guardsmen on May 4, 1970, during the Kent State demonstrations.

Controlling Cambodia's destiny

Lon Nol (LEFT) ousted Prince Sihanouk, shown (ABOVE) meeting Mao Tse-tung.

Norodom Sihanouk was installed as King of Cambodia by the French in 1941, when he was only 19 years old. At the Geneva Conference in 1954, Cambodia was granted independence, upon which Sihanouk renounced the throne, created his own political party, and was swept to power.

For the next 16 years, he tried to maintain his country's neutrality. When the North Vietnamese seemed to be prevailing in South Vietnam, he allowed the NVA to set up bases in eastern Cambodia; when they were weakened by Tet in 1968, he shifted allegiance to the Americans, allowing President Nixon to carry out secret bombings of the NVA enclaves. By March, 1970, Cambodia was becoming an extension of the Vietnam war zone; when Sihanouk traveled abroad, he was ousted by his prime minister, Lon Nol, after which the prince moved to China, allying himself to the Communist Khmer Rouge.

When Lon Nol seized power in Cambodia, he inadvertently condemned his country to civil war, foreign interference, and eventually Communist takeover. Born in 1913, Lon rose through the ranks of the Cambodian Army and government under Sihanouk's tutelage and was appointed prime minister in 1969. By the time of the coup a year later, he was in poor health and this, coupled with his limited grasp of international politics, allowed him to be manipulated by outside powers. In 1970, he was not fully informed of the U.S. decision to mount cross-border operations against NVA bases in eastern Cambodia; by 1971, he had lost control of much of his country to both the NVA and Khmer Rouge. When Phnom Penh fell in 1975, Lon fled to Hawaii, leaving Cambodia to Pol Pot.

Lam Son 719 began at 0700 hours on February 8, when the lead elements of the 1st Armor Brigade, equipped with U.S. M-41 light tanks and M-113 APCs crossed the border along the narrow, terrain-restricted and unrepaired Route 9. At the same time, U.S. helicopters of the 223d Combat Aviation Battalion and 158th Aviation Battalion left Khe Sanh packed with men of the 1st Infantry, 1st Airborne, and 1st Rangers.

On the southern escarpment, the insertions went smoothly, despite NVA antiaircraft fire: by the end of the day ARVN battalions, with artillery, had been established at LZs Blue and Hotel. On the northern flank, opposition was tougher, costing the Americans seven helicopters destroyed, but LZs were carved out at Hill 30, Hill 31, Ranger North, and Ranger South. It was a good start.

However, problems soon developed. Although 1st Armor reached Aloui, about 13 miles inside Laos, on February 10 (where they were joined by the 9th Airborne Battalion, helicoptered in at 1900 hours), they failed to advance any farther. Route 9 had deteriorated alarmingly as they moved forward from the border, and all wheeled vehicles had been left at LZ Bravo, unable to proceed because of the poor state of the road. No engineers were sent forward to effect repairs, leaving the tanks and APCs at Aloui dependent on helicopters for supply. A combination of misty, wet weather, and NVA antiaircraft fire meant that this could not always be guaranteed.

1st Armor just sat there, unsure what to do next.

This played into the hands of the NVA, giving them time to concentrate forces against the incursion. By February 12, all ARVN positions were coming under probing attacks, preparatory to a determined Communist counterattack in the north, where the firebases were spread out and vulnerable. Ranger North came under pressure first: on February 20, NVA infantry breached the perimeter wire and, after a night of vicious hand-to-hand fighting, the Rangers were forced to take shelter in the neighboring jungle, leaving 130 wounded behind.

U.S. rescue helicopters flew in on February 21, only to be swamped by panic-stricken South Vietnamese, some

The secret bombings

On March 18, 1969, in response to pleas from General Abrams, the MACV commander, to be allowed to use U.S. airpower against NVA bases in eastern Cambodia, President Nixon ordered B-52 Stratofortress bombers to initiate Operation Menu. Carried out in the strictest secrecy—the pilots, for example, were told merely to react to ground-control radar units and were not aware of their precise targets—the bombings continued until May 26, 1970. By then, the B-52s had flown 4,308 sorties and dropped a total of 120,578 tons of bombs on NVA supply dumps and base areas in Cambodia.

But the air actions did not end there. In late May, 1970, the operational codename was changed to Freedom Deal and the campaign opened up to USAF tactical aircraft, flying in support of Cambodian troops who were by now fighting an estimated 40,000 Communists northeast of the city of Phnom Penh.

Between July 31 and August 9, 1970, for example, 182 fighter-bomber and 37 gunship attacks prevented the fall of Kompong Thom, while similar strikes allowed Lon Nol's forces to recapture the town of Skoun. But the Cambodian Army was weak and, as the Communists closed in on the capital, USAF planes and Army helicopters continued to lend support. Freedom Deal was to continue until August 15, 1973, when, under intense political and public pressure, Nixon accepted Congressional calls for a halt under Public Law 93–52, which cut off all funds. Less than two years later, Phnom Penh fell to the Khmer Rouge led by the infamous Pol Pot.

Armed with 20mm cannon, bombs, rockets, and napalm, the A-1 Skyraider, shown flying over Pleiku (ABOVE) and on an aircraft carrier (TOP), played a crucial role in the covert bombing of Cambodia.

A North Vietnamese infantryman at the time of Lam Son 719. He wears the standard NVA green uniform with extra camouflage provided by a "shawl" of leaves hung around his neck. His helmet, modeled on the European colonial pith helmet, is ideally suited to jungle conditions, as are his rubber-and-canvas shoes. He is armed with an AK-47 Kalashnikov and carries three reserve "banana" bullet clips in his chest pouches.

of whom clung desperately to the skids of the overloaded choppers, only to fall to their deaths as the pilots struggled back to the border.

The same happened at Hill 31, attacked by over 2,000 NVA, backed by 20 Soviet-built PT-76 tanks, on February 25. As the 400 men of the 3d Airborne Battalion fought for their lives, two battalions of armored cavalry were ordered to leave Aloui and move north, through the jungle, to relieve them. Ambushed less than 2,000 yards from Hill 31, the APCs stopped and, in the absence of positive orders, went no farther.

U.S. airstrikes had been called in, but, when one of the Phantoms was shot down and its two-man crew seen to bail out, the entire air-support operation was diverted to rescue them. Only 55 ARVN from Hill 31 made it to safety. Now even more isolated, Ranger South and Hill 30 had to be abandoned, effectively closing down the northern arm of Lam Son 719.

General Lam, aware of the possibility of defeat, flew to Saigon on February 28 for urgent talks with Thieu. Together, they decided to revitalize the attack by concentrating on the southern arm, where 1st Infantry's firebases were still intact. On March 3, the 3/1st ARVN Infantry Regiment was helicoptered forward to a new LZ, codenamed Lolo, in the first of a series of "leapfrog" assaults toward Tchepone.

The NVA were waiting, and, as the first pair of Hueys touched down at Lolo, "all hell broke loose." Seven of the first ten helicopters were hit by rocket, mortar, or machine-gun fire, although this did not deter the U.S. pilots. All day they flew in, deposited troops, then (if still intact) went back to the border for another load. By nightfall, over 500 ARVN had been delivered, at a cost of seven helicopters destroyed and 35 damaged.

Such determination clearly surprised the NVA, who did relatively little to prevent ARVN landings farther west, at LZs Liz and Sophia II, on March 4/5. On the 6th, the entire 2d ARVN Infantry Regiment was brought in by helicopter from South Vietnam—a distance of 48 miles—to take LZ Hope to the northeast of Tchepone. There was little opposition, enabling the ARVN to claim a victory of sorts by taking the town.

But this success presented Lam with a hard decision. From the experiences so far on the northern flank and at LZ Lolo, it was obvious that the NVA was prepared to fight. If the ARVN was to continue deeper into Laos, casualties would be sure

157

The Ho Chi Minh Trail

In 1959, the Hanoi government decided to help the VC in South Vietnam by opening a supply line to them. At first, it was felt that this would be best achieved using a fleet of coastal vessels. But, as the enemy responded to this, the emphasis shifted to a 1,000-mile network of jungle and mountain trails—known collectively as the Ho Chi Minh Trail—which wound through eastern Laos and into Cambodia, crossing the border into South Vietnam.

Beginning in the North around the Mu Gia and Ban Karai passes, the trail zigzagged its way south inside a corridor up to 30 miles wide, within which parallel trails, connected by cross-tracks, granted a degree of immunity to aerial attacks. In the early years, the journey from the North took about six months; but as the war escalated improvements were made. Permanent way stations were set up as supply dumps and rest centers, and antiaircraft batteries were deployed. In the early 1960s, only about 400 tons of supplies a week could be moved into the South, mainly on porters' backs; ten years later, the trail had become a highway, capable of carrying over 10,000 trucks at any one time.

TRUCKS - MU GIA PASS AREA
8 FEBRUARY 1967

75 TRUCKS

ROUTE 15

MU GIA PASS

LAOS

NVA trucks (LEFT) head south along one of the roads of the Ho Chi Minh Trail. With the destruction of one of the trail's bridges (ABOVE) by American bombers, NVA engineers have created two by-pass fords to keep the traffic flowing.

to rise and the chances of a complete defeat increase. Rather than risk the political and military consequences of such an outcome, Lam ordered his men to disengage and fall back to the border.

The withdrawal began on March 11/12, when LZs Hope and Sophia II were abandoned without incident, but they were the exceptions. On March 16, it was the turn of LZ Lolo, by now containing all four battalions of the 1st ARVN Infantry Regiment. Three of them pulled

back on foot, leaving the 4th Battalion (420 men) as a rearguard. As soon as the main body had left, the NVA struck with overwhelming force: the 4/1st fought well for nearly two days, but by March 18, they were down to only 88 effectives, commanded by a sergeant. When helicopters of the 223d CAB went in to rescue them, they were mobbed; only 36 men were brought to safety, landing in bullet-ridden choppers at Khe Sanh, where the press was waiting. Reports of an ARVN disaster swept around the world.

These stories were reinforced by the experiences of the 1st Armor Brigade, ordered to pull back down Route 9 early on March 19. As they set out, towing 17 damaged tanks and APCs, promised support from two U.S. air-cavalry helicopter units failed to materialize (they had been diverted to support ARVN airborne forces in the mountains), leaving the column to proceed with no protective screen. As the lead tanks—four M-41s—crossed a stream to the east of Aloui at 0800 hours, they came under NVA rocket fire from the jungle fringe. One tank was disabled, causing the crews of the other three (with the accompanying ARVN paratroopers) to abandon their vehicles and flee down the trail, heading east.

The tanks effectively blocked the way for the rest of the column, which came under sustained NVA attack. It took three hours to maneuver APCs forward under fire to remove two of the tanks, after which the column started moving again, although without the 17 vehicles previously under tow. They were later destroyed by U.S. Cobra gunships.

The withdrawal rapidly became a rout, for although the 1st Armor column eventually made it back to the border, the NVA infiltrated forces along Route 9 in front of it. This in turn threatened the U.S. firebases in Vietnam, which had to be withdrawn, under tank escort, along what soon became known as "Ambush Alley." Meanwhile, South Vietnamese Marines had pulled back under fire from LZs Blue and Hotel, occupied when the 1st Infantry moved forward to Tchepone. Lam Son 719 was officially terminated on April 6. By then, the ARVN had lost 1,529 men killed and 5,483 wounded, while U.S. losses were 219 killed and 1,149 wounded as well as 107 helicopters destroyed and 618 damaged.

Like most operations, success was claimed—it was estimated, for example, that the NVA had suffered nearly 20,000 casualties and had been prevented from mounting an offensive into MRI—but no one could disguise the poor performance of the South Vietnamese. Without U.S. air and artillery support, their losses would have been even greater, while various shortcomings—in command initiative, inter-unit cooperation, and tactical skills—had been highlighted.

The problems of Vietnamization

After the shock of the 1968 Tet Offensive, U.S. political leaders desired that the South Vietnamese armed forces be bolstered, allowing more U.S. troops to be sent home. The ARVN had responded to the crisis of Tet well and there were hopes that a competent military force was emerging.

Unfortunately for the allies, Vietnamization did not run smoothly. Because of the pressures for U.S. withdrawal, the process was rushed, with little time available for the ARVN to prove itself in battle while the Americans were still present in strength. Also, the emphasis was firmly on creating a duplicate U.S. Army trained by U.S. officers, such as the one shown (BELOW) with ARVN soldiers, complete with U.S. weapons, equipment, and air support, but often at the cost of basic military training. Despite U.S. efforts, the ARVN, by 1971, was little more than a facade: it looked strong and could, in the right circumstances, fight well, but political corruption and endemic desertion denied it any staying power. It was to operate well against the NVA Easter Offensive in 1972, but had the advantage of U.S. air support. Once that had gone, the ARVN became little more than a shell.

THE WAR YEARS

March 18, 1970	Prince Sihanouk overthrown as head of state in Cambodia by Lon Nol.
April 29/ June 30, 1970	ARVN incursions into the "Parrot's Beak" and U.S./ARVN incursions into the "Fish Hook," eastern Cambodia, trigger demonstrations in the U.S.
May 4, 1970	National Guardsmen open fire on antiwar protestors, Kent State, Ohio: four students killed.
June 24, 1970	U.S. Senate repeals the 1964 Gulf of Tonkin Resolution.
Jan. 30/ Feb. 7, 1971	U.S. forces carry out Operation Dewey Canyon II to clear Route 9 to the Laotian border in MRI.
April 19/ 26, 1971	Vietnam Veterans Against The War stage a series of demonstrations in Washington.
Aug. 18, 1971	Australia and New Zealand decide to withdraw their forces from South Vietnam by the end of the year.
Nov. 12, 1971	President Nixon announces a further U.S. troop withdrawal of 45,000 men, bringing the total of U.S. forces in South Vietnam down to 139,000.

AN LOC

April 8–July 11, 1972

ESPITE THE SUCCESS OF THE NVA in blunting the South Vietnamese incursion into Laos in early 1971, the government in Hanoi could not be satisfied with the progress of the war. Over the previous few years, any hopes of winning a "People's War," based on the Maoist model of subversion, guerrilla pressure, and open battle, had faded; and the Communists had been forced to accept a steady reduction of influence in key areas of South Vietnam.

The U.S.-backed policy of pacification, coupled with the crippling of the VC in the Tet Offensive of 1968, had allowed the Saigon authorities to reclaim control of all but 10 of their 45 provinces. A U.S. withdrawal may have been effected, but the campaign in the South, from the Communist point of view, had stagnated.

Hanoi could, of course, rebuild the VC using North Vietnamese "fillers" infiltrated down the Ho Chi Minh Trail. This would take time, however, during which the South's armed forces—already increased to more than a million men under Vietnamization—would be greatly improved and strengthened.

An alternative was to take immediate advantage of the U.S. withdrawal, hitting the ARVN while it was still psychologically dependent on the Americans, and gambling on the fact that U.S. politicians would be unlikely to authorize a recommitment of force now that their involvement in an unpopular war was running down. As 1972 was a U.S. presidential election year, during which no candidate would dare to alienate public opinion, arguments in favor of a full-scale conventional invasion of the South during that year seemed persuasive.

Le Duan, First Secretary of North Vietnam's ruling Lao Dong party, put such arguments to the Soviet leadership when he visited Moscow in the spring of 1971. They were sympathetic, recognizing that, if the South was defeated, it would not only put President Nixon at a disadvantage in forthcoming superpower

> **"Hold them and I'll kill them with airpower. Give me somebody to bomb and I'll win."**

MAJOR GENERAL JAMES HOLLINGSWORTH, SENIOR U.S. ADVISER, ARVN III CORPS, APRIL, 1972

talks, but would also create a unified Vietnam indebted to the Soviet Union and obliged to act as a counter to Chinese influence in Southeast Asia. Le Duan received promises of substantial aid, chiefly in terms of modern arms.

By the end of the year, the NVA had been transformed from an essentially guerrilla army into a modern conventional force, equipped with T-34, T-54/55 and PT-76 tanks, long-range 130mm artillery pieces, mobile SAMs, and fleets of trucks. To make full use of the latter, the Ho Chi Minh Trail was widened, supply dumps were located at key points close to intended invasion routes, and forces were built up along the borders of South Vietnam. Ominously for the South, General Vo Nguyen Giap, Minister of Defense in Hanoi and victor of Dien Bien Phu, was put in overall command.

Giap's plan was a complex one. Instead of concentrating his substantial forces—over 200,000 men—in one place, he divided the assault into three separate operations, designed to confuse and weaken the ARVN response. The attack would begin around the DMZ, with a full-scale multidivisional advance south toward Hue and Da Nang, with other forces pressing in from the A Shau valley in the west. This, it was argued, would force President Thieu to commit reserves to protect his northern provinces, upon which a second assault would emerge from Cambodia to threaten Saigon through Tay Ninh and Binh Long provinces, while other forces entered the Mekong Delta.

Once again, ARVN reserves would have to be committed, leaving few available to face the third and final attack, through the Central Highlands to take Kontum and aim for the coast in Binh Dinh province. This would split South Vietnam in two, leading to its collapse or, at the very least, a peace agreement on Hanoi's terms.

The plan had certain basic flaws—particularly in its failure to concentrate NVA forces, leaving them vulnerable to

Off-duty ARVN soldiers (ABOVE) inspect an abandoned NVA tank in a street of An Loc. With the help of massive U.S. air support, South Vietnamese troops managed to prevent a strong Communist force from overrunning the town during the 1972 Easter Offensive.

Advancing on foot and atop APCs, ARVN troops cross marshland in an operation to clear Route 13, the main road connecting Saigon with the besieged defenders of An Loc.

An ARVN APC moves down a street in Quang Tri City, which has been devastated by bombardments and airstrikes during the battle for its control. The ARVN eventually managed to recapture the battered town in September, 1972, more than four months after it had fallen to the Communists.

piecemeal defeat—and it took little account of the potential impact of U.S. and South Vietnamese air attack. Indeed, the offensive was affected by airpower before it began, for as early as December, 1971, the NVA buildup was monitored and selected strikes were carried out against force concentrations and supply

dumps close to the DMZ. By then, the allies were convinced that the North would attack during the Tet celebrations in February, 1972; when they passed off peacefully, the ARVN relaxed. At the same time, American (and world) attention shifted to China, where Nixon's historic visit dominated the news. It was just what Giap wanted.

The offensive began at noon on Thursday, March 30, 1972, on the eve of the Easter weekend. ARVN firebases just south of the DMZ were suddenly swamped with artillery fire, chiefly from Soviet-supplied M-46 130mm field guns north of the border, beyond the range of the U.S.-built 105mm and 155mm pieces in ARVN hands. Simultaneously, three NVA divisions—a total of 30,000 men, backed by up to 200 tanks—swept across the DMZ to overwhelm outposts manned by the inexperienced ARVN 3d Division, which fell back in great confusion about ten miles toward Dong Ha on the Mieu Giang River.

The situation was saved by the destruction of the Dong Ha bridges—blown up, in the absence of precise orders, by prudent U.S. advisers—and by the arrival of the ARVN 20th Tank Regiment, equipped with U.S. M-48s. Blocked at Dong Ha, the NVA shifted some 12 miles west to Cam Lo, aiming to cross the river and link up with the NVA 324thB Division, already moving east from the A Shau valley.

Despite a lack of air support because of poor weather, the ARVN appeared to have consolidated a defense line, but it did not last. On Easter Sunday, April 2, the firebase at Camp Carroll, subjected to a deluge of artillery shells and rockets, suddenly collapsed, opening up a huge gap at just the point where the NVA divisions advancing south and east were aiming to link up. They poured through the gap, taking the bridge at Cam Lo and forcing the ARVN to pull back again, this time to the east, creating a new defense line that stretched in an arc from the Cua Viet River near the coast, through Dong Ha to the Thach Han River close to Quang Tri City.

Refugees were already clogging the roads leading south to Hue but, despite panic in the ARVN 3d Division, the line held, shored up by Vietnamese Marines, the crack ARVN 1st Division, and the ubiquitous 20th Tank Regiment. Furthermore, as the weather cleared, Nixon authorized the commitment of U.S. airpower, sending fighter-bombers north of the DMZ for the first time since 1968 and ordering air reinforcements into the war

Nixon's visit to China

President Nixon's visit to Peking in late February, 1972, was an indication of U.S. awareness of the growing importance of international power politics to the Vietnam War. Throughout the 1960s, North Vietnam enjoyed virtually unlimited support from the two Communist "giants"—China and the Soviet Union—by portraying the conflict in the South as a "war of independence" against "lackeys of the imperialist West."

The situation began to change in 1968, as a Sino-Soviet split emerged. A series of events—the Soviet invasion of Czechoslovakia, the announcement of the Brezhnev Doctrine outlining the "right" of the Soviet Union to intervene in the affairs of "deviant" Communist states, the Cultural Revolution in China—led in 1969 to a buildup of forces on both sides of the Sino-Soviet border. The United States recognized an opportunity for driving a wedge between Hanoi and its supporters, particularly China. Although Nixon, shown (RIGHT) meeting Mao Tse-tung, produced no concrete proposals concerning Vietnam from his visit, it was obvious to the North that

China was prepared to seek a rapprochement with the United States that could only result in a cut in support levels. When, less than three months later, Nixon visited Moscow with new arms control proposals, the Soviets appeared to be following a similar line, fearful that Sino-American links would surround the U.S.S.R. Although both Communist powers still provided arms and equipment, Hanoi was being forced to the conference table.

Tank action at Dong Ha

By March 31, 1972, the NVA attack south of the DMZ in MRI had overrun outlying ARVN firebases and was approaching the Mieu Giang River, northwest of Quang Tri City. The ARVN commander, General Vu Van Giai, hastily established a defense line on the south bank of the river. Included in his formations was the newly formed 20th Tank Regiment, equipped with U.S.-supplied M-48A3s—one of which is shown (RIGHT), trapped in a crater in Quang Tri.

Initially deployed to guard bridges over the river at Dong Ha, the regiment got off to a good start when it hit an NVA column moving south along Route 1, destroying nine PT-76 and two T-54 tanks for no loss. This threw the NVA into confusion, disrupting their advance until April 2, when they tried to by-pass Dong Ha to the west, through Cam Lo. On that occasion, the South Vietnamese tankers destroyed a further 16 T-54s.

The NVA paused to build up their forces and to bring forward Soviet-supplied AT-3 Sagger wire-guided antitank missiles. On April 27, under heavy artillery support, the

Communists renewed their attack all along the line. The 20th Tank Regiment, ordered to move west to plug a reported gap, began to suffer losses. These were exacerbated by a lack of supplies and a general panic among other ARVN units in the area. By May 2, the regiment had been forced to retreat south of Quang Tri City, having lost or abandoned all its vehicles. Nevertheless, its actions had helped to disrupt the NVA advance.

By April 13, 1972, Communist forces, made up of the NVA/VC 9th Division and the NVA 7th Division, had the defenders of An Loc (**7**) in a stranglehold. Six days before, Communist troops had taken Quan Loi airfield to the east of An Loc, giving them the valuable high ground from which to shell the town.

Communist T-54 tanks (**8**), accompanied by infantry, rumbled into An Loc from the northeast.

The ARVN defenders reacted quickly and knocked out the lead T-54 with an M72 Light Antitank Weapon. The enemy armor was then

The next assault (**1**) came at 1015 from the northwest, with Communist tanks and infantry advancing (**2**) into the south of the town. Again, however, formidable airpower (**3** and **5**), including USAF A-37s from Bien Hoa, blunted the enemy advance.

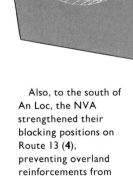

Also, to the south of An Loc, the NVA strengthened their blocking positions on Route 13 (**4**), preventing overland reinforcements from Saigon. At dawn on April 13, six engaged by three U.S. Army Cobra helicopters (**6**) whose high-explosive rockets destroyed four more tanks and stalled the attack.

163

On March 30, 1972, the NVA Easter Offensive began with the aim of destroying the ARVN and overthrowing the Thieu government of South Vietnam. The NVA initially achieved rapid success as they swept over the DMZ and, later, east into the Central Highlands and south toward Saigon.

The NVA 7th Division moved south of An Loc, cutting Route 13 and the town's connection with Saigon. By April 7, An Loc was surrounded—a bitter 95-day siege had begun.

As NVA artillery began raining shells down on An Loc on April 12, ARVN troops prepared themselves for the inevitable assault. By this time, the town was being defended by the battered ARVN 5th Division and four Ranger battalions.

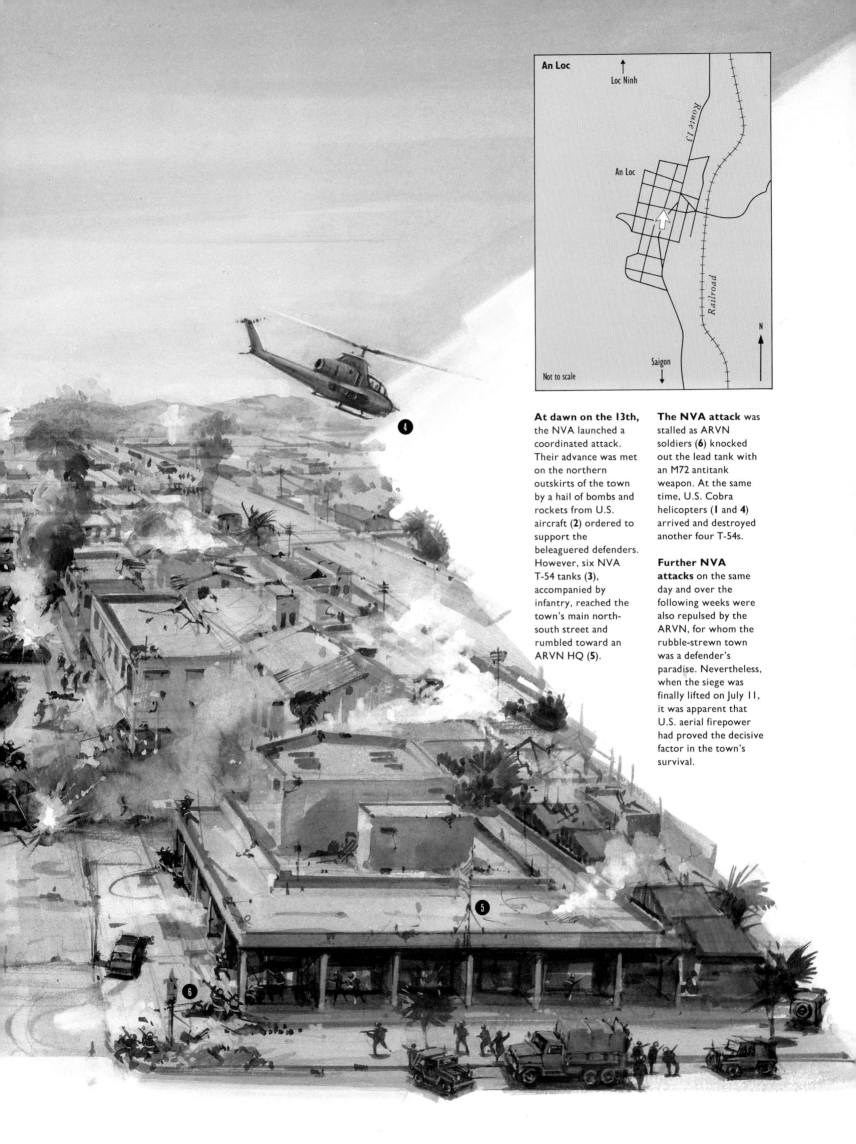

An Loc

Loc Ninh

Route 13

An Loc

Railroad

Saigon

Not to scale

N

At dawn on the 13th, the NVA launched a coordinated attack. Their advance was met on the northern outskirts of the town by a hail of bombs and rockets from U.S. aircraft (**2**) ordered to support the beleaguered defenders. However, six NVA T-54 tanks (**3**), accompanied by infantry, reached the town's main north-south street and rumbled toward an ARVN HQ (**5**).

The NVA attack was stalled as ARVN soldiers (**6**) knocked out the lead tank with an M72 antitank weapon. At the same time, U.S. Cobra helicopters (**1** and **4**) arrived and destroyed another four T-54s.

Further NVA attacks on the same day and over the following weeks were also repulsed by the ARVN, for whom the rubble-strewn town was a defender's paradise. Nevertheless, when the siege was finally lifted on July 11, it was apparent that U.S. aerial firepower had proved the decisive factor in the town's survival.

zone. By April 6, additional USAF squadrons were on route to Southeast Asia, while four extra carriers joined the Seventh Fleet task force off the coast.

This was just as well, for, by now, Giap's second assault had materialized. On April 2, NVA/VC forces crossed the border from Cambodia, threatening Tay Ninh City. Thieu hurriedly committed reinforcements from the Mekong Delta (itself about to be attacked), only to discover that this was a feint. On April 5, a much more dangerous attack began, as the NVA/VC 9th Division suddenly advanced on Loc Ninh to the east. Defended by an infantry regiment and a Ranger battalion, the town fell in less than 24 hours, opening up a direct route to

Saigon—Route 13 through An Loc and Lai Khe.

Realizing the danger, Thieu ordered his 5th Division into An Loc, with the ARVN 21st Division and parts of the 9th Division—withdrawn from the Delta—entering Lai Khe to create a second line of defense. He was only just in time: as the ARVN 5th Division completed its move, reinforced at the last moment by two Ranger battalions, the NVA 7th Division swept in from the west, cutting Route 13 to the south, between An Loc and Lai Khe. As the NVA/VC 9th Division closed in from the north and east, taking the outpost of Quan Loi and its important airfield on April 7, An Loc was surrounded. NVA commanders confidently

predicted that they would be in Saigon itself by the 20th.

NVA artillery began to soften up An Loc on April 12, causing some damage, but forcing the ARVN defenders—by now reinforced by a further two Ranger battalions, flown in on the 10th—to dig in. Major General James Hollingsworth, senior U.S. adviser to the ARVN III Corps, did all he could to help, persuading MACV commander General Creighton Abrams to provide maximum air support. Thus, when the Communists moved out of the surrounding hills and rubber plantations to attack An Loc at dawn on April 13, they did so through a deluge of bombs, rockets, and cannon shells delivered by U.S. aircraft.

Nevertheless, a group of six T-54 tanks, accompanied by infantry, did survive to penetrate the town's perimeter, lumbering down the main street from the northeast toward the ARVN headquarters. The lead tank was hit and disabled by an ARVN soldier using a U.S.-supplied M72 LAW (Light Antitank Weapon) and, as the other five tried to maneuver around it to continue the advance, three U.S. Army AH-IG Cobra gunships appeared overhead. Firing their 2.75in armor-piercing rockets, they disabled a further four tanks, scattering the infantry and halting the attack.

The NVA tried again at 1015 hours, this time with 10 tanks advancing from the northwest, but the combination of

LAWs and Cobra gunships, joined by USAF A-37 Dragonfly ground-attack aircraft from Bien Hoa, took its toll. As the streets of An Loc filled with burning enemy tanks, ARVN morale soared, but not for long: despite the U.S. airstrikes, Communist troops pressed on relentlessly, seizing the vital airstrip and reducing the defenses to an area less than a mile square.

Thieu ordered his personal guard, the ARVN 1st Parachute Brigade, to reinforce An Loc (they arrived by parachute late on the 13th), but the defenders were beginning to wilt. Without U.S. air support—including B-52s, committed to strike NVA concentration areas in the surrounding countryside—An Loc

U.S. tactical air support, 1972

When the NVA Easter Offensive began on March 30, 1972, President Nixon was swift to offer support to the embattled ARVN. No U.S. ground combat units were available, but tactical airpower was. Within hours, USAF fighter-bombers and B-52s from Thailand and Guam, plus USN and Marine aircraft from the Seventh Fleet offshore, had been committed to the fray.

The NVA had been expecting such a reaction. All their units committed to the South had Soviet-supplied surface-to-air missiles (SAMs) and antiaircraft guns attached, while the offensive had been timed to coincide with overcast skies. But the Americans were by now extremely experienced, and their countermeasures were both swift and effective. F-4 or F-105 "Wild Weasels" flew SAM-suppression missions, while OV-10 Bronco FACs (Forward Air Controllers) called in wave after wave of fighter-bombers, gunships, and attack helicopters.

At the same time, in a rerun of the earlier Arc Light strikes, B-52s—operating in three-aircraft "cells"—flew from Thailand and Guam to deliver devastating weights of high explosives. On May 11/12, for example, during the battle of An Loc, B-52 cells appeared over the battle area every 55 minutes for 30 consecutive hours. Elsewhere, newly developed laser-guided "smart" weapons enhanced accuracy and proved particularly useful against NVA armor. In the northern provinces of South Vietnam between April 1 and August 15, it was estimated that U.S. aircraft destroyed 285 tanks. The NVA had no effective response.

F-4 Phantoms, shown (LEFT) in formation with an RB-66, played an important role in

U.S. tactical air support for ARVN forces in 1972.

Thieu and Ky: leading the South

Born in Annam in 1923, Nguyen Van Thieu (BELOW RIGHT) graduated from the Vietnamese Military Academy in 1949 and attended the U.S. Command and General Staff College at Fort Leavenworth in 1957. By 1963, Thieu was commanding the ARVN 5th Infantry Division, participating in the coup to overthrow President Diem.

In 1965, as one of the "Young Turks," he played a leading role in overthrowing General Khanh, after which he was appointed Chairman of the National Leadership Committee. When elections were held in 1967, he became President of South Vietnam. Reelected in 1971, he faced the difficult task of preserving his country as the U.S. made peace with the North and withdrew. In 1975, when the NVA invaded, Thieu made a series of military decisions which proved disastrous, allowing the Communists to advance rapidly toward Saigon. On April 21, he resigned and fled.

Nguyen Cao Ky (BELOW LEFT) was born near Hanoi in 1930 and first saw military service in 1950, when he was drafted into the Vietnamese National Army, established by the French. He was subsequently trained as a pilot, and his promotion was rapid in the postindependence air force. By 1965, when he participated in the "Young Turk" rebellion, he was already a lieutenant general. He was elected to the Armed Forces Council as prime minister, a post he continued to fill, despite howls of protest from Buddhists and other political factions he suppressed, until the elections of 1967, when he became vice-president under Thieu. However, Ky refused to stand in the presidential elections of 1971, accusing Thieu of vote rigging; instead, he reverted to his military rank of air marshal. In April, 1975, he fled Saigon, and settled in California.

M-48A3 Patton Medium Tank (U.S.)

Weight	47.2 tons
Crew	4
Max speed	30mph
Armament	90mm main gun; one 30-cal coaxial machine gun and one 50-cal cupola-mounted machine gun

Tanks in Vietnam

Although South Vietnam was not ideal tank country, lacking the wide open spaces for deployment of massed formations, both sides in the conflict used tanks with some success. On the Allied side, American M-41s (and some M-48s) were issued to the ARVN, while U.S. Marine and Army units used the M-48 (ABOVE and LEFT), M-60, and M-551 Sheridan, the latter a light reconnaissance vehicle with a sophisticated gun/missile armament. The Australians used British-designed Centurions. NVA units deployed Soviet- or Chinese-built PT-76 amphibious tanks as early as 1968, which by 1972 had been joined by T-54/55s with heavier armor and armament, although both types proved vulnerable to U.S. airpower.

T-54 Main Battle Tank (NVA)

Weight	36 tons
Crew	4
Max speed	30mph
Armament	100mm main gun; one 7.62mm or 12.7mm turret-mounted machine gun

would probably have fallen, leaving the road to Saigon protected by little more than the ARVN 21st Division. As that formation was displaying a distinct lack of effectiveness in its efforts to push north from Lai Khe, the situation would have been desperate.

In the event only one regiment (belonging to the ARVN 9th Division) made any progress, by-passing NVA roadblocks to the east, but it soon found itself caught in a no-man's-land swept by enemy fire. Only 120 survivors—all of them wounded—broke through to An Loc on April 15, leaving the road still blocked behind them. The NVA settled down to conduct a siege, reducing An

Loc to rubble as they poured artillery fire down from the nearby hills. USAF C-130s had to be brought in to drop supplies to the battered defenders, while fighter-bombers, gunships, and B-52s offered round-the-clock support.

With NVA assaults in both north and south apparently stalled, it looked as if Thieu had made the right responses. But Giap still had a final card to play—his third attack, through the Central Highlands. As early as April 12, the NVA gave notice of their intentions in this area by attacking "Rocket Ridge" overlooking Dak To. They followed this up on the 23rd with a full-scale assault on isolated ARVN outposts, defended by elements of

the 22d Division, at Tan Canh, Dak To II, and Ben Het. The offensive caught the ARVN commander, Colonel Le Duc Dat, unprepared. As a result, despite the presence of the vastly experienced John Paul Vann, now chief adviser to the ARVN II Corps, the outposts quickly fell. As ARVN survivors pulled back toward Kontum, Vann (soon to be killed in a helicopter crash) took it upon himself to organize a defense of the city, moving ARVN Rangers and units of the 23d Division from elsewhere in MRII. By early May, Kontum was under siege, its survival dependent on U.S. air support.

Any hope of reinforcing Kontum was dashed by events farther north. On April

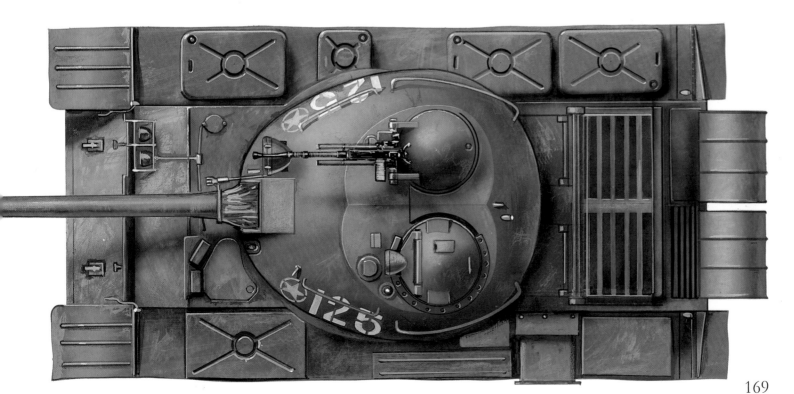

27, the NVA began to probe the Cua Viet-Thach Han defense line, achieving an unexpected success when the already demoralized ARVN 3d Division collapsed.

Amid rumors that the enemy had broken through to the west, ARVN soldiers abandoned their positions to flee south toward Quang Tri City. Instead of investigating the truth of such rumors, Lieutenant General Hoang Xuan Lam, commander of the ARVN I Corps, ordered the 20th Tank Regiment to move to the west: when the M-48s began to leave Dong Ha, units on their flanks joined the withdrawal, convinced that the end was near.

Looters (LEFT) scavenge in a shell-torn street of Dong Ha during the NVA Easter Offensive.

Men of the ARVN 21st Division fight their way along Route 13 toward the beleaguered town of An Loc.

The 3d Division commander, Brigadier General Vu Van Giai, tried to stop the panic, but to no avail. By May 1, the NVA had seized Quang Tri City, adding to the chaos by shelling Route 1 to the south, by now jammed with soldiers, civilians, and abandoned equipment. An estimated 20,000 people died.

Ironically, the fall of Quang Tri City highlighted the central flaw in Giap's strategy. Because of the attacks elsewhere—by this time stalled around An Loc and Kontum—there were no NVA reserves available to exploit what could have been a decisive thrust in the northern provinces.

Instead, Thieu was given time to restore order by sacking Lam, arresting Giai, and turning I Corps over to Lieutenant General Ngo Quang Truong, one of the South's most experienced commanders. He formed a new defensive line about 25 miles north of Hue, on the My Chanh River, halting the panic by threatening to shoot all deserters and looters. Lacking the strength to pursue their advantage, the NVA had no choice but to allow this consolidation to take place.

This pattern was repeated elsewhere, for while the crisis was occurring in the northern provinces, NVA assaults in Binh Long province and the Central Highlands were being blocked, then turned back, using a combination of U.S. airpower and ARVN resolve. At An Loc, the NVA/VC 5th Division—tasked with

destroying the town when it was obvious that the 9th Division had failed—mounted a major assault on May 9.

In response, Hollingsworth called in the B-52s, and for the next five days, they appeared over the battle area to pulverize enemy approach routes. By the 14th, the Communists had had enough; although they did not pull back from An Loc or Lai Khe (the siege of An Loc was not officially lifted until July 11, after 95 days), they tried no more open assaults. Around Kontum, U.S. air support prevented an NVA victory, even though small groups of sappers did manage to infiltrate the city. By late May, the worst was over.

Fighting continued, especially in the north, until September, when Quang Tri City was reoccupied by the ARVN after a particularly tough battle. But by then it had been obvious for some time that Giap's strategy had failed. His inability (or unwillingness) to concentrate his forces gave the South the opportunity to blunt and then counterattack each NVA offensive in turn, while the weight of U.S. fire support was decisive.

In the northern provinces alone, ships of the Seventh Fleet fired over 160,000 tons of shells against land targets between

April and September, while over South Vietnam as a whole some 700 U.S. fighter-bombers and 170 B-52s had been on constant call. With An Loc and Kontum acting as rocks in the stream of the Communist advance, Giap's chances of victory were slim.

By September, 1972, the North Vietnamese had lost about half their committed force—an estimated 100,000 men—against a South Vietnamese casualty figure half that size. The NVA remained in possession of a 10-mile strip of territory just south of the DMZ, as well as a few enclaves close to the Cambodian border, but this was small compensation for such enormous losses. As long as the Americans were prepared to commit their air (and naval) assets to the protection of the South, Hanoi could not hope to win, particularly when elements of those assets were also being used to bomb North Vietnam itself. It was, indeed, a lesson learned the hard way.

THE WAR YEARS

Feb. 21, 1972	President Nixon begins an official visit to China.
March 30/ April 1, 1972	The NVA Easter Offensive begins with an attack south from the DMZ toward Quang Tri City.
April 5, 1972	The NVA open up a second offensive from Cambodia into Binh Long province, north of Saigon.
April 8	The NVA open up a third offensive from Laos and Cambodia into the Central Highlands. In Binh Long province, An Loc is surrounded.
May 8, 1972	President Nixon orders the mining of North Vietnamese ports and increased bombing of "war-related" targets in Operation Linebacker.
May 13	USAF F-4 Phantoms use laser-guided bombs to cut the Thanh Hoa bridge in North Vietnam.
May 20	Summit meeting in Moscow between President Nixon and First Secretary Leonid Brezhnev.
June 28, 1972	The ARVN, with U.S. air and naval support, begin a counteroffensive in Quang Tri province.
July 11, 1972	Siege of An Loc ends; NVA pulls back.

Communist soldiers captured during the offensive grimace with discomfort.

The NVA lost an estimated 100,000 men during the hard-fought campaign.

THANH HOA BRIDGE

May 13, 1972

T HE AMERICAN AIR RESPONSE TO the North Vietnamese invasion of the South in 1972 was not confined to the battlefield alone. President Nixon's immediate reaction was to consider hitting NVA supply dumps and lines of communication north of the DMZ—a plan of action that seemed justified when the nature of the invasion was realized.

Before 1968, NVA forces in the South had needed no more than 400 tons of supplies a week to survive, but the large-scale conventional army of 1972 required an estimated 10,000 tons a week. The bulk of such supplies had to be received in Hanoi or Haiphong from the North's foreign backers, then transported south toward the battle area. Ports, railroads, roads, and bridges were clearly vulnerable targets; their destruction would have an immediate effect on the ability of the NVA to fight.

By April 6, 1972, Nixon had more than 1,000 fighter-bombers and 200 B-52s available in or around Southeast Asia. A large proportion of them would need to be committed to the battlefield if the ARVN was to survive, and this fact—coupled with a political desire not to jeopardize forthcoming superpower talks with the Soviet Union—initially restricted the scope of any new campaign against North Vietnam.

Under the codename Freedom Dawn, fighter-bombers were kept below the 20th parallel, hitting supply lines and storage areas close to the DMZ, but when this strategy had no discernible effect, Nixon went one stage further. On April 16, 17 B-52s launched a nighttime raid against POL storage facilities around Haiphong. It was the first time the Stratofortresses had been deployed that far north and was a portent of things to come.

This was only part of the campaign. If NVA supplies were to be disrupted quickly, certain targets in the North seemed ideal, particularly the road and rail bridges linking Hanoi to the ports and

> ### "The [North Vietnamese] have never been bombed like they're going to be bombed this time."
>
> PRESIDENT RICHARD M. NIXON, APRIL, 1972

carrying supplies toward the DMZ. Chief among them were the Paul Doumer, a huge 5,532-foot bridge east of Hanoi, and the Ham Rung ("Dragon's Jaw"), a smaller 540-foot structure that spanned the Ma River near Thanh Hoa, south of the capital.

Both bridges had been attacked during Operation Rolling Thunder (1965–68) and, in August, 1967, spans of the Paul Doumer had been destroyed, but the raids had been costly to the Americans and had inflicted little permanent damage. Enormous concentrations of enemy antiaircraft and SAM defenses had taken a steady toll on the attackers, damage had been quickly repaired, and supplies had continued to flow. During the bombing halt after November, 1968, repairs had been made more permanent.

By April, 1972, the Americans had access to "smart" weapons which promised to achieve more instantaneous and decisive results. Electro-optical guided bombs (EOGBs) and laser-guided bombs (LGBs) used new technology to guarantee pinpoint accuracy—the former by TV guidance, the latter by "locking on" to a laser beam directed at the target—while a variety of electronic aids enhanced the survivability of any attacking force. When the bridges appeared on the strike lists for Freedom Dawn in early April, the USAF was confident of success and organized immediate attacks on the targets.

The first of these attacks, against the Thanh Hoa bridge, took place on April 27. Preceded by four F-4 Phantoms, which laid a "chaff" corridor to confuse enemy radars, eight F-4s of the 8th Tactical Fighter Wing (TFW) commanded by Colonel Carl S. Miller, set out from Ubon Royal Thai Air Base laden with 2,000-pound guided weapons. When they arrived over the target, the weather was not clear enough to "illuminate" the bridge for LGBs, but five EOGBs were successfully launched despite a barrage of antiaircraft and SAM fire. Post-raid reconnaissance showed

An F-4 Phantom (ABOVE) drops a Paveway laser-guided bomb (LGB) toward its target. The LGB was one of a new generation of "smart" weapons which totally revolutionized air warfare. In simple terms, the target was illuminated by a laser beam from a Pave Knife laser designator attached to the underside of the aircraft. The bomb was then released and would "ride the beam" to the target, using its laser seeker unit.

The formidable B-52 Stratofortress bombers (RIGHT) were unleashed by President Nixon as part of the Linebacker bombing campaign over North Vietnam in 1972. Carrying a bombload of up to 70,000 pounds each, the B-52s launched a series of particularly devastating attacks (unofficially codenamed Linebacker II) on previously restricted targets in the Hanoi/Haiphong area from December 18 to 30.

173

Boeing B-52D Stratofortress

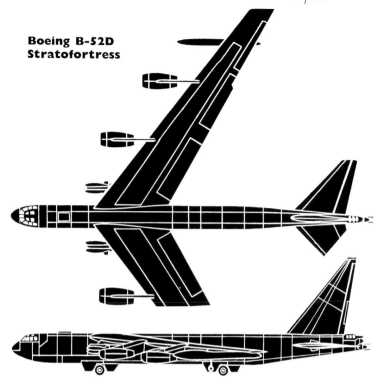

Weight	450,000 lb (loaded)	Max speed	630mph
		Range	6,200 miles
Bombload	up to 70,000 lb of "iron" bombs		

General Dynamics F-111A

Weight	91,500 lb (loaded)	Max speed	1,450mph (Mach 2.2) at 35,000 ft; 800mph (Mach 1.2) at low level
Bombload	18,000 lb (24 × 750 lb bombs) normal load over North Vietnam	Range	3,165 miles

The B-52 and the F-111A were both used to bomb Hanoi and Haiphong in December, 1972, during the Linebacker II raids. This allowed the B-52 to assume its originally intended role as a strategic aircraft. Up to this point, it had been used only for tactical strikes. The swing-wing F-111A could fly at low level in all weathers to hit precise targets. Together they made a formidable strike package.

damage to the bridge, although not enough to destroy it entirely. Another raid was needed.

Before that attack could be carried out, the 8th TFW was tasked to hit the Paul Doumer bridge as part of an elaborate strike package involving more than 50 assorted aircraft. Organized into flights of four, 16 F-4s launched a total of 22 LGBs and 7 EOGBs against the target on May 10, achieving a number of hits which destroyed one span and damaged several more. Twenty-four hours later, a single flight returned to the scene, releasing eight LGBs which completed the job: by the end of the day, three more spans were down, and the Paul Doumer was effectively out of action. No U.S. aircraft had been lost.

Confidence among the F-4 crews was high when, on May 13, they were ordered to return to the Dragon's Jaw. This time, the strike force consisted of 14 aircraft, carrying a total of nine 3,000-pound and fifteen 2,000-pound LGBs as well as

HANOI THERMAL POWER PLANT

BEFORE

16 NOV 72

forty-eight 500-pound conventional bombs. The aircraft flew from Thailand across Vietnam to the Gulf of Tonkin before swinging northwest to approach the bridge from the sea. Skies were clear and, despite an intense antiaircraft/SAM response, the guided weapons were successfully launched from an altitude of 14,000 feet some two or three miles from the target. Laser illumination was effective: as the smoke and dust cleared, the western span of the bridge lay twisted and broken. Again, no U.S. aircraft were lost.

By this time, peace negotiations in Paris had broken down, and Nixon had authorized a more sustained bombing campaign. Codenamed Operation Linebacker, it was initiated on May 8 when the President, in a special TV broadcast to the American nation, announced his intention to mine North Vietnamese ports and to release his aircraft—including the B-52s—to hit war-related targets all over the country. It was a calculated gamble, designed to exploit the desire for détente among Hanoi's foreign backers, but it was not just a rerun of Rolling Thunder.

The basic aim of Linebacker—to reduce North Vietnam's capability to wage continued war in the South—was familiar; but by concentrating on supply targets, it was achievable. In addition, as the decision to mine the ports implied, Nixon was prepared to be much more ruthless, and this hardline attitude was manifested in a relaxation of the tight political control that had characterized the earlier campaign. Under Linebacker, the air commanders were allowed to choose their targets more freely and to design the appropriate strike packages.

This system was essential if the USAF, Marine, and USN aircraft committed to the bombing were to survive what was by now a highly sophisticated air-defense system in the North. Attack aircraft—usually 32 F-4s carrying guided weapons and conventional bombs—were protected by 20 to 40 support aircraft, including F-4 or F-105 "Wild Weasels"

HANOI THERMAL POWER PLANT

AFTER

The two aerial reconnaissance photos (OPPOSITE PAGE and LEFT) show the Hanoi Thermal Power Plant before and after a U.S. bombing raid during Operation Linebacker in 1972. The fact that the damage was effectively limited to the power plant indicates the use of "smart" bombs, whose pinpoint accuracy added a new dimension to U.S. aerial offensives.

The peace merchants

Born of Jewish parents in Germany in 1923, Henry Kissinger (ABOVE RIGHT) attended Harvard University and was awarded a doctorate in 1954. Specializing in international politics, he was appointed National Security Adviser to Richard Nixon in early 1969. Kissinger spent much of the next four years negotiating peace terms with the North Vietnamese, often in private meetings with Le Duc Tho in Paris. But these sessions did not stop him from supporting military actions designed to pressurize Hanoi into making an agreement. A settlement was achieved in January, 1973, earning both chief negotiators the Nobel Peace Prize. Appointed U.S. Secretary of State in September, 1973, Kissinger served under President Ford (1974–76), then returned to academic life.

Born in 1911, Le Duc Tho (ABOVE LEFT) was a founder member of the Indo-Chinese Communist Party, with Ho Chi Minh, in 1930. In the mid-1960s, he moved into South Vietnam to coordinate the politico-military campaign against Saigon, but in 1968, he was ordered to travel to Paris as chief negotiator at the peace talks. Closely associated in the public eye with Henry Kissinger, he conducted private talks with the latter that ran parallel to the more open sessions. Together, the two men hammered out an agreement, signed in January, 1973.

Thanh Hoa Bridge

Railroad

Thanh Hoa Bridge

Ma River

N

Thanh Hoa

176

Under clear skies and at a height of about 14,000 feet, the lead F-4 (**5**) banked away, having delivered its LGB some two or three miles from its target. As a second F-4 (**1**) prepared to unleash its bomb, a massive explosion (**3**) signified a direct hit on the western span of the bridge.

After a partially successful raid on the Thanh Hoa bridge on April 27, 1972, the F-4 Phantoms of the 8th Tactical Fighter Wing returned on May 13 to finish the job. A total of 14 F-4s, carrying both laser-guided bombs (LGBs) and conventional bombs, set off from their base in Thailand.

Despite heavy antiaircraft fire and SAMs (**2** and **4**) directed at them from the cratered moonscape around the heavily defended bridge, no American planes were lost during the mission. Later reconnaissance photographs showed that the LGBs had destroyed the bridge's western span. The Dragon's Jaw, which had survived previous U.S. raids, was now finally broken.

In response to the NVA invasion of the South in 1972, President Nixon decided to bomb the North's vital supply lines north of the DMZ. Particularly vital targets were rail

and road bridges, the foremost being the Paul Doumer, east of Hanoi, and the Ham Rung ("Dragon's Jaw")— a bridge spanning the Ma River near the town of Thanh Hoa.

By this time, U.S. aircraft were using "smart" bombs whose accuracy made the Americans confident of destroying their targets.

"Smart" weapons

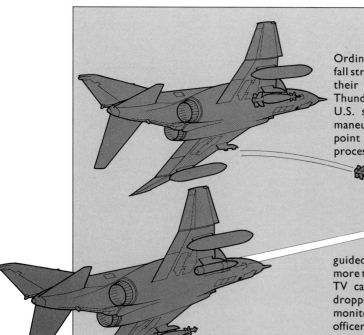

Ordinary bombs dropped from an aircraft fall straight down without direction toward their target. During Operation Rolling Thunder (1965–68), attempts were made by U.S. scientists to introduce methods of maneuvering or directing bombs with pinpoint accuracy. The U.S. Navy began the process with the Walleye electro-optical

The laser-guided bomb (LGB) system.

guided bomb (EOGB), which was nothing more than a conventional bomb with a small TV camera mounted on the nose. As it dropped, the camera relayed pictures to a monitor in the aircraft, where a weapons officer could alter its path by electronically steering the tail fins.

The USAF went for a more sophisticated system, shown in the diagram. Laser energy was used to illuminate the target, upon

which a laser-guided bomb (LGB) would be directed to "ride the beam." Known by the codename Paveway, the system called for an attacking aircraft to identify the target by means of a small onboard TV camera, then to fire a Pave Knife laser designator before

releasing the bomb. The bomb would then follow the beam using a laser seeker unit. Both designator and bomb could be carried on the same aircraft (an F-4 Phantom), but over North Vietnam it was found to be more effective to use two aircraft, one to designate and the other to drop the weapon, usually from an altitude of 12,000–14,000 feet. With a circular error probable (CEP) of less than 30 feet—in other words, a guarantee that 50 percent of all LGBs would land within that distance of the target—the system represented a quantum leap in air-weapons technology.

U.S. military commitment and combat deaths, 1960–72

Year*	Military Commitment	Combat Deaths
1960	875	
1961	3,164	
1962	11,326	759
1963	16,263	
1964	23,310	137
1965	184,300	1,369
1966	385,300	5,008
1967	485,600	9,378
1968	536,100	14,592
1969	475,200	9,414
1970	334,600	4,221
1971	156,800	1,380
1972	24,000	300

*Taken as of December 31

Total combat deaths	46,558
Total non-combat deaths in Vietnam	10,390

In addition, it is estimated that at least 300,000 U.S. servicemen were wounded (and the figure could be much higher) and 2,494 servicemen and civilians were listed as "missing in action" between 1960 and 1972.

Operation Homecoming

According to the Paris Agreements of January 27, 1973, all "captured military personnel and foreign civilians" of the signatory powers were to be returned to their respective homelands. To the Americans, this meant primarily the PoWs held in North Vietnam. They were to be released progressively, in line with U.S. troop withdrawals from the South: as soon as the last U.S. soldier left Vietnam, the last PoW would be set free. The Communists provided a list of 587 American citizens in their charge (a figure amended later to 591 as the Chinese agreed to release men held

by them). Operation Homecoming began on February 12, 1973, when the first batch of PoWs was handed over. Hanoi soon fell behind schedule, however, and it was only after President Nixon had suspended U.S. troop withdrawals that the process continued smoothly, ending on March 29. Meanwhile, in Vietnam itself, Saigon officials released 26,508 NVA and VC prisoners, while the Communists repatriated about 5,000 South Vietnamese. Since 1973, there have been persistent rumors of U.S. prisoners still in Communist hands, as part of the total of 2,494 servicemen and civilians missing from the Vietnam War era.

Lieutenant Colonel Robert L. Strim is welcomed home by his family in March, 1973. An enormous outpouring of public emotion accompanied the return of the PoWs to the U.S.

for SAM suppression, hunter-killer teams to destroy ground defenses, "chaff" dispensers to create a "sanitized radar environment," and fighters to take on the MiGs. Add to these the ECM (electronic countermeasures) aircraft, tankers, and rescue helicopters essential to any raid, and the elaborate nature of Linebacker may be appreciated. At the same time, the B-52s were mounting their own attacks.

Results were impressive. By October 23, when Nixon suspended bombing north of the 20th parallel in response to an apparent willingness of the North Vietnamese to resume meaningful peace negotiations, the Americans had delivered 155,500 tons of bombs and inflicted widespread damage. Industrial and supply-stockpile targets had been destroyed, the replenishment of such supplies from outside sources had been curtailed, most of the bridges linking Hanoi to China, Haiphong, and the war zone to the south had been cut, and North Vietnam's air defenses had been disrupted. It had cost the Americans 44 aircraft.

But this was not the end of the campaign. By December, 1972, the peace negotiations had stalled yet again, with each side accusing the other of prevarication. In an effort to break the deadlock and to guarantee that any agreement would allow the Americans to withdraw from the war "with honor," Nixon threatened Hanoi with massive aerial destruction. When this failed to have any effect, on December 18 the President released his full air strength over the North in a short, devastating campaign known unofficially as Linebacker II.

The bombing was carried out over a 13-day period, December 18–30, which included a 36-hour Christmas "pause." During that time, over 20,000 tons of bombs—guided as well as conventional—were dropped, chiefly onto Hanoi and Haiphong, and for the first time in the war, the B-52s were allowed to contribute without restriction.

Indeed, their involvement symbolized Nixon's resolve. Flying at night from Thailand and Guam, anything up to 150 bombers could be committed against specific targets, preceded by fighter-bomber strikes against air-defense systems and "chaff" sorties to clear the way. The North Vietnamese responded with a formidable display of antiaircraft fire, which included nearly 1,000 SAMs, and the Americans did suffer losses (26 aircraft, of which 15 were B-52s), but as missile stockpiles ran out, there was little the North could do to prevent widespread destruction.

Citizens of Hanoi pick their way through bomb craters and wreckage as they inspect damage inflicted by a U.S. bombing raid.

By December 30, when Nixon again pulled his aircraft back below the 20th parallel, U.S. fighter-bombers and B-52s had inflicted more damage on the North in 13 days than in the whole of the preceding eight years. Railyards, barracks, and warehouses had been flattened, fuel storage depots set ablaze, and electrical power plants put out of action. It was enough to persuade Hanoi to return to the conference table. Although it is perhaps naïve to say that bombing alone achieved peace, there is no doubt that it made a major contribution.

On January 23, 1973, an agreement was initialed by U.S. negotiator Henry Kissinger and his opposite number from Hanoi, Le Duc Tho, to come into effect four days later. It allowed for the withdrawal of U.S. forces from South Vietnam, an exchange of prisoners, and a ceasefire based on territory held. The last component angered President Thieu, for it left the NVA in possession of South Vietnamese territory close to the DMZ, but he was placated by Nixon's promise to provide air and naval support in the event of a future crisis. It was a promise that was not to be kept.

THE WAR YEARS

Oct. 8/11, 1972	A sudden flurry of activity in Paris implies that a breakthrough has been made in the peace negotiations.
Nov. 7, 1972	Richard Nixon is reelected U.S. President.
Dec. 18/30 1972	In the absence of a peace settlement, President Nixon releases the B-52s over Hanoi and Haiphong in Operation Linebacker II.
Jan. 27, 1973	"An Agreement Ending the War and Restoring Peace in Vietnam" is signed by the U.S., North and South Vietnam, and the VC in Paris. All remaining U.S. troops to be withdrawn from the South within 60 days. Secretary of Defense Melvin Laird announces an end to the U.S. draft.
June 4, 1973	U.S. Senate approves a bill to block funds for any U.S. military activities in Indochina.
Nov. 7, 1973	Congress overrules President Nixon's veto of the War Powers Resolution, designed to limit presidential ability to commit U.S. forces abroad.
Aug. 9, 1974	Richard Nixon resigns as President.

179

THE FALL OF THE SOUTH

March 11–April 30, 1975

THE PARIS AGREEMENTS OF January, 1973, did not end the fighting. As a means of allowing the Americans to disengage from the war with honor, they may have been effective, but to the South Vietnamese, forced to accept an NVA presence on territory south of the DMZ, they were humiliating and disastrous.

The ARVN therefore continued their counterattacks along the Cua Viet River in the northern province of Quang Tri and maintained pressure on NVA enclaves elsewhere. By the end of 1973, despite the presence of an International Commission for Control and Supervision (ICCS), appointed by the Paris signatories to monitor and report ceasefire violations by both sides, the South Vietnamese had recovered about 15 percent of the disputed land.

This outcome was not unexpected. In the days leading up to the January agreements, the Americans had poured military equipment worth an estimated $1 billion into the South, turned over a plethora of fully operational facilities to the Saigon authorities and made repeated pledges of renewed support if the Communists resumed their offensive. ARVN commanders, already boosted by their victories at An Loc, Kontum, and Quang Tri City in 1972, remained confident and fought accordingly. They did so against an enemy significantly weakened by recent losses on the battlefield and by the impact of the Linebacker raids.

However, as time went on, this imbalance was seen to be a sham. Although U.S. equipment was delivered in vast quantities in early 1973, much of it was secondhand—F-5 aircraft, for example, were transferred to Saigon from South Korea and Taiwan, not from American stockpiles—and spare parts were in short supply. More significantly, U.S. financial aid did not materialize in the quantity or with the frequency promised in 1973. Congress, intent on preventing renewed U.S. commitment, progressively cut the amount of money voted for Saigon—in

> "The Americans abandoned us. They sold us out. . . . A great ally failed a small ally."

PRESIDENT NGUYEN VAN THIEU, APRIL 21, 1975

1974, for example, a military aid package worth $1.6 billion was reduced to $700 million and requests for further aid in that fiscal year were refused.

Also, in November, 1973, the War Powers Act came into force, requiring the U.S. President by law to consult with Congress before military forces were allowed to be committed abroad for longer than 90 days. Nine months later, as Nixon resigned rather than face impeachment over Watergate, the affairs of Indochina ceased to enjoy priority.

Few in Saigon seemed prepared to face this new reality, clinging to the belief that no U.S. President would dare watch the South fall. But they did little to help themselves. Between 1973 and 1975, South Vietnamese politics moved further away from the democratic ideal, as President Thieu lost popular support.

The burden of the continued fighting fell on the peasants, many of whom wanted nothing more than an end to what was now nearly 30 years of war. Also, the middle classes resented the endless demands for taxes to pay for the large armed forces.

Indeed, when it was realized that much of the money was being used to line the pockets of corrupt politicians and incompetent military commanders, leaving the armed forces so weak that desertion rates were outstripping those of conscripted recruitment, any confidence that the people still had rapidly disappeared. Facing an enemy intent on political as well as military victory, Thieu was making a grave mistake: he was alienating the very people he needed to act as a buffer against Communist aggression.

All these factors unavoidably affected the efficiency of the ARVN, which declined alarmingly once the Americans left. In retrospect this was hardly surprising, for despite Vietnamization and the victories of 1972, the South Vietnamese were poorly prepared to stand alone. Throughout the "main-force war" (1965–72), the Americans had dominated the conduct of military operations, with MACV

ARVN airborne troops wait to be lifted into the Xuan Loc area, 40 miles east of Saigon, during the NVA invasion of the South, which began in March, 1975. The battle for Xuan Loc involved three NVA divisions trying to dislodge the ARVN 18th Infantry Division.

The ARVN fought heroically, but eventually conceded defeat on April 18, 1975, a month after the battle had begun. The road to Saigon was now open.

With the fall of the South an inevitable outcome, in April, 1975, panic seizes Saigon as crowds of people (LEFT), desperate to be evacuated, try to breach the U.S. embassy wall.

Under Operation Frequent Wind the Americans managed to evacuate about 8,000 people during the final days of the South's existence. But as the last U.S. helicopter left Saigon on April 30, thousands of South Vietnamese were left to their fate.

181

headquarters, backed by the sophisticated intelligence agencies of a superpower, virtually dictating the strategy and—whether intentionally or not—imposing its own tactical doctrine.

This was fine as long as U.S. advice, troops, weapons, and money were freely available; once these had been withdrawn or cut, the ARVN were left with a tradition of warfare ill-suited to the situation they faced. South Vietnamese formations were organized along American lines and trained to fight using a combination of firepower and air sup-

port, both of which were badly affected once the money ran out.

By late 1974, for example, artillery ammunition stockpiles in the South were about 20 percent of their 1972 levels, while 11 out of 66 South Vietnamese Air Force squadrons had been disbanded for lack of fuel, in desperately short supply since the quadrupling of oil prices on world markets in the aftermath of the October 1973 Arab-Israeli War.

As the South Vietnamese armed forces declined, so those of the North recovered. Slowly but surely, the Hanoi government

rebuilt its divisions and, free from U.S. air interference, improved the Ho Chi Minh Trail to guarantee more rapid logistical support to the battle areas of the South. Lost equipment was replaced, fresh recruits were absorbed, and preparations for a new offensive made. By 1974, the North Vietnamese had 19 divisions in the field, 12 of them actually on territory south of the DMZ, captured in 1972. All that was needed was an opportunity for them to strike.

The chance came unexpectedly, as a result of a mishandling of the situation by

Operation Frequent Wind

As the NVA closed in around Saigon in April, 1975, the Americans faced a dilemma. If they began to pull their people out of the embassy and other city locations too early, all confidence in the South Vietnamese government would disappear; if they left it too late, they risked losing their nationals to the enemy as hostages. President Ford decided to delay full-scale evacuation as long as possible, although this did not prevent a steady flow of refugees escaping through Tan Son Nhut airport. They were mainly prosperous or influential South Vietnamese, but included nearly 3,000

orphans of mixed U.S.-Vietnamese blood, taken to the United States for adoption.

On April 29, however, the airport came under NVA artillery fire and had to be closed to fixed-wing traffic, leaving President Ford with no choice but to initiate Operation Frequent Wind. Sixty CH-53 helicopters from a Seventh Fleet task force in the South China Sea flew into Saigon to

Authorized personnel and civilians gather at the U.S. embassy in

Saigon for a last-minute evacuation from the city on April 29, 1975.

pick up U.S. citizens (and some South Vietnamese) from preselected rooftop locations. All day, and throughout the night, the helicopters flew back and forth, chiefly from the embassy. There, under Marine protection, embassy staff and a select number of South Vietnamese were lifted out, while the building itself was besieged by other Vietnamese, desperate to escape. Altogether, about 8,000 people were rescued, but many loyal Vietnamese were abandoned. The last helicopter, carrying the Marine guard, flew out early on April 30, leaving Saigon to its fate.

the Saigon authorities. Since 1975, fighting had continued in the northern provinces of South Vietnam—in 1974, it was estimated that the ARVN suffered 15,000 casualties in Quang Nam province alone—and this had led to a "top heavy" deployment of ARVN units.

Five divisions, including the Marine and Airborne elements of Thieu's forces, were packed into the northern provinces, leaving the rest of the country poorly defended. The Communists, realizing this, decided to maintain the pressure in the north, keeping the ARVN pinned down, while mounting a series of offensives elsewhere to grab territory preparatory to a decisive attack on Saigon. In January, 1975, the first of these offensives succeeded in taking the province of Phuoc Long, northeast of the capital, at very small cost. The Americans, significantly, did not react.

Planners in Hanoi, aware of just how vulnerable Thieu now was, called for a more general offensive before the monsoon began in May, aiming for total victory in 1976. General Van Tien Dung was placed in command and, mindful of Giap's shortcomings in 1972, he decided to concentrate his forces against the Central Highlands, both to threaten to split the South in two and to exploit the "top heavy" ARVN deployment.

Three NVA divisions moved toward Ban Me Thuot in early March, laying siege to the town in a manner reminiscent of Kontum or An Loc in 1972. But by 1975 the strategic situation had changed. With no U.S. air support available, ARVN defenders were on their own: Ban Me Thuot fell on March 11.

Thieu could have survived this setback, but instead he ordered an immediate redeployment of forces. His Airborne Division was directed to move south to protect Saigon, while other units in the northern provinces pulled back to the coast in case they needed to be evacuated quickly from a region under threat of isolation. At the same time, Major General Pham Van Phu was ordered to withdraw units from Pleiku and Kontum in the Central Highlands, preparatory to a counterattack against Ban Me Thuot.

It is hard to imagine a more disastrous set of orders. As Phu's forces began their withdrawal, aiming for Tuy Hoa on the coast, they triggered a panic among the civilian population, which blocked the only available road—Route 7. But it had been neglected for years, and, as the "Column of Tears" moved slowly east, delayed by broken bridges, the NVA closed in. By April 1, the column had

Why did America not help?

Despite the promises made by President Nixon at the time of the Paris Agreements in early 1973, the U.S. made no move to help the South two years later. With a new president and a Congress intent on preventing a recommitment of U.S. forces to Southeast Asia, this was hardly surprising. But they were merely reflecting a deeper reason for inaction: after the traumas of the previous decade, the American people lacked the patience for a protracted, undeclared war.

ceased to exist, leaving the Central Highlands in Communist hands. ARVN forces to the north, threatened with encirclement, had already joined the rout: amid scenes of mass hysteria, Hue had fallen on March 25 and Da Nang four days later.

The NVA made the most of the situation, redeploying their Central Highlands divisions to mount an immediate advance on Saigon known as the Ho Chi Minh campaign. Some ARVN units stood firm—the 18th Division held Xuan Loc, east of the capital, until April 18—but it was a lost cause. On April 21 Thieu

President Nixon resigns

On June 13, 1971, the *New York Times* began to print the "Pentagon Papers," a collection of confidential government documents on the Vietnam War leaked by David Ellsberg, a former employee of the Department of Defense. President Nixon, shown (ABOVE) with Vice President Spiro Agnew in 1973, was concerned that such revelations would undermine the peace negotiations then going on but failed to halt publication. Convinced that the leak was part of a wider antigovernment plot, he authorized a lawyer, David Young, and a White House assistant, Egil "Bud" Krogh, to investigate the affair, stating "I don't want to excuses. I want results . . . whatever the cost."

Young and Krogh set up a clandestine team—"the plumbers"—and recruited other experts such as former CIA man E. Howard Hunt and ex-FBI agent G. Gordon Liddy. They compiled a list of Nixon's "enemies," producing dossiers on each, but their actions soon degenerated into illegality—culminating with their breaking into the Democratic National Committee offices in the Watergate Hotel in Washington. In June, 1972, members of the team were arrested. Nixon denied all knowledge of their existence, but rumors quickly spread that White House tapes, incriminating the President, existed. When he refused to release them, the House of Representatives Judiciary Committee started impeachment proceedings. Rather than face such public humiliation, Nixon resigned on August 9, 1974.

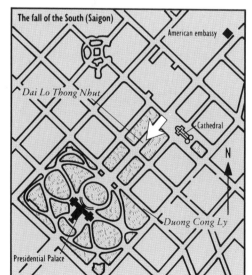

The Paris Agreements of January, 1973, gave the United States the chance to pull out of Vietnam with a degree of honor. But they also sanctioned the presence of the NVA just south of the DMZ—a situation that the South Vietnamese found intolerable. Shortly after the Agreements, therefore, the South mounted a series of counterattacks on these NVA enclaves and, by the end of the year, they had recovered about 15 percent of the disputed territory.

This limited military success was achieved with the help of enormous stockpiles of military hardware bequeathed to the ARVN by the Americans. But, as time passed, the ARVN's advantage over the NVA in equipment and supplies diminished. As the political situation in the U.S. changed, with Congress anxious to prevent the country becoming reembroiled in the war, financial support for the South waned.

At the same time, general dissatisfaction with President Thieu's regime increased. Desertions from the ARVN by war-weary peasants exceeded conscripted recruitment. Deprived of U.S. tactical advice, air support, military intelligence, and firepower, the South Vietnamese armed forces went into decline.

Since the withdrawal of the Americans, the NVA had been steadily building up its strength, ready to invade the South if the opportunity should present itself. The moment to strike eventually came in January, 1975. With ARVN forces concentrated in the northern provinces, the North attacked and seized the poorly defended province of Phuoc Long, northeast of Saigon. The Americans did not react, and, encouraged by this, the NVA planned a bigger offensive in the Central Highlands to split the South in two. In early March, 1975, with no U.S. aircraft to hinder them, NVA forces captured the town of Ban Me Thuot.

The fall of the South (Saigon)

American embassy

Dai Lo Thong Nhut

Cathedral

N

Duong Cong Ly

Presidential Palace

President Thieu reacted to this setback with a redeployment of forces that created widespread panic among the civilian population. The NVA took full advantage of the situation: the Central Highlands soon fell, and, as ARVN troops in the north succumbed to the mass hysteria sweeping the country, Hue was taken on March 25 and Da Nang four days later. The northern provinces were quickly lost.

For the people of Saigon and for South Vietnam, the writing was now on the wall. On April 21, Thieu resigned and General Duong Van Minh eventually took over the doomed presidency. On April 30, the last U.S. evacuation helicopters took off at dawn: hours later, the first NVA T-54 tanks and trucks began to rumble into Saigon.

There was an eerie calm and air of desolation in Saigon. Streets were littered with rubbish and discarded weapons and uniforms. One or two pockets of ARVN resistance remained, but nothing could prevent the NVA advance toward Doc Lap, the Presidential Palace.

At about midday, NVA Tank 843, camouflaged with palm branches, advanced along Dai Lo Thong Nhut Boulevard, slightly ahead of the other tanks in the column. Drawing near to the palace (1), Tank 843 (2) speeded up and burst through the ornamental gates. Watching this historic moment was a small group of ARVN soldiers (4), standing under trees on the palace lawns, waiting to surrender.

As the other T-54s (3) in the column advanced toward the gates, Tank Leader Bui Quang Than jumped from the turret of Tank 843 and rushed forward waving the gold-starred National Liberation Flag. Within minutes this flag would be raised above the palace: the Second Indochina War was over.

185

resigned, opening the way for the appointment of General Duong Van Minh ("Big Minh") to the presidency in the hope that he could negotiate with Hanoi. It was not to be: by the end of the month, with the Americans hastily evacuating the city by helicopter and news of the fall of Phnom Penh to the Khmer Rouge fresh in their minds, the people of Saigon faced disaster.

At 0500 hours on April 30, NVA armored columns moved in for the kill, entering Saigon from all directions. The Eastern Column, led by Tank 843, had the key task—the seizure of the Presidential Palace—and it pushed forward against minimal opposition along streets strewn with abandoned military equipment. Two ARVN M-41 tanks tried to block the way on Hong Thap Tu Street, only to

be destroyed; Tank 843 moved left into Mac Dinh Chi Street, then right into Dai Lo Thong Nhut Boulevard. Passing the cathedral on its left, it gathered speed as the palace gates loomed ahead. With other T-54 tanks close behind, having arrived by a slightly different route, Tank 843 crashed through the gates and slewed to a halt at the palace steps. As a crewman rushed forward with a large Communist

"Year Zero"—Pol Pot's revolution

When the defense of Phnom Penh collapsed on April 16, 1975, after four months of Communist siege, Cambodia entered a nightmare. At dawn the next day, hard-faced Khmer Rouge soldiers marched into the city, shown (BELOW) devastated by the siege, and immediately began to impose a ruthless authority. Their leader, Pol Pot (RIGHT), had decreed that the entire population of Phnom Penh—anything up to two million people—was to be moved forcibly to the countryside, "class enemies" (interpreted as anyone who was not of peasant stock) were to be weeded out and executed, and Cambodia was to be transformed into an agricultural state.

Pol Pot called it "Year Zero," the start of a completely new society. Many reasons were put forward for such a drastic change—the need to rid the country of the corruption associated with city life, the desperate need for food after so many years

of war, and an ideological desire for a return to the "purity" of peasant life—but the results were catastrophic. As the columns of city-dwellers moved into the countryside, many died of hardship, neglect, and disease. Once attached to a "collective," others succumbed to back-breaking work and meager rations; yet more were killed or tortured at the whim of their guards. Families were split up, individual freedoms disappeared, and, as the economy faltered, the Khmer Rouge leadership demanded even more work. By December, 1978, when the Vietnamese invaded what was then the Democratic Republic of Kampuchea, an estimated one million people had died.

flag, ARVN soldiers, dejected and broken, looked on.

NVA Colonel Bui Tin was one of the first into the palace. Racing upstairs, he confronted President Minh, who said, "I have been waiting since early this morning to transfer power to you." Colonel Tin's reply was appropriately terse: "You cannot give up what you do not have." Communist victory was complete.

THE WAR YEARS

March 11/
April 1,
1975
NVA seize Ban Me Thuot, capital of Darlac province in the Central Highlands; as President Thieu orders the Central Highlands to be abandoned, South Vietnam is cut in two.

March 25/
29, 1975
Hue and Da Nang, in the northern provinces of South Vietnam, are abandoned to the NVA.

April 8/18,
1975
As NVA forces advance south toward Saigon, the ARVN 18th Division fights for Xuan Loc, east of the capital, but fails to hold the town.

April 12/16
Phnom Penh falls to the Khmer Rouge: their leader, Pol Pot, seizes power.

April 21
Nguyen Van Thieu resigns as President of South Vietnam and flees. General Duong Van Minh is appointed President on April 28.

April 29/30
Operation Frequent Wind: U.S. evacuates about 8,000 people from Saigon by helicopter.

April 30
Saigon falls to the Communists, marking the end of the Second Indochina War.

May 12/15,
1975
The *Mayaguez* Incident: U.S. Marines are committed to rescue the crew of the cargo ship *Mayaguez*, seized by the Khmer Rouge in the Gulf of Thailand.

Jan. 21,
1977
Jimmy Carter, elected U.S. President in November, 1976, pardons most of the draft evaders of the Vietnam War era.

Dec. 25,
1978
Vietnamese invasion of Kampuchea (Cambodia); Pol Pot overthrown when Phnom Penh falls on January 7, 1979.

Feb. 17/
March 5,
1979
Chinese attacks on northern Vietnam.

The *Mayaguez* Incident

On May 12, 1975, President Gerald Ford faced a new threat to U.S. interests in Southeast Asia. An American cargo ship, the *Mayaguez*, was seized by a Khmer Rouge gunboat in international waters some 40 miles off the Cambodian coast, and its 39-man crew was accused of "spying." Ford condemned the action as "piracy" and ordered an immediate rescue mission. A battalion of Marines was flown from Okinawa to U Tapao in Thailand while U.S. aircraft monitored the *Mayaguez*, by now at anchor under guard off the island of Koh Tang. Before dawn on May 15, eight USAF CH-53 helicopters left U Tapao with a Marine assault group, destined for Koh Tang.

The mission ran into serious difficulties. As the first helicopter landed on the island's northern neck, it came under intense fire; although the Marines dismounted, the CH-53 was forced to crash-land in the sea. A second helicopter was so badly hit that it had to turn back, while the third and fourth were brought down on the beach. One burst into flames, killing 13 men on board. Reinforcements were flown in, only to be pinned down by the Khmer Rouge. They were extracted that night, by which time the *Mayaguez* had been liberated by a separate Marine party and its crew released by the Cambodian authorities. By the end of the day, 18 U.S. servicemen were dead.

U.S. Marines (ABOVE) stand on board the *Mayaguez* following the recovery of the ship. Later, two officers, Major Ray Porter and Captain Walter Wood (LEFT), raised the Stars and Stripes.

THE CONTINUING WAR

B Y THE END OF 1975, THE WHOLE of Indochina was under Communist rule. The process had cost an estimated three million lives and had taken 30 years, during which two major outside powers—France and the United States—had been humiliated. It seemed like the end of a nightmare.

But hopes of prolonged peace were quickly dashed. Although the revolutionaries in Vietnam, Laos, and Cambodia may have appeared to the Americans to be of the same political persuasion, it soon became obvious that, once in power, they had different beliefs, made worse by a resurgence of traditional ethnic and territorial rivalries. At the same time, their emergence as victors altered the balance of power in Asia, with the two Communist superpowers—China and the Soviet Union—interfering to gain or maintain their own particular influence. Far from becoming a region of peace and harmony, Indochina rapidly degenerated into a cauldron of continued conflict.

Ethnic differences were apparent from the start. In Vietnam, victorious Northerners imposed harsh conditions on the defeated South. All political and military supporters of President Thieu were rounded up and, if not executed, sent to special "reeducation camps": altogether, over 200,000 may have been affected, plus thousands more who were "reeducated" on a local basis.

Simultaneously, over a million city-dwellers, chiefly from Saigon (renamed Ho Chi Minh City in July, 1976), were relocated to "New Economic Zones" in the countryside, where their "corrupt' Western ways were sweated out in hard labor. Religions, such as Buddhism and Catholicism, were attacked and those involved in "bourgeois trade"—mainly ethnic Chinese—were persecuted.

The results were predictable: Chinese-Vietnamese trekked north to China in their thousands or took to the high seas, often in flimsy, open boats in search of a safe haven. Joined by anti-Communist

"*Vietnam, the body and conscience of our time, the dragon still defiantly breathing fire on two frontiers.*"

BRITISH VIETNAM PHOTOGRAPHER TIM PAGE, AFTER THE WAR

Vietnamese, principally from what had been the South, the latter soon became known as the "boat people." Their sudden arrival in neighboring states helped to create one of the worst refugee problems of the modern world.

However, even this pales into insignificance next to events in Cambodia (renamed Democratic Kampuchea in 1975, with reversion to the more familiar name 14 years later). Once Pol Pot's Khmer Rouge took over, they began an extraordinary policy of "social restructuring," forcing the entire population of Phnom Penh to move into the countryside, where a combination of hard labor, poor diet, and extreme cruelty cost at least a million lives. Once again, the response of many was to escape: by August, 1979, some 320,000 refugees had fled to Vietnam and 150,000 to Thailand, drawing both countries into Cambodian affairs.

Many of those who entered Vietnam were in fact ethnic Vietnamese, singled out by Pol Pot for persecution not just because the Khmer Rouge resented Hanoi's acceptance of peace in 1973—something which had allowed American bombers to concentrate on Cambodia for nearly eight months—but also as a reflection of age-old ethnic antipathy.

This was manifested in border clashes between Cambodia and Vietnam, as well as a deterioration in their relations. It culminated on December 25, 1978, when, in response to Khmer Rouge incursions, Hanoi committed 120,000 troops (many equipped with captured U.S./South Vietnamese gear) to a full-scale invasion. The Khmer Rouge were not strong enough to stand and fight, so they pulled back to guerrilla bases on the Thai border. Phnom Penh fell to the Vietnamese on January 7, 1979.

This triggered a Chinese response. As supporters of Pol Pot, they could not stand idly by and watch him defeated, but there was more to it than that. Hanoi's preference for the Soviet Union—sealed on November 3, 1978, by a formal treaty which included the right of Soviet

A young boy (LEFT) stands next to the skulls of Cambodians who died because of Pol Pot, leader of the Khmer Rouge. After Phnom Penh fell in 1975, Pol Pot ordered the population of the city to be herded into the countryside so that Cambodia could become an agricultural state. Thousands died from disease and hardship.

A veteran (OPPOSITE PAGE) reads the name of a comrade inscribed on the Vietnam Memorial in Washington, D.C. The memorial marked a change in public attitudes toward the war.

In a cemetery (BELOW) near Xuan Loc, northeast of Saigon, relatives tend the graves of just a few of the Communist soldiers who died in the war.

The boat people

Between April, 1975, and August, 1979, an estimated 675,000 people left Vietnam as refugees. Of these, about 250,000 were ethnic Chinese, who moved overland to China when the Hanoi regime began a deliberate policy of persecution. The rest, such as those (ABOVE), fled in open boats, taking to the sea in search of refuge in the non-Communist world, despite the danger of storms, shipwreck, and pirates.

International reaction to the boat people was initially sympathetic. In 1979, a United Nations conference in Geneva decided that

Western nations should absorb many of the refugees, with the United States, Canada, Australia, France, and Britain all agreeing to take their share. But the flow did not cease. A fresh round of anti-Chinese repression in 1984, coupled with a failing Vietnamese economy, led to a new exodus: in 1986, 19,500 Vietnamese chose to take their chances as boat people, followed by another 28,000 in 1987, and 45,500 in 1988. By then, many of the countries in which they had initially sought asylum—notably Thailand, Singapore, Malaysia, and the British colony

of Hong Kong—were running out of patience, particularly when it became clear that the majority were not strictly refugees escaping political persecution, but "economic migrants" searching for a better life. In Hong Kong, the new arrivals were placed in detention camps, screened, and encouraged to return to Vietnam. When this failed to stem the flow, forcible repatriation was introduced. In the light of renewed negotiations with Hanoi, this was not pursued, but it was yet one more sad legacy of Vietnam's recent history.

warships to use the former U.S. facility at Cam Ranh Bay—reinforced Chinese fears that their Communist superpower rival was using Vietnam as part of an elaborate strategy of encirclement.

As soon as Vietnam moved into Cambodia, therefore, Peking threatened retaliation. When this had no discernible effect, the Chinese attacked northern Vietnam. On February 17, 1979, up to 200,000 Chinese troops crossed the

border, aiming for the provincial capitals of Lao Cai, Cao Bang, and Lang Son. Local Vietnamese forces bore the brunt of the assault and, on March 5, having lost a reported 20,000 casualties, the Chinese withdrew. They had not been defeated— Peking described the incursion as a "punishment" successfully carried out— but if it had been designed to force Vietnam to pull out of Cambodia, it failed. The war against Pol Pot (joined

now by a variety of non-Communist nationalist groups) went on.

Nevertheless, it soon became obvious that the maintenance of Vietnamese forces in Cambodia was proving politically difficult to Hanoi. The pursuit of guerrillas across the border led to clashes between the Vietnamese and Thais, the number of refugees in Thailand increased alarmingly, and Vietnamese efforts to create a new, pro-Vietnam, government

Vietnam veterans

Between August, 1964, and January, 1973, 2,594,000 U.S. servicemen were posted to South Vietnam, the vast majority on tours lasting 365 days. Of that number, perhaps 80 percent were exposed to enemy attack, although only about 40 percent participated in ground skirmishes. Those who survived, such as the group of veterans (ABOVE), were returned to civilian life without ceremony. Unlike the veterans of earlier wars, they were not given warm public welcomes; instead, many returned to taunts of "baby killer" and were advised not to wear their uniforms or medals in public.

The majority of veterans managed to reintegrate successfully into society, but to some the experience of both Vietnam and their return home proved too much to absorb. Facing a country seemingly indiffer-

ent to their sacrifices and feeling guilty at having survived where their friends had not, these men found it difficult to settle back into a normal pattern of living, suffering a disproportionate incidence of social and personal problems. Psychiatrists who dealt with them dubbed their condition Post Traumatic Stress Disorder (PTSD), characterized by insomnia, reenactment of disturbing experiences from Vietnam, acute depression, and an inescapable feeling that the war had been a waste.

Changing public attitudes in the United States, manifested in the dedication of the Vietnam Memorial in Washington, D.C. in November, 1982, have done much to help the situation. But to a significant number of veterans, their Vietnam tour of duty remains a constant nightmare.

THE WAR YEARS

July 22, 1979	Vietnam claims "total victory" over Pol Pot and the Khmer Rouge in Cambodia (Kampuchea), but guerrilla clashes continue.
March 9, 1980	China pledges support for Khmer Rouge guerrillas fighting the Vietnamese.
Nov. 13, 1982	Vietnam Memorial, commemorating U.S. servicemen killed or missing, is dedicated in Washington, D.C.
Jan. 14, 1985	Hun Sen is elected Premier of Cambodia by Vietnam-backed National Assembly.
May 2, 1988	Vietnam announces it will withdraw 50,000 troops from Cambodia by the end of the year, leaving 50,000 in place.
Oct. 12, 1988	Vietnam agrees to take back any boat people from Hong Kong who wish to return.
April 5, 1989	Vietnam announces that it will withdraw all its remaining troops from Cambodia by the end of September.
Sept. 30, 1989	Withdrawal of Vietnamese troops from Cambodia is complete; Khmer Rouge offensive opens in the northwest to fill the vacuum.
Dec. 11, 1989	Britain forcibly repatriates 51 boat people from Hong Kong to Vietnam.
Jan. 7, 1990	Khmer Rouge threaten the city of Battambang in northwestern Cambodia.

in Phnom Penh were thwarted by international refusals to grant it formal recognition. In addition, the continuing war was an expensive drain on human and economic resources, affecting the ability of Hanoi to solve its domestic problems.

In May, 1988, the Vietnamese announced their intention to cut their occupation force by half, following this up in September, 1989, by a complete withdrawal. The fact that almost immediately the Khmer Rouge and their allies launched an offensive toward the city of Battambang in the northwest of the country merely showed that the fighting was far from over. Indochina, after 45 years of virtually non-stop war, is perhaps no nearer finding a lasting peace.

The Khmer Rouge, 14 years after their victory against Lon Nol's forces in the battle for Phnom Penh (RIGHT) in 1975, threatened to repeat their efforts in 1990 after the withdrawal of Vietnamese forces the year before.

191

GLOSSARY

AAA Antiaircraft artillery
AATTV Australian Army Training Team Vietnam
ACAV Armored Cavalry Assault Vehicle
Airmobility The use of helicopters to ensure self-contained tactical movement and support
Ap Vietnamese word for village/hamlet
APC Armored Personnel Carrier
Area warfare A military strategy used by the NVA in which infiltration and ambush were preferred to set-piece battles
ARVN Army of the Republic of (South) Vietnam
ATC Armored Troop Carrier
ATF Australian Task Force
Body count The number of enemy dead on a particular battlefield
BLT (U.S. Marines) Battalion Landing Team
CCB Command and Control Boat
CIA Central Intelligence Agency
CIDG Civilian Irregular Defense Group
CinCPAC Commander in Chief, Pacific
Claymore Antipersonnel land mine
COIN Counterinsurgency
CORDS Civil Operations and Rural Development Support
COSVN (Communist) Central Office for South Vietnam
CTZ Corps Tactical Zone (applied to any of the four areas into which South Vietnam was divided for military purposes and designated with a Roman numeral, e.g. ICTZ); in July, 1970, the CTZs were renamed Military Regions (MRs)
DER Destroyer Escort Radar
DEROS Date eligible to return from overseas
DMZ The demilitarized zone which separated North and South Vietnam at the 17th parallel
DOD Department of Defense
Dust-off Medical evacuation helicopter or mission
DZ Drop zone
ECM Electronic countermeasures
FAC Forward Air Controller
FSB Fire Support Base
Frag To kill or try to kill with a fragmentation grenade (also a euphemism for the deliberate killing of unpopular officers or NCOs)
Free Fire Zone An area, usually uninhabited or under enemy control, for which permission was not needed before firing on it could begin
Grunt Slang for U.S. infantryman (from the noise made when shouldering heavy packs)
Ho Chi Minh Trail A network of trails extending from North to South Vietnam via Laos and Cambodia used by the NVA to transport supplies
JCS (U.S.) Joint Chiefs of Staff
KIA Killed in action

LAW Light Antitank Weapon
LRRPs Long Range Reconnaissance Patrols (pronounced "Lurps")
LVT Landing Vehicle Tracked
LVTP Landing Vehicle Tracked, Personnel
LZ Landing zone
MAAG Military Assistance Advisory Group
MACV Military Assistance Command, Vietnam
MACV-SOG Military Assistance Command, Vietnam-Studies and Observation Group
MEB Marine Expeditionary Brigade
Medevac Medical evacuation by helicopter
MIA Missing in action
MR Military Region. See CTZ
MRF Mobile Riverine Force
NDP Night defensive position
NVA North Vietnamese Army
NVAF North Vietnamese Air Force
OPLAN Operation Plan
Pacification Policy of countering VC influence in the villages of South Vietnam
PACV Patrol Air Cushion Vehicle
PBR Patrol Boat, River
POL Petroleum, oil and lubricant
R and R Rest and Recreation
RAR Royal Australian Regiment
RF/PF (South Vietnamese) Regional and Popular Forces ("Ruff-Puffs")
RIF Reconnaissance-in-force
RPF River Patrol Force
RPG Rocket-propelled grenade
SAM Surface-to-air missile
SAS (Australian) Special Air Service
SEALORDS Southeast Asia Lake, Ocean, River, and Delta Strategy
SEATO Southeast Asia Treaty Organization
TACAIR Tactical Air Control Airborne
TFW Tactical Fighter Wing
Tunnel Rat A U.S. soldier who specialized in searching enemy tunnel complexes
VC Viet Cong
Vietnamization The process of turning responsibility for the war from U.S. forces to the South Vietnamese
VNAF South Vietnamese Air Force
War Zones C and D Two VC-occupied areas located to the north of Saigon

BIBLIOGRAPHY

Albright, John, Cash, John A. and **Sandstrum, Allan W.** *Seven Firefights in Vietnam* Office of the Chief of Military History, United States Army, Washington D.C., 1970
Anderson, Charles R. *The Grunts* Presidio Press, California, 1976
Baker, Mark *Nam: The Vietnam War in the Words of the Men and Women Who Fought There* William Morrow, New York, 1981; Abacus, London, 1982
Berger, Carl (ed) *The United States Air Force in Southeast Asia 1961–73* Office of Air Force History, Washington DC, 1977
Bonds, Ray (ed) *The Vietnam War: The Illustrated History of the Conflict in Southeast Asia* Crown Publishers, New York; Salamander, London, 1983
Bowman, John S. (ed) *The Vietnam War: An Almanac* World Almanac Publications, New York, 1985
Broughton, Colonel Jack *Thud Ridge* J.B. Lippincott, New York, 1969
Buckingham, William *Operation Ranch Hand: The United States Air Force and Herbicides in Southeast Asia, 1961–1972* U.S. Government Printing Office, Washington D.C., 1982
Burstall, Terry *The Soldiers' Story: The Battle at Xa Long Tan Vietnam 18 August 1966* University of Queensland Press, Queensland, Australia, 1986
Butler, David *The Fall of Saigon: Scenes from the sudden end of a long war* Simon and Schuster, New York, 1985; Sphere Books, London, 1986
Caputo, Philip *A Rumor of War* Holt, Rinehart and Winston, New York; Macmillan, London, 1977
Charlton, Michael and **Moncrieff, Anthony** *Many Reasons Why: The American Involvement in Vietnam* Scolar Press, London, 1978
Chinnery, Philip D. *Life on the Line: Stories of Vietnam Air Combat* Blandford Press, London, 1988
Cincinnatus *Self Destruction: The Disintegration and Decay of the United States Army during the Vietnam Era* W.W. Norton, New York, 1978
Coleman, J.D. *Pleiku: The Dawn of Helicopter Warfare in Vietnam* St Martin's Press, New York, 1988
Collins, Brigadier General James Lawton *The Development and Training of the South Vietnamese Army, 1950–1972* Vietnam Studies, Department of the Army, Washington D.C., 1975
Croizat, Colonel Victor *The Brown Water Navy: The River and Coastal War in Indo-China and Vietnam, 1948–1972* Blandford Press, Blandford, Dorset, 1984
Davidson, J. *Indo-China: Signposts in the Storm* Longman Malaysia, 1979
Donovan, David. *Once a Warrior King: Memories of an Officer in Vietnam* Weidenfeld and Nicolson, London, 1986

Drendel, Lou *And Kill MiGs: Air to Air Combat in the Vietnam War* Squadron/Signal Publications, Carrollton, Texas, 1984
Dung, General Van Tien *Our Great Spring Victory* Monthly Review Press, New York, 1977
Dunn, Peter M. *The First Vietnam War* C. Hurst, London, 1985
Dunstan, Simon *Vietnam Tracks: Armor in Battle, 1945–1975* Presidio Press, California; Osprey Publishing, London, 1982
Eckhardt, Major General George S. *Command and Control, 1950–1969* Vietnam Studies, Department of the Army, Washington D.C., 1974
Emerson, Gloria *Winners and Losers: Battles, Retreats, Gains, Losses, and Ruins from the Vietnam War* Random House, New York, 1976; Penguin Books, London, 1985
Estes, Jack *A Field of Innocence: A Memoir of the Vietnam War* Breitenbush Books, New York, 1987; Headline Books, London, 1989
Ewing, Michael *The Illustrated History of the Vietnam War: Khe Sanh* Bantam Books, New York and London, 1987
Fall, Bernard B. *Street Without Joy: Insurgency in Indochina, 1946–63* Stackpole Books, Harrisburg, Pennsylvania, 1963
— *Hell in a Very Small Place: The Siege of Dien Bien Phu* J.B. Lippincott, New York, 1966
— (ed) *Ho Chi Minh on Revolution: Selected Writings, 1920–66* Frederick A. Praeger, New York, 1966
Fulton, Major General William B. *Riverine Operations 1966–1969* Vietnam Studies, Department of the Army, Washington D.C., 1973
Giap, General Vo Nguyen *People's War, People's Army* Frederick A. Praeger, New York, 1967
— *Big Victory, Great Task* Frederick A. Praeger, New York, 1968
Glasser, Ronald J. *365 Days* Longman, London, 1972
Gregory, Barry *Vietnam Coastal and Riverine Forces Handbook* Patrick Stephens, Wellingborough, Northamptonshire, 1988
Gunstan, Bill *Aircraft of the Vietnam War* Patrick Stephens, Wellingborough, Northamptonshire, 1987
Hackworth, Colonel David H. and **Sherman, Julie** *About Face* Simon and Schuster, New York; Sidgwick and Jackson, London, 1989
Halberstam, David *The Best and the Brightest* Random House, New York, 1972
Hay, Lieutenant General John H. *Tactical and Materiel Innovations* Vietnam Studies, Department of the Army, Washington D.C., 1974
Heiser, Lieutenant General Joseph M. *Logistic Support* Vietnam Studies, Department of the Army, Washington D.C., 1974

Herr, Michael *Dispatches* Knopf, New York; Pan Books, London, 1978
Hosmer, Stephen T., Kellen, Konrad and Jenkins, Brian M. *The Fall of South Vietnam: Statements by Vietnamese Military and Civilian Leaders* Crane, Russak, New York, 1980
Johnson, Lyndon B. *The Vantage Point: Perspectives of the Presidency 1963–1969* Popular Library, New York, 1971
Karnow, Stanley *Vietnam: A History* Viking, New York; Century Publishing, London, 1983
Kelly, Colonel Francis J. *U.S. Army Special Forces 1961–1971* Vietnam Studies, Department of the Army, Washington D.C., 1985
Kinnard, Douglas *The War Managers* Avery Publishing, Wayne, New Jersey, 1985
Kissinger, Henry *The White House Years* Little Brown, Boston, Mass., 1974
Kolko, Gabriel *Vietnam: Anatomy of War 1940–1975* Random House, New York; Allen and Unwin, London, 1986
Lacouture, Jean *Ho Chi Minh: A Political Biography* Random House, New York, 1968; Penguin Books, London, 1969
Lanning, Michael Lee *The Only War We Had: A Platoon Leader's Journal of Vietnam* Ivy Books, New York, 1987
— *Vietnam, 1969–1970: A Company Commander's Journal* Ivy Books, New York, 1988
Larsen, Lieutenant General Stanley Robert and Collins, Brigadier General James Lawton *Allied Participation in Vietnam* Vietnam Studies, Department of the Army, Washington D.C., 1975
Lewy, Guenter *America in Vietnam* Oxford University Press, London and New York, 1978
Lifton, Robert Jay *Home From The War: Vietnam Veterans: Neither Victims Nor Executioners* Wildwood House, London, 1974
Lunn, Hugh *Vietnam: A Reporter's War* University of Queensland Press, Queensland, Australia, 1985
Maclear, Michael *Vietnam: The Ten Thousand Day War* St Martin's Press, New York; Eyre Methuen, London, 1981
Mangold, Tom and Penycate, John *The Tunnels of Cu Chi* Hodder and Stoughton, London, 1985
Marshall, S.L.A. *Bird: the Christmastide Battle* Cowles, New York, 1968
— *Battles in the Monsoon: Campaigning in the Central Highlands South Vietnam Summer 1966* Morrow, New York, 1968
— *Ambush: The Battle of Dau Tieng War Zone C, Operation Attleboro, and other Deadfalls in South Vietnam* Cowles, New York, 1969
— *The Fields of Bamboo: Dong Tre, Trung Luong and Hoa Hoi, Three Battles Just Beyond The South China Sea* Battery Press, Nashville, Tennessee, 1984

Mason, Robert *Chickenhawk* Viking Press, New York, 1983; Corgi Books, London, 1984
Mason, Steve *Johnny's Song: Poetry of a Vietnam Veteran* Bantam Books, New York, 1986
McAulay, Lex *The Battle of Long Tan* Arrow Books, London, 1987
McChristian, Major General Joseph A. *The Role of Military Intelligence 1965–1967* Vietnam Studies, Department of the Army, Washington D.C., 1974
Middleton, Drew (ed) *Air War-Vietnam* Arno Press, New York; Arms and Armour Press, London, 1978
Nixon, Richard *The Memoirs of Richard Nixon* Grosset and Dunlap, New York, 1978
Nolan, Keith William *Battle for Hue: Tet 1968* Presidio Press, California, 1983;
— *Into Laos: The Story of Dewey Canyon II/Lam Son 719* Presidio Press, California, 1986
— *Death Valley: The Summer Offensive I Corps August 1969* Presidio Press, California, 1987
Oberdorfer, Don *Tet! The Turning Point in the Vietnam War* Doubleday, New York, 1971
O'Brien, Tim *If I Die in a Combat Zone* Calder and Boyars, London, 1973
O'Neill, Robert J. *General Giap: Politician and Strategist* Frederick A. Praeger, New York; Cassell Australia, 1969
Ott, Major General David Ewing *Field Artillery 1954–1973* Vietnam Studies, Department of the Army, Washington D.C., 1975
Page, Tim and Pimlott, John (ed) *NAM: The Vietnam Experience 1965–1975* Hamlyn, London, 1989
Palmer, Dave *Summons of the Trumpet: U.S.-Vietnam in Perspective* Presidio Press, California, 1979
Parrish, John *12, 20 and 5: A Doctor's Year in Vietnam* E.P. Dutton, New York, 1972; published in Britain as *Journal of a Plague Year* André Deutsch, London, 1973
Pearson, Lieutenant General Willard *The War in the Northern Provinces* Vietnam Studies, Department of the Army, Washington D.C., 1975
Peers, William *The My Lai Inquiry* W.W. Norton, New York, 1979
Pentagon Papers, The Gravel Edition (5 vols) Beacon Press, Boston, Mass., 1971
Petersen, Barry and Cribbin, John *Tiger Men: An Australian Soldier's Secret War in Vietnam* Sidgwick and Jackson, London, 1988
Pimlott, John (ed) *Vietnam: The history and the tactics* Orbis Publishing, London; Crescent Books, New York, 1982
Ploger, Major General Robert R. *U.S. Army Engineers 1965–1970* Vietnam Studies, Department of the Army, Washington D.C., 1974

Robbins, Christopher *The Invisible Air Force: The True Story of the CIA's Secret Airlines* Macmillan, London, 1979
— *The Ravens: Pilots of the Secret War of Laos* Corgi Books, London, 1989
Rogers, Lieutenant General Bernard William *Cedar Falls-Junction City: A Turning Point* Vietnam Studies, Department of the Army, Washington D.C., 1974
Rosie, George *The British in Vietnam* Panther Books, London, 1970
Rosser-Owen, David *Vietnam Weapons Handbook* Patrick Stephens, Wellingborough, Northamptonshire, 1986
Rutledge, Howard and Rutledge, Phyllis *In the Presence of Mine Enemies: 1965–1973 A Prisoner of War* Fleming H. Revel, New Jersey, 1973; William Collins, London, 1974
Santoli, Al *Everything We Had: An Oral History of the Vietnam War* Random House, New York, 1981
— *To Bear Any Burden: The Vietnam War and its Aftermath in the Words of Americans and Southeast Asians.* E.P. Dutton, New York, 1985; Abacus, London, 1986
Schell, Jonathan *The Real War* Corgi Books, London, 1989
Schemmer, Benjamin F. *The Raid* Harper and Row, New York, 1976; Macdonald and Jane's, London, 1977
Scholl-Latour, Peter *Death in the Rice Fields: Thirty Years of War in Indochina* Orbis Publishing, London, 1981
Sharp, Admiral Ulysses S. Grant and Westmoreland, William C. *Report on the War in Vietnam (as of June 1968)* U.S. Government Printing Office, Washington D.C., 1968
Shawcross, William *Side-Show: Kissinger, Nixon and the Destruction of Cambodia* Simon and Schuster, New York; André Deutsch, London, 1979
Sheehan, Neil *A Bright Shining Lie: John Paul Vann and America in Vietnam* Jonathan Cape, London, 1989
Shore, Captain Moyars S. *The Battle for Khe Sanh* History and Museums Division, Headquarters, U.S. Marine Corps, Washington D.C., 1969
Shulimson, Jack and Johnson, Major Charles M. *U.S. Marines in Vietnam: The Landing and the Buildup 1965* History and Museums Division, Headquarters, U.S. Marine Corps, Washington D.C., 1978
Snepp, Frank *Decent Interval: The American Debacle in Vietnam and the Fall of Saigon* Random House, New York, 1977; Penguin Books, London, 1980
Stanton, Shelby L. *The Rise and Fall of an American Army: U.S. Ground Forces in Vietnam, 1965–1973* Presidio Press, California, 1985
— *Green Berets at War: U.S. Army Special Forces in Southeast Asia 1956–1975* Presidio Press, California; Arms and Armour Press, London, 1986

— *Vietnam Order of Battle* Galahad Books, New York, 1987
— *Anatomy of a Division: 1st Cav in Vietnam* Presidio Press, California, 1987
Starry, General Donn A. *Mounted Combat in Vietnam* Vietnam Studies, Department of the Army, Washington D.C., 1978.
Summers, Colonel Harry G. *On Strategy: A Critical Analysis of the Vietnam War* Dell Publishing, New York, 1982
— *Vietnam War Almanac* Facts on File Publications, New York, 1985
Terry, Wallace *Bloods: An Oral History of the Vietnam War by Black Veterans* Ballantine Books, New York, 1985
Terzani, Tiziano *Giai Phong! The Fall and Liberation of Saigon* St Martin's Press, New York; Angus and Robertson, London, 1976
Tolson, Lieutenant General John J. *Airmobility 1961–1971* Vietnam Studies, Department of the Army, Washington D.C., 1973
Uhlig, Frank *Vietnam: The Naval Story* Naval Institute Press, Annapolis, Maryland, 1986
Vietnam Experience, The (multi vols) The Boston Publishing Company, Boston, Mass., 1981–87
Westmoreland, General William C. *A Soldier Reports* Doubleday, New York, 1976
Zaffiri, Samuel *Hamburger Hill: May 11–20, 1969* Presidio Press, California; Arms and Armour Press, London, 1988

INDEX

Page numbers in **bold** print indicate major references to a subject; illustrations, diagrams and supplementary text are shown with page numbers in *italics*: *col* is added to references for supplementary text contained in the "War Years" column, and *gl* is added to references to the glossary.

A

A Loui 140
A Shau valley *42*, *71col*, *127*, *151*; Hamburger Hill **140–7**; NVA invasion (An Loc): **160–71**
A Shau village 140
AATTV 60
AB–141: 72
Abrams, Creighton Williams *34*, *127col*, **140–7**, **143**, *156*, 166
ACAVs *101*, 105–7
ACOUSIDS (Acoustic/Seismic Intrusion Detectors) 119
ADSIDS *119*
Agency for International Development *34*
Agent Orange **102**
Agnew, Spiro: photo *183*
AID *34*
Ainslie, Peter 68
Air-Delivered Seismic Intrusion Detectors (ADSIDS) *119*
air warfare, 26, *47col*, *71col*, 78, 118, 125–6; air support for infantry **81**; in Cambodia 148–50, *154*, **156**; coastal patrols *114*; during Easter Offensive **160–71**; in NV "selective bombing" 32, 35–9, Rolling Thunder 38, *59col*, **84–95**, *107*, Freedom Dawn **172–9**; Niagara **126**; rescue of pilots 90
aircraft: of USN 90; A–1 Skyraider *81*, 90, *126*, *144*, **156**; A–3 Skywarrior 90; A–4 Skyhawk ("Scooter") *81*, 84–95, 90, *122*; A–6 Intruder 90, *126*; A–7 Corsair II: 90; A–37 Dragonfly *163*, 167; B–26: *17*; B–52 Stratofortress (Boeing): 59, *139col*, 140, *156*, 167, 171, 172, *173*; B–52D: 84–95, *126*, 148–50, *154*, **174**; B–57: 84–95; B–66 Destroyer *86*; C–123 Provider *102*, *103*, *122*, 124; C–130 (Hercules) 116, *122*, *123*, 124, 169; EB–66 ECM 92; F–4 Phantom *85*, 86, 90, *167*, 171, 172, *173*; F–4C Phantom *71col*, *83col*, 90, 91, *167*, 175–9; F–8 Crusader 84–95, 90; F–8E Crusader *34*, 35, 36; F–100 Super Sabre 74, 84–95, *85*; F–105 Thunderchief ("The Thud") 84–95, *86*, **92**; F–105 "Wild Weasel" 86, 90, *167*, 175–9; F–105F 90,

92; KC–135 tanker 90; KC–135A tanker 92; L–19 spotter plane *28*, *30*; MiGs (Mikoyan/Gurevich) *85*, 86–92; MiG–17 "Fresco" *71col*, **92–3**, MiG–21: *83col*, 91; O–1 Bird Dog (Cessna) *81*; O–2A (Cessna): *81*; O–1E Bird Dog 125; OV–10 Bronco *81*, *167*; P2V Neptune *114*; P3A Orion (Lockheed) *114*; P5M Marlin (Martin): *114*; RB–66: *167*; RC–121: 92; TA–4 *122*; *see also* gunships; helicopters
aircraft carriers, USN 90; *Forrestal* *95col*; *Ticonderoga* 34, 36
AirLand Battle 10
airmobility 10, *35*, *38*, 48–54, *50*, *54*, *192gl*
Alcala, Raoul H. *101*, 105–7
Algerians 8, *15*
Allied Land Forces French Indochina 19
Allied leaders conference, Manila (1966) *83col*
Aloui, Laos *153*, 155–9
Alvarez, Everett 94
ambush: Australian SAS **66**; Communist area warfare 72, *78*, 81–3, *82*; U.S. LRRPs *83*
An Cuong (1): 43–7
An Cuong (2): *45*, 46, 47
An Khe 48, 59, *59col*
An Loc (and Easter Offensive) 98, 105, *143*, *159*, **160–71**, 180
An Thoi *45*, 46, 47, 114
Annam *11*, 12, *31*, 130
"Anne-Marie" strongpoint *15*, 16, 20–3
antiaircraft defenses **86–92**, 105, 172
antitank vehicles, Ontos: Starlite 40, *41*, *45*, 46, 47; Tet Offensive *133*, 137, 138
"ap" *192gl*
Ap Bac **24–31**
Ap Bac hamlet 30
Ap Bau Bang 107
Ap Bau Bang II: **100–1**, 105
Ap Bia **140–7**
Ap Gu 107
Apache Snow, Operation 140–3
APCs *see* Armored Personnel Carriers
"Arc Light" strikes *126*, *167*
area warfare (NVA/VC): 8–10, 72–4, *77*, *78*, 81–3, *82*, *192gl*
Armed Forces Council *95col*, *167*
Armored Cavalry Assault Vehicles (ACAVs): *101*, 105–7
Armored Personnel Carriers (APCs; M–113s, M–113A1s): 26, **30**, 60, 69–70, *78*, 110; An Loc *161*, *162*; Ap Bac *25*, *28*, 30, *31*; Lam Son 719: *153*, *154*, 155–9
Armored Troop Carriers (ATCs): 110; Rach Ba Rai River 108, 110, *112–13*
Army Aircraft Requirements Review Board *50*
Army of the Republic of South Vietnam (ARVN): *95col*, 138;

allied aid 60, U.S. 26, 40, *40* (at Ap Bac) **26–31**, *30*; corruption and weaknesses 40, 51, 72, 74, 128, 148, *159*, 160, Ap Bac 26, 28, 29, 30, intelligence gathering *83*, after U.S. withdrawal 180–2; coups: against Diem 31, *31*, 32, against Kanh 38; Joint General Staff Command building attacked 128; mutiny 72; special responsibilities 72, 108; Vietnamization *see separate entry*. Ap Bac **24–31**; Starlite 40; Ia Drang 51–2, *59col*; Khe Sanh 118, 124, 126; Tet Offensive **128–39**; Hamburger Hill **142–7**; Lam Son 719: **148–59**, 170–1; An Loc and Easter Offensive **162–71**; after Peace Agreement, fall of the South **180–7**.
Units: 1st Corps **151–9**, 170–1; 2d Corps 169; 3d Corps 166; 1st Div 130–4, 140–3, 162; 1st Airborne Div 151–9; 1st Infantry Div 151–9; 3d Div 162, 170–1; 5th Infantry Div *164*, 166–7, *167*; 7th Div 26–31, *28*; 9th Div 166–9; 18th Infantry Div *181*, 183; 21st Div 166–71, *170*; 22d Div 169; 23d Div 169; 1st Infantry Regt 157–8; 2d Infantry Regt 157; 3d Regt: 2/3d **140–7**; 20th Tank Regt **162–71**, *163*; 1st Armor Bde 151–9; 1st Parachute Bde *167*; "Black Panther" Co. 138; Regional Force Co. 118; Marines 151, 162; Rangers 124, 126, 151–9, *164*, 166–71; 9th Airborne Btn 155; Special Forces 51–2, 59
Army Tactical Mobility Requirement Board *50*
Assault Support Patrol Boats (ASPBs): 110
ATCs 110; Rach Ba Rai River *108*, 110, *112–13*
ATF *192gl*
Attleboro, Operation **72–83**
Australia, and Australian forces 27, 60, 72, *83col*, 168, 190; ATF 60, *192gl*; Long Tan **60–71**; Special Air Service (SAS): 62; **62**, **66**; withdrawal *159col*

B

Bac (hamlet, ie Ap Bac) 30; Battle of Ap Bac **24–31**
Ban Me Thuot *83*, 128; fall of the South **183–7**, *187col*
Bao Dai, Emperor *23col*, 24
Battambang, Cambodia 191, *191col*
Bau Bang *101*, 105, 107
"Beatrice" strongpoint *15*, 16, 22, assault on 23
Ben Cat 96–8, 105
Ben Het 169
Ben Long 110
Ben Suc 96–8
Bien Hoa 38, *47col*, 60, 61, 74, *102*, 167

Binh Ba 71
Binh Dinh province 51, 74; NVA invasion 160–71
Binh Long province: NVA invasion 160–71, *171col*
Binh Thai 40, *137*
Binh Xuyen pirates 24
Blackburn, Donald *95*
Blastout 1, Operation 42–3
BLU–1 and BLU–27: *125*
"boat people" 188, **190**, *191col*
boats *see* riverine craft
body count **75**, *192gl*
Bolo, Operation *83col*, **84–95**
Bomb Live Units *125*
bombs 74, *81*, *101*, *107*; "Daisy Cutter" *54*; "smart" weapons (EOGBs and LGBs) *167*, 172–9, *173*, *178*
booby traps (VC) 42, 78–9, *98*
Breeding, Earle *122*, 124
Brezhnev, Leonid: summit meeting (1972): *171col*
Brink Hotel, Saigon 38
Britain, and British forces: in Vietnam before partition 12, **19**; refusal to send forces 60; Vietnamese refugees *190*, in Hong Kong *190*, *191col*
Brown, Thomas W. 55, 59
Buddhists 24, 31, 38, *71*, *71col*, *167*, 188; priest's suicide 31, *31*, *31col*
Buick, Bob 70–1
Buon Enao: Montagnards *58*
Burma: "Domino Theory" 27

C

Ca Lu 126
Calley, William L. **137**
Cam Lo 162
Cam Ne (1) 42–3
Cam Ranh *34*, *59col*, 104
Cam Ranh Bay *82*, 190
Cam Son Secret Zone 108
Cambodia 8–11, 12, *23*, 27
Cambodia, and the Vietnam War: indigenous groups aid U.S. *58*, *83*; NVA/VC sanctuaries 59, 74, 78, 83, NVA attacks from 160, 171, *171col*; NVA/VC supply route *42*, 59, *102*, *114*, *158*, *see also* Ho Chi Minh Trail; Sihanouk and Lon Nol 148–50, *150*, **155**, *156*, *159*, *159col*; U.S./ARVN activities in border region (War Zone C) 74–9, 96–107; U.S./ARVN incursions *139*, *139col*, 148–50, *154*, **156**, *159*, *159col*, 188
Cambodia, and the Khmer Rouge 148, **150**, *155*, 186; "Democratic Republic of Kampuchea" **186**, reverts to "Cambodia" 188; *Mayaguez* Incident **187**; Pol Pot's revolution *156*, **186**, *187col*, **188–91**, Vietnamese invasion (1978): *186*, *187col*
Camp J.J. Carroll 116, *126*, *126*, *127*, 162
Camp Holloway 38, *38*
Cao Bang 190

Cao Bang-Lang Son ridge 18
Cao Dai sect 24
Carter, Jimmy *187*
Castor, Operation *13, 16*, 20
Castries, Christian Marie Ferdinand de la Croix de *15*, 20–3, *22*
casualty figures (U.S.) **178**
Cat Bi 90–2
Cau Do River 42
ceasefires 128, 179, 180
Cedar Falls, Operation *83col*, **96–8**, *99*
Central Intelligence Agency 24, *26*, 31, 32; after Diem 34, *36*, 86, 148–50, *183*
Central Office for South Vietnam (COSVN): Junction City 98, 103–5, 107
Cheatham, Ernest C. 128*q*, 134–7
chemicals *see* Agent Orange; gas; defoliants; napalm
China, and Indochina 8–11, 12, 26
China, under Mao 14, *14*, **19**, 22, *23col*, 26, *155*; involvement in Vietnam War *71col*, 84, 86, *87*, 91, *139*, 179, peace negotiations and agreement *139*, *178*, the continuing war 188–90, *191col*, Chinese-Vietnamese persecuted, and "boat people" 188, **190**, *191col*; Mao and Nixon *139, 143*, 162, **162**, *171col*; Sino-Soviet split 160, **162**, 188–90
Cholon, Saigon: Diem killed *31*
Chu Lai 40, 43, 72
Chu Luc 20
Chu Pong Mountain **48–59**
CIA *see* Central Intelligence Agency
CIDGs *see* Civilian Irregular Defense Groups
CinCPAC *34*, 35, 42, *192gl*
Civil Guard 20, *58*; at Ap Bac **26–31**; NV peasant militia *87*
Civil Operations and Rural Development Support (CORDS): *34*, 148
Civilian Irregular Defense Groups (CIDGs): *58*, 98, 116, 123; at Lang Vei 116, 122, 123, **127**
civilians (NV): *94, 95*; militia *87*
civilians (SV): *82*, 139, 148; at fall of the South *181, 183, 185*, "corrupted" citizens relocated 188; My Lai *115*, **137**
"Claudine" strongpoint *15*, 20–3
Clifford, Clark 27, *107col*, *115col*, *127col*, 134
Cochin China *11*, 12
COIN **70–1**
Colleton, USS 110
Combined Intelligence Center *99*
Combined Military Exploitation Center *99*
Combined Military Interrogation Center *99*
Comer, Andrew G. *45, 47*
Command and Control Boats (CCBs): 108, 110, *110*
Commander in Chief, Pacific (CinCPAC): *34*, 35, 42, *192gl*

Communism, in Southeast Asia **8–11**, 22, *23col*, 26, 27, *58, 162*, 188; SEATO formed (1954): *31col*; *see also* Khmer Rouge; Pathet Lao
Communism, in Vietnam 8*q*, 12, 14, *14, 19*; First Indochina War (1946–54): **12–23**, *31col*, Geneva Accords *23, 23col*, 24, 26, *155*; in Vietnam War *see* infiltration; insurgency and counterinsurgency; Viet Cong
Con Thien *95col*
Condor, Operation *18*
CORDS *34*, 148
Coronado, Operation **108–15**
Corps Tactical Zones (CTZs; later Military Regions): *9 (map)*, 150, *192gl*
"corrupted" citizens relocated 188
corruption (SV): 24, *30, 31, 83col*; *see also* Army of the Republic of South Vietnam (corruption and weaknesses)
COSVN: Junction City 98, 103–5, 107
counterinsurgency *see* insurgency and counterinsurgency
coups (SV): against Diem 31, *31*, 32; against Khanh 38
Cronkite, Walter *130*
CTZs (later MRs, Military Regions) *9 (map)*, 150, *192gl*
Cu Chi 72, *98*
Cua Viet River 162, 169–71, 180

D

Da Krong valley *139col*, 140
Da Nang 38, *71col*, 72, 84, *104, 107*, *114*; An Loc 160–71; Starlite **40–7**, Da Nang in flames **42**; taken by NVA after Peace Agreement 183, *185*
Dabney, William 116–8, *121*, 122
Dai, Bao *23col*, 24
Daily News (NY): report *39*
"Daisy Cutter" bombs *54*
Dak To *58*, 169; Battle of Dak To *107col*
Dak To II: 169
Dat, Le Duc 169
Dau Tieng 79
David, Bert A. 110–14
Davis, Sammy, Jr. *104*
Davis, Wilbert *113*, 114
Davy Crockett, Operation 74
Dean, Arthur 27
Deane, John R. Jr. *102*
defoliants *83col*, **102**, *103*
"De Lattre Line" 19
Delaware, Operation 140
Delaware/Lam Son 216, Operation *127col*
Demilitarized Zone (DMZ): *23*; McNamara Line *95col*, *119*; NVA action 74, An Loc 160–71, territory held 171, 179, 180; U.S./ARVN action 32, 84–6, *95col*
democracy (SV): *see* elections, free

DePuy, William E.: Attleboro 77, 82–3; El Paso **74–9**
DeSaussure, Edward H.: Attleboro **76–83**
deserters: ARVN 148, *159*, 170–1, *170*, 180; NVA/VC 43, 57, *99*, 118; U.S. *143*
De Soto missions 32–9
Destroyer Escort Radar *114*
Dewey Canyon, Operation *139col*, 140
Dewey Canyon II, Operation 151, *159col*
Diem, Can 24
Diem, (Jean-Baptiste): Ngo Dinh *23col*, 24, 26, *26*, 31, **31**, *31*, *31col*; ARVN generals' coup 31, *31*, 32, *167*
Diem, Madame Nhu 24
Diem, Nhu 24, *30*, 31, *31*
Diem, Thuc, Archbishop 24
Dien Bien Phu: battle **12–23**, and Khe Sanh 116, **118**, 122, 124
Dien Bien Phu village 20
DMZ *see* Demilitarized Zone
"Dominique" strongpoint *15*, 16, 20–3
"Domino Theory" **27**, 188
Don Dien Michelin rubber plantation: Attleboro **76–83**
Dong A Tay 140
Dong Ha 162, **163**, 170, *170*
Dong Khe 18
Dong Tam 108, 110
Dong Thoung bridge 86
Dong Xoai *47col*
Doty, Mercer M. 110–14
Double Eagle, Operation 74
draft and evasion (U.S.), *106, 107col*, *139, 179col, 187col*; cards burnt *59col*, 106
"Dragon's Jaw" (Ham Rung): bridge **172–9**
drug abuse: U.S. forces *104, 143*
Duan, Le 160
Duc, Quang *31, 31col*
Duc Co 51
Dung (VC squadron leader): *29*
Dung, Van Tien 183
Duong Son (1): 42
"Dust-Off" missions *57*

E

Easter Offensive (and An Loc): 98, 105, *143, 159*, **160–71**, 180
ECM (electronic countermeasures) to missiles 86–90, 92, 172, 179
Edwards, Robert H. *48q*
Eisenhower, Dwight D., President *23col*, 24, **27**
El Paso, Operation *71col*, **74–9**; Phase Two *71col*
elections, free *23*, 24, 32, *83col, 95col, 107col*, *167*; democratic ideal loses support 180; local elections *95col*, 148
electronic countermeasures (ECM) to missiles 86–90, 92, 172, 179
electronic detectors 10, *99, 119*
electro-optical guided bombs

(EOGBs): 172–9, **178**
"Eliane" strongpoint *15*, 16, 20–3
Ellsberg, David **183**
EOGBs 172–9, **178**
ethnic peoples: blacks in U.S. forces **147**; Indochinese 188; Vietnamese: Chinese-Vietnamese refugees ("boat people") 188, **190**, *191col*, used by Special Forces *58, 71, 83*
Ewell, Julian J. *75*

F

FACs *81*
Festa, Roger A. 105–7
Filhol Plantation 96–8
Fire Support Bases (FSBs) **54**, *67*; Junction City 98, 105, 107
firing villages 42–3, *71*; *see also* "search and destroy" operations
"Fish Hook" 148–50, *154, 159col*
flamethrowers 30, 47
Flaming Dart, Operation 38
Flaming Dart II, Operation 38
Ford, Gerald, President *106*, *182*, *187*
Forrestal, U.S. carrier *95col*
Fort Bragg, N. Carolina: 5th Special Forces Group *31*
Forward Air Controllers *81*
foxholes (VC) *28*, 30
"fragging" *143, 192gl*
France: in Indochina (1945–54): **8–11**, 12, 24, 26, *155*, effects of World War II: 12, *19*, 22, U.S. involvement 22, *23col*, 26; First Indochina War (1946–54) 10, **12–23**, *31col*, 1st and 2d Airborne Battle Groups *16*, 20, Geneva Accords *23, 23col*, 24, 26, *155*
France, and Vietnam War ("Second Indochina War"): de Gaulle condemns U.S. policies *83col*; Vietnamese refugees (1979) *190*
"Francoise" strongpoint *15*
Free Fire Zone *192gl*
Freedom Dawn 172
Freedom Deal, Operation **156**
French Foreign Legion 13, 23
Frequent Wind, Operation *174*, **182**
FSBs **54**, *67*; Junction City 98, 105, 107
fuel supplies (NV): POL storage sites 86, 172; *see also* supplies (NVA/VC)
Fulton, William B. 108–10

G

"Gabrielle" strongpoint *15, 16*, 20–3
Gadsden, Operation 98–102
"Garry Owen" Brigade 55
gas: CS gas *98*, 122, 137
Gaulle, Charles de 12, *249, 83col*
Geneva Accords (1954) *23, 23col*, 24, 26, *155*
Gia Lam 90–2
Giai, Vu Van *163*, 171
Giap, Vo Nguyen 12, **15**, *15*; An Loc **160–71**; Dien Bien Phu **14–23**

195

Godard, Colonel (at Dien Bien Phu): *18*
GPES *122*
Gracey, Douglas **19**
Gravel, Marcus J. 134–7
"Greek-Letter Projects" *83*
Green Beach *46*
Green Berets *see* United States Special Forces
Greene, Wallace M. *40q*
grenades 29, 30, *30*, *45*, 137; attached to trip wires *78–9*; at Dien Bien Phu *14*, *21*; "fragging" *143*; grenade launchers *57*, *111*, 114; NVA RPGs 143; rifle-grenade rockets 105; smoke grenades *124*
Ground Proximity Extraction System *122*
Gruening, Ernest 38
Grunt, and *Grunt Free Press 146*
Guam *95col*, 167, 179
guerrilla warfare 8–10; *see also* area warfare
Gulf of Tonkin Incident **32–9**
Gulf of Tonkin Resolution 35–8; repealed 150, *159col*
guns and artillery: at Dien Bien Phu *18*, *20*, *21*, *22*; dropped in blankets from helicopters *70*; on rescue helicopters *90*; VC ammunition dumps *79*; antiaircraft defenses **86–92**, 172; antitank weapons 114, *163*, LAWs 127, *163*, *165*, *167*; flamethrowers 30, 47; heavy guns, cannon *67*, 108, *110*, *111*, 116, *156*, 105mm *67*, 105, *126*, *163*, 155mm 62, *126*, *163*, at An Loc 160, *162*, *163*, 167; howitzers *54*, *67*, *73*, *97*; machine guns 22, 47, *57*, *87*, *90*, *110*, 134–7, 143, *168*; 7.62mm *20*, *61*, *63*, 50-caliber *41*, *105*, *111*, on M-113 APCs *30*, *31*, *69*, M60 ("The Pig") 114, **115**, *133*; mortars *18*, 62, 66–8, 105, *126*, 81mm *42*, 108, *110*, 134–7, at Khe Sanh 118, 122, 123, 125; recoilless rifles *41*, *42*, *44*, *45*, 62, 66–8, 105, 137, 143; rifle power (assault rifles) *75*, *87*; AK-47 Kalashnikov *42*, **75**, 143, *157*, M-14 *73*, M-16 Colt **75**, *99*, 114, *117*, *119*, 124, 137, 148, M-16AI Colt **75**; homemade VC rifle **75**; sub-machine guns *20*, 107, MAT-49: *18*, Owen *63*, *69*; *see also* grenades; missiles; rockets
gunships, esp. AC-47 Spooky *81*, 107, *127*

H
Haig, Alexander M. *96*
Haiphong *71col*, 84, 86, 172–9; First Indochina War 12–14
Ham Rung ("Dragon's Jaw") bridge **172–9**
Hamburger Hill **140–7**
"hammer and anvil" operations

96–8, 108–10
Hanoi: French center of government 12, 14, 19, *31col*; Hoa Lo PoW compound *94*; strategic bombing 172–9, Rolling Thunder *71col*, *83col*, 84, 86, 90, 95, Thermal Power Plant *175*; *see also* North Vietnam, government
Harrington, Myron C. 138
Hastings, Operation 74
Haszard, Sidney S. *101*, 107
Hawaii: CinCPAC *34*, 35, *42*, *192gl*; conferences in Honolulu 40, 43, *47col*, *59col*; Lon Nol *155*
"hearts and minds" campaign 71, *71*
helicopter(s): 26, 48, **57**, 140, 148; airmobility 10, *35*, *38*, 48–54, *50*, *50*, *54*, *192gl*; deployed 43–7, *95*, *113*, *182*, Ap Bac 26–31, Ia Drang **48–59**, Junction City 96, 98, 102, *102*, Khe Sanh *121*, 122, *123*, 124–6, Lam Son 719: 155–9, Saigon evacuation *182*, Tet Offensive 130, *134*; Medevac *57*, *142*, *146*; 57th Medical Detachment *57*; rescue of downed pilots *90*; AH-1G Cobra *56*, *156*, 159, *163*, *165*, 167, *169*; CH-21 Shawnee "Flying Bananas" *25*, *28*, *30*; CH-46: 30, *122*, *123*, 124–6; CH-47 Chinook (Boeing-Vertol) 48, CH-47A *57*; CH-53: *121*, 124–6, *182*, *187*; CH-54 Tarhe Flying Crane 48, *54*, 57, CH-54A *56*; HH-3: *90*, *95*; HH-3E *95*; HH-53C *95*; OH-6A Cayuse Loach (Hughes) *56*; OH-13 Sioux 48; UH-1 Iroquois Huey (Bell) *25*, *28*, *30*, 54, *70*, *122*; UH-1A *25*, *57*; UH-1D *57*; UH-1E 48, 124–6
Herr, Michael: *Dispatches 127*
Herren, John D. *53col*, 56–9
Hill 30: *45*, *46*, 47, 155–7
Hill 31: 155–7
Hill 43: *44*, *46*, 47
Hill 327: *42*
Hills 800, 900, 916: 140
Hill 937 ("Hamburger Hill"): **140–7**
Hill Fights (Hills 64, 558, 861, 861A, 881North, 881South): Khe Sanh **116–27**
Ho Bo Woods 96–8
Ho Chi Minh 12, 14, **14**, *14*, **20**, **22**, *23*, *23col*, 24; Communist ideals *8q*, *14*, 19; takes over in Hanoi (1954): *31col*, death *147col*
Ho Chi Minh City 188; *see also* Saigon
Ho Chi Minh Trail 24–6, *158*, 160, *182*; defoliants *102*; VC supply line *114*, **158**; *see also* infiltration
Hoa Binh 19
Hoa Hao sect 24
Hoa Lo PoW compound, Hanoi *94*
Hollingsworth, James *160q*, 166, 171

Homecoming, Operation **178**
Hon Gai, NV 35, *94*
Hon Me, NV 34, *36*
Hon Ngu, NV 34, *36*
Honeycutt, Weldon 142–7, *146*
Hong Kong: ICCP founded *14*; Vietnamese refugees 190, *191col*
Honolulu: conferences 40, 43, *47col*, *59col*
Hope, Bob: Bob Hope Show *104*
hovercraft: PACVs *110*, *111*
Howze, Hamilton, and Howze Board *50*
Hue: An Loc **160–71**; Tet Offensive **130–9**; after U.S. withdrawal 183, *185*
"Huguette" strongpoint *15*, *16*, 20–3
Humphrey, Hubert *139*
Hunt, E. Howard *183*
Huong Giang (Perfume River) **130–8**

I
Ia Drang Campaign **48–59**
Ia Drang valley *42*
ICCP 12, *14*, **20**, *175*
Indian unit: 20th Indian Division 19
Indochina: French rule **8–11**, 12
Indochina War, First (1946–54): 10, **12–23**, *31col*; Geneva Accords **23**, *23col*, 24, 26, *155*
Indochina War, Second (ie Vietnam War): *179col*, *185*, *187col*, continuing war 10, **188–91**
Indo-Chinese Communist Party 12, *14*, **20**, *175*
Indochinese Federation 12
infiltration and subversion 8–10, *14*, *19*, 26, 74; from NV *42*, 72, 74, *79*, *83*, 84, 86, 95, *95col*, Ia Drang **48–59**; Khe Sanh *115col*, **116–27**, 128, *see also* Ho Chi Minh Trail; into Cambodia *155*; into Laos 150, *see also* insurgency and counterinsurgency
insignia, badges: Australian *61*, *62*, MACV *34*; U.S. *33*, *49*, *73*, *97*, *109*, *141*
insurgency and counterinsurgency 8–10, *15*, 24, 26, 32, 40, 42, 72–4, 148; CIDGs *see separate entry*; COIN **70–1**; operations *68*, *95*, *98*
intelligence gathering *58*, *79*, *83*, *98*, *99*; Australians 62, *62*; VC *68*
International Armistice Commission for DMZ *23*
International Commission for Control and Supervision 180
"International Tribunal", Stockholm (1967): *95col*
Iron Hand 86, 92
Iron Triangle *83col*, **96–8**, **105–7**
"Isabelle" strongpoint *15*, 20–3

J
Jackson, O.D. 60–6
"Jacob's Ladders" *54*

James, Daniel "Chappie" *92*
Japan, in Indochina 12, *19*, 22, *23col*
Jason Group: McNamara Line *119*
Jenkins, Homer K. 47
John Paul Jones, Operation 74
Johnson, Lyndon Baines, President *39 col*, *83*, *115*, **134**, *139*, 148, *159*; *see also* United States, and Vietnam War policy, under Johnson
Junction City, Operation *95col*, **96–107**
jungle and forest 50, *58*, *78*, 86, *157*; A Shau valley 140, 143–7; Attleboro 77, 79, 81; defoliants *83col*, 102, *103*; Junction City 96–8, *99*, 107
"Juno" strongpoint *15*, 23

K
Kampuchea, Democratic Republic of (1975–89): *186*, *187col*, **188–91**; name changed *186*, reverts to "Cambodia" 188; *see also* Cambodia
Karch, Frederick J. 40
Katum camp 98, 102, *103*, 105
Kendall, Geoff *64*, 66–9
Kennedy, Edward: antiwar 147, *147col*
Kennedy, John F., President 24, 27, 32, *39col*, *102*; *see also* United States, and Vietnam War policy, under Kennedy
Kennedy, Robert: death *127col*
Kent State, Ohio 150, **154**
Kep 90–2
Khanh, Nguyen 32, 38, *39*
Khanh Hoi *147*
Khe Sanh *115col*, **116–27**, 128, 151, 158
Khe Sanh village 116, 118
Khmer Rouge (Cambodian Communists) *see under* Cambodia
KIA *192gl*
Kien An 90–2
Kinnard, Harry W. O. 48–59, **50**
Kissinger, Henry *147col*, **175**, 179
Kontum 51, *59*, *107col*, 128, 180, 183; NVA invasion (An Loc) **160–71**
Korea, South: Vietnam War 60, *75*, *83col*
Korean War 22, *23col*, *35*, 50, *125*
Krogh, Egil "Bud" *183*
Ky, Nguyen Cao 38, *47col*, *71col*, *95col*, *107col*, **167**

L
Lahue, Foster C. 130–4
Lai Chau 20
Lai Khe *101*, 105, 107, 166–71
Laird, Melvin *139col*, *179col*
Lam, Hoang Xuan 151–9, 170–1
Lam Son 719, Operation **148–59**
land use 24, *26*, 148; "Strategic Hamlets" 26, *30*
landing craft *26*, **110**
landing zones (LZs) *54*, , 74, 98, 126; Ia Drang 48, 51, 55, 56, 59,

LZ X-Ray *48q*, 49, *50*, *53*, 56–9;
  Lam Son 719: 155–9; Starlite 43,
  47
Lang Son 190
Lang Vei 116, *122*, 123, **127**
Lansdale, Edward 24, *26*
Lao Cai 190
Lao Khe 18
Laos 8–11, 12, 20, **23**, 27, 188;
  Pathet Lao (*Neo Lao Hak Sat*;
  Lao Liberation Front): 20, **150**,
  188
Laos, and the Vietnam War *58*, *119*,
  139, *159*; ARVN/U.S. incursions
  116, **159**; border action 116, 126,
  140–7, **148–59**; Ho Chi Minh
  Trail *42*, *102*, *150*, *158*; NVA
  bases 150, *171col*
LAPES *122*, *123*
laser-guided bombs (LGBs): *167*,
  172–9, *173*, **178**
Lattre de Tassigny, Jean de 19
LCMs **110**
Le My village 42
League for the Independence of
  Vietnam 12; *see also* Viet Minh
Leary, Timothy *136*
LGBs *167*, *172–9*, *173*, **178**
Liddy, G. Gordon *183*
Lindbergh-Hughes, James *94*
Linebacker, Operation 90, *94*, 173,
  175–9, 180
"Linebacker II", Operation *173*,
  174, 179, 180
Lo Go village 102
Loan, Nguyen Van Ngoc *130*
Loc Ninh 74, 78, *78*, 128, 166
logistic flow (U.S.) **82**
Lon Nol 148–50, **155**, *156*, *159*
Long Binh 72
Long Phuoc village 62
Long Range Reconnaissance Patrols
  83
Long Tan **60–71**
Long Tan village 62, *63*
Lorraine, Operation 19
Low Altitude Parachute Extraction
  System *122*, *123*
Lownds, David 116–8, *121*
LRRPs ("Lurps"): **83**
LVT *45*, *46*, 47
LVTPs **40–7**, **47**
LZs *see* landing zones

M
M-113s *see* Armored Personnel
  Carriers
MAAG 22, *23col*, *31col*
Ma River 172
McCloy, John 27
McNamara, Robert S. 32, 48, *50*,
  72, *83col*, 86, 95, *95col*;
  McNamara Line *95col*, **119**;
  resignation *107col*
MACV 26, *31col*, **34**, 35, 38, *114*,
  130–4, 180–2; CIDGs *58*,
  intelligence role 99; MACV–
  SOG *83*, *83col*; Priority Areas 72;
  Westmoreland hands command
  to Abrams *127col*

Maddox, USS **32–9**
Man, Chu Huy **48–59**
Manila Conference (1966) *83col*
Mao Khe 19
Mao Tse-tung *14*, **19**, 22, *23col*,
  162
"Market Time" **114**
Masher/White Wing, Operation
  59col, 74
Massachusetts Striker, Operation
  140
May, Allen 68
May Tao hills 60, 62, 71
Mayaguez Incident **187**
Meadows, Richard J. *95*
medals and awards 47, *49*
medical matters *50*, 54, *57*, 82, *98*;
  casualty figures (U.S.) *178*;
  Hamburger Hill *142*, 146, *146*;
  jungle *78–9*; Medevac **57**; Tet
  wounded *131*, *134*
Medina, Ernest *137*
Mekong Delta 26, 72; Ap Bac
  24–31; NVA invasion **160–71**;
  Rach Ba Rai River *107col*,
  108–15
Meloy, Guy S. *73*, **76–83**
Menu, Operation *139*
Michelin: Don Dien plantation
  76–83
Midway: Nixon meeting with Thieu
  147
Mieu Gang River *162*, *163*
"Mike" (CIDGs) *58*
Military Assistance Advisory
  Group 22, *23col*, *31col*
Military Assistance Command,
  Vietnam *see* MACV
Military Regions (MRs; formerly
  CTZs): *9* (*map*); 150, *192gl*
militia units 20, *58*; Civil Guard at
  Ap Bac **26–31**; NV peasant
  militia *87*
Millar, David *59col*
Miller, Carl S. 172–4, *177*
mines *15*, *30*, *54*, *78–9*, *119*, *171col*;
  Claymore *66*, *79*; Saigon harbor
  mined 108, 110, *112–3*, 114
Minh, Duong Van, "Big Minh" 32,
  183–7, *187col*
Minh, Ho Chi *see* Ho Chi Minh
Minh Thanh 102
"Mini-Tet" *127col*
missiles: air-to-air 86–90, *89*, 92;
  surface-to-air 38, SAMs 86, *87*,
  89, 92, 160, *167*, 172, *175–9*;
  electronic countermeasures
  (ECM): 86–90, 92, 172, 179;
  Rolling Thunder **86–95**, 172
Mobile Riverine Force **108–17**
monitors *109*, *110*, *111*, *112–13*
monsoon: effects 69, 78, *78*, 86, 118,
  124, 137; Dien Bien Phu *14*, *17*,
  23
Montagnard tribesmen: Ia Drang
  51, *58*
Moore, Harold G. *53*, 55–9
morale: SV population 38, 84, 128,
  180; U.S. forces **143**
MRF **108–17**

"Mutter's Ridge" (Nui Cay Tre) 74,
  83col
My Lai Massacre **137**

N
Na San 20
Nam Yen *45*, *46*, 47
Nam Yum River *17*, 23
napalm 28, *81*, *101*, 107, 118, **121**,
  125; French use 19; used on
  Cambodia *156*
National Liberation Front (NV) 26
National Priority Areas 72–4
National Security Action
  Memorandum 273: 32
nationalists 8–11, 12, 24, *31*
naval warfare: Gulf of Tonkin
  Incident **32–9**; coastal patrol
  114; Mobile Riverine Force
  108–17
Navarre, Henri 20
NDP *192gl*
Neo Lao Hak Sat (Pathet Lao) 20,
  150, 188
"New Economic Zones" 188
New York: demonstrations *95col*
New York Times: Pentagon Papers
  183; War reports *83col*, *183*
New Zealand 27, 60, 68–9, *83col*,
  159col
newspapers, press 23, *39*, *83col*, **130**,
  146, 147, 158; Pentagon Papers
  183; Rolling Thunder 92–5; Tet
  Offensive 128, *129*, 139; for U.S.
  forces **146**, *146*
Nglia Lo ridge 19
Nghe An, Annam 14
Nguyen ai Quoc (b. Nguyen Tat
  Thanh; later Ho Chi Minh) 12,
  14; *see* Ho Chi Minh *for full entry*
Nguyen Hoang bridge 134
Nha Trang *58*, *114*
Nhu: Madame Nhu 24
Niagara, Operation 125–6. *126*
Niotis, John D. 138
Nixon, Richard Milhous, President
  139, *139col*, **143**, *179col*;
  superpower talks: China *159col*,
  162, **162**, *171col*; Soviet Union
  160, *171col*, 172; resignation
  179col, 180, **183**
Nol, Lon 148–50, **155**, *156*, *159*
North Vietnam: government 24, 38,
  86, 95, 128, *147*, 180–7, *see also*
  Ho Chi Minh; partition 8, *9*
  (*map*), **23**, 26, *see also* Indochina
  War, First; U.S. action in NV
  71col, *83col*, 139, *171col*, Rolling
  Thunder *see separate entry*,
  renewed bombing (1972) 90, *143*,
  162–6, *171col*, **172–9**
North Vietnamese Air Force
  (NVAF) 86; *see also* aircraft
  (MiGs)
North Vietnamese Army (NVA) 40,
  172; general strategies, area
  warfare 8–10, *19*, 72, 74, 160;
  Infantryman *157*; fall of the
  South **180–7**; after U.S.
  withdrawal 148, 182, occupied

territory 179, 180, 182; *see also*
  Cambodia; Easter Offensive;
  infiltration; insurgency; Laos;
  Tet Offensive
NVA units: 5th Div (NVA/VC)
  171; 7th Div *163*, 166–71; 9th
  Div (NVA/VC) *163*, **166–71**;
  304th Div 118, 126; 324thB Div
  162; 325thC Div 118, 123, 126;
  29th Regt **140–7**; 90th Regt
  95col; 101st Regt 98, 102
NSAM 32
NSCM *23col*
Nui Cay Tre 74, *83col*
Nui Dat **60–71**
Nuong tribesmen 51
NVA *see* North Vietnamese Army

O
Ogier, Herbert L. *32*, 34, *39*
Ohio National Guard 150, *154*
Olds, Robin *89*, **90–2**
Ontos antitank vehicles: Starlite 40,
  41, *45*, *46*, 47; Tet Offensive *133*,
  137, 138
operations *see* individual operations
Operations Plan (OPLAN) 34A: 32,
  34
Owen: "Garry Owen" Brigade 55

P
pacification 60, 148, 160, *192gl*
PACVs *110*, *111*
Page, Tim *188q*
parachutes: Junction City landings
  102, *102*, Para-Jumpers (for
  rescue) 90; supplies *119*, *122*,
  124
paratroopers: French parachute
  battalions, Dien Bien Phu *13*, *14*,
  16, 18, 19, 20, *21*, 23
Paris: peace talks 95, *139col*, *147col*,
  175, Paris Peace Accords (1973)
  94, *143*, *175*, *178*, 179, *179col*, 180,
  182, 188
"Parrot's Beak" 148–50, *154*, *159col*
Pathet Lao 20, **150**, 188
Patrol Air Cushion Vehicles *110*,
  111
patrol boats: P4s 32–9; PBRs *110*,
  111
patrols 67, **71**, *71*, **78–9**, *78*, **83**;
  coastal patrols *114*
Patton, Colonel George S. 74
Paul Doumer bridge 172, 174, *177*
PBRs *see* patrol boats
peace 84, 86, 95, *136*; negotiations
  95, *127col*, 128, *139col*, *147col*, 175,
  183; Paris Peace Accords (1973)
  94, *143*, *175*, *178*, 179, *179col*, 180,
  182, 188
peasants *47col*, 62, **71**, 180; during
  French rule 8, *11*, 12, *14*, 19, 24;
  favor US Communists *35*,
  42–3, 128, morale in SV 38, 84,
  128, 180; "Strategic Hamlets"
  26, *30*, *71*; "Village War" 72; *see
  also* militia units
Pegasus, Operation *122*, 126, *127*
"people sniffers" *119*

Perfume River (Huong Giang) **130–8**
Peterson, Lee 40
Philippines 27, 60, *83col*, 114
Phnom Penh, Cambodia *150*, *155*, *156*, 186, *186*, *187col*, **188–91**
Phoenix program 148
Phu, Pham Van 183–7
Phu Bai 40, 72, 130–4
Phu Cam Canal 134–7
Phu Cuong 78
Phu Hoa Dong village 99
Phuc Yen 89, 90–2
Phuoc Long province 183
Phuoc Tuy province 60–71, 108; "Phuoc Tuy's Own" 68
Phuong Hoang 148
Pierce Arrow, Operation 34, **35–9**, 90, 94
Pin Feather, Operation 63
pirates: Binh Xuyen 24
Plain of Jars, Laos 20
Plain of Reeds 26, 108
Plei Me 50, 51–4, 59
Pleiku 38, *38*, 48, 51, 52, 72, 128, *156*
Pol Pot *156*, **186**, *187col*, 188–91
POL supplies campaign 86, 172
Post Traumatic Stress Disorder *191*
Porter, Ray 187
Prairie, Operation 74
Prek Lok camp 98, 102–3
prisoners of war 86, **94**, *99*, *171*, **178**, 179
Projects Delta, Gamma, Omega and Sigma *83*
propaganda: antiwar media reports *95col*, 128, *129*, **130**, 139, 147, U.S. Marines burning huts 42–3; *see also* protests
propaganda, Communist *19*; COSVN leaflets 103–5; U.S. PoWs paraded *94*
prostitution *104*, *147*
protests, antiwar *59col*, *95col*, **136**; (esp. on college campuses) against bombing of Cambodia 150, **154**, *156*; against napalm *125*; draft cards *59col*, *106*, "Stop the Draft Week" *107col*; in Washington *107col*, **136**, *159col*
protests, by Buddhists *71*, *71col*
PTSD *191*
public attitudes, morale, in South Vietnam 10, 38, 84, 128, 180
public opinion, reactions (international) 8, *59col*, 60, *95col*
public opinion, reactions, in U.S. 38, **136**, *139*, 160; Hamburger Hill *145*, 147; Rolling Thunder 86, 92–5; after Tet Offensive 128–30, *130*, 139; troop morale affected *143*; Vietnam Veterans Against the War **136**, *159col*; *see also* propaganda; protests; after Peace Agreement *183*; attitude to veterans *178*, **191**; War Memorial (Washington) *189*, *191*, *191col*

"Puff the Magic Dragon" *81*
punji-stakes *78–9*

Q
Quan Loi 78, 105, *163*, 166
Quang Khe, NV 35
Quang Tri 116, **160–71**, 180
Qui Nhon 38, 40, 72, 74, *114*

R
R and R **104**, *147*
race *see* ethnic peoples
Rach Ba Rai River *107col*, **108–15**
radar 86, *87*, 92, *114*, 125–6, 172, 179
Radeker, Walter S. III: 92
Ranch Hand, Operation **102**
Rao Quan River and valley 116
Raspberry, Everett T., Jr 92
Reasoner, Frank S. *47col*
Red Beaches, 40, 110, *113*, 114
"reeducation camps" 188
refugees 162, 188, 190, **190**, *191col*
Regional and Popular Forces ("Ruff-Puffs") 148
Rest and Recreation **104**, *147*
Rhodes, F. E. "Dusty", Jr. 110–15
Ridenhour, Ronald 137
riverine craft: Armored Troop Carriers (ATCs) *110*, Rach Ba Rai River *108*, 110, *112–13*; Assault Support Patrol Boats (ASPBs) *110*; Command and Control Boats (CCBs) 108, 110, *110*; landing craft *26*, LCMs *110*, Landing Vehicle Tracked Personnel (LVTPs) 40–7, *47*; monitors *109*, *110*, *111*, *112–13*; Patrol Air Cushion Vehicles (PACVs) *110*, *111*; River Patrol Boats (PBRs) *110*, *111*; Swift 138
"Roadrunners" *83*
roads *78*, *78*, *82*, 84, 86, 140, 172–9; *see also* routes
Roberts, Adrian 69
"Rocket Ridge" 169
rockets 19, *57*, *81*, 130, 134–7, *143*, *163*; at Khe Sanh *118*, *121*, 123, 125
Rockpile 116, 126, *126*, 127
Rogers, Gordon B. *50*
Rolling Thunder, Operation 38, *59col*, *83col*, **84–95**, 107, 172; bombing ends 139, *139col*
Roman Catholics 24, 26, 31, 188
Routes: 1: 130–4, *163*, 171; 4: 98, 102; 7: 183; 9: 116, 126, *127*, 151–7, *159col*; 13: An Loc *161*, *163*, 166, *170*; Junction City 96, *101*, 105; 19: 48; 246: 105; *see also* Ho Chi Minh Trail
RPG *143*, *192gl*
rubber, rubber plantations 22, **76–83**, 96–8, 105–7; Long Tan **60–8**; patrolling *78*
Rung Sat Special Zone: VC base 108
Rusk, Dean 27

S
Sabben, David *63*, 64, 66–70

"safe bases" of peasant support 12, *19*
Saigon 11, 22, 31, 82, *107*; attacked 128–30, *129*, *139col*, 160, Brink Hotel 38, harbor mined 108, after Peace Agreement and U.S. withdrawal **181–7**, Fall *185*, 186–7, evacuation *174*, **182**; British and Allied forces 12, *19*; National Priority Area 72; Attleboro **74–83**; Cedar Falls *83col*, 96–8; R and R **104**, *147*; punishment of anti-Communists 188, boat people 188, **190**, *191col*; renamed Ho Chi Minh City 188; riots *71col*
Saigon River: Junction City 96–8, 105–7
Salan, Raoul 19
Sams, Ken and *Grunt* 146
SAMS *see under* missiles
San Francisco: demonstrations *95col*
SAS (Aus) 62, **62**, *66*, *192gl*
Savage, Clyde E. 59
Scanlon, Jim 30
seaborne supplies: NVA/VC 86, *114*; U.S. 82
SEALORDS 115, *192gl*
Seaman, Jonathan O. **96–107**
"search and destroy" operations 10, 42–3, *67*, 71, 74, *78*; Attleboro 79–83; Cedar Falls 96–8, *99*
SEATO: founded *31col*, *192gl*
seismic devices: on McNamara Line **119**
Sen, Hun *191col*
17th parallel: partition **23**, 24
Seward, Operation 74
Sharp, Gordon 64, 66–70
Sharp, Ulysses S. Grant 33
Short, Harlan E. 105
Sigholtz, Robert H. 102
Sihanouk, Prince Norodom, of Cambodia 148–50, *150*, **155**, *159col*
Simons, Arthur "Bull" *95*
16th parallel: Chinese/British divide 12
Skoun, Cambodia *156*
Slingshot, Operation *115*
"smart" weapons (EOGBs, LGBs) *167*, 172–9, *173*, **178**
Smith, Harry 64, 66–70
smoke 122, *125*
"Snoopy's Nose" *113*, 114
Snoul, "Fish Hook" 150
Somerset Plain, Operation 140
Son Tay raid *94*, **95**
"Soulsville" *147*
South Vietnam: partition 8, *9* (*map*), Geneva Accords *23*; public attitudes, morale 10, 38, 84, 128, 180; after Peace Agreement, territory held by NVA 179, 180, *182*; fall of the South **180–7**; *see also* Easter Offensive; Saigon; Tet Offensive
South Vietnamese forces 148, 182, 183; Army *see* Army of the Republic of South Vietnam;

General Mobilization law *127col*, 128, 148; Navy *114*; Special Forces 140–7
Southeast Asia *83col*, 172; Communism **8–11**, 22, 24; "Domino Theory" **27**, 188; SEATO founded *31col*; U.S./SV allies 60
Soviet Union 8–11, 26, involvement, support for NV: during Rolling Thunder 84, 86, *87*, military equipment *127*, 157, *163*; *see also* aircraft (MiGs); guns and artillery (rifles, Kalashnikov); Sino-Soviet split 160, **162**, 188–90; U.S.: Nixon and détente *139*, *143*, 160, 172, visit to Moscow 162, *171col*, 172
"Sparrowhawk" strongpoint *15*, 23
Special Air Service (Aus) 62, **62**, *66*
"Spooky" *see under* gunships
Srok Dong, Battle 78
Stanley, Morrie 68–9
Starlite, Operation **40–7**, 116
Statrum, Leroy *154*
"stay behind" parties (Viet Minh) 24–6, 26
Stockholm: "International Tribunal" condemns U.S. *95col*
Stone, John B. 89, 92
Stoner, Eugene *875*
strategic bombing *see* air warfare (under NV "selective bombing")
"Strategic Hamlets" 26, **30**
Strim, Robert L. *178*
Suoi Da 98; Attleboro **79–83**
Suoi Da Bang River 69, 70
Suoi Tre 107
"Super Gaggle" 122, 125
supplies (NVA/VC) 19, 79, **114**, 150, *156*, **158**, 172; in tunnels 97, **98**; U.S. attacks **114**, 140–7, Rolling Thunder *83col*, 84, 86, Thanh Hoa bridge 172–9
supplies (U.S.): dropped, wrapped in blankets 70; for Khe Sanh **122**, *123*, 124–5; U.S. logistic flow **82**
Swift (river boats) 138

T
Ta Bat 140
Tactical Air Control Airborne (TACAIR) **81**, 125
T'ai units 20
Tan Canh 169
Tan Son Nhut airfield *71col*, 84, 102, *182*
Tan Thoi **26–31**
tanks 71, *101*, 148; at An Loc 160, *161*, 162, *163*, *165*, 167; antitank weapons 114, *163*, LAWs *127*, *163*, *165*, 167; *see also* Ontos antitank vehicles; flame-thrower tanks *45*, *47*;
tanks: Centurion *168*; M-24 Chaffee *17*; M-41: *153*, *155*, 158–9, *168*, 186; M-48: *78*, 105–7, *133*, 134–8, 162, *168*, 170, 40, *43*, *45*, 46, *47*; M-48A3 Patton

168; M-551 Sheridan *168*; M-60: 168; PT-76: *127*, 160, *163*, *168*; T-34: 160; T-54: 160, *163*, *165*, 167, **168**, *185*, 186–7; T-55: 160, *168*

Tau-O: 78

Tay Ninh province and City 72, 78, *78*, 79–84; An Loc 160–71; Junction City 96–8, *97*, *105*, 107

Taylor, Maxwell 38

Tchepone, Laos 151–7

television reports 42–3, *94*, *130*

Tet celebrations 128, 162

Tet Offensive (1968) 35, 95, **128–39**; and Khe Sanh *115*, *119*, 122, 124, 126; MRF, and Coronado Operations 114–5; aftermath *159*, 160, 172

Thach Han River 162, 169–71

Thai Nguyen industrial complex (NV) 95, *95col*

Thailand: after peace, continuing war in Indochina 188–91, *190*; *Mayaguez* Incident *187*; military ally 60, *83col*, *107col*; U.S. forces 95, *147col*, USAF operations 84–6, 90, 92, *167*, 172, 175, 179

Than, Bui Quang *185*

Thanh, Nguyen Tat (later Nguyen ai Quoc, *and* Ho Chi Minh) 12, 14; *see* Ho Chi Minh *for full entry*

Thanh Dien Forest 96–8

Thanh Hoa bridge 86, **172–9**, *171col*

That Khe 18

Thi, Lt. General: dismissed *71col*

Thi Tinh River 96

Thien Ngon *123*

Thieu, Nguyen Van 38, *147col*, 157, **167**; election *95col*, *107col*; General Mobilization law *127col*, 128, 148; An Loc 160–71; reaction to peace negotiations 179; fall of the South 180–7, *180q*; resignation 183–6; supporters punished 188

Tho, Le Duc *175*, 179

Thompson, Robert H. 138

Thua Thien province 137, **140–7**

"Thunder Runs" **78**

Ticonderoga, USS *34*, 35, *36*

Tin, Bui *187*

Tone, La Than 118

Tonkin *11*, 12, 18

torpedoes: Gulf of Tonkin Incident 35, *37*, *39col*

Townsend, Colin 69–71

TPQs 125–6

Tra Bong River 43–7, *46*

tribesmen *see* ethnic peoples

Truman, Harry, President: policy 22

Truong, Ngo Quang 130, 137–8, 171

Tu Do, Saigon *147*

Tucson, Operation 98–102

tunnels, and tunnel rats 96–8, *97*, *98*, 102

TURDSID *119*

Turner Joy, USS 35, *37*, *39col*

Tuy, Xuan: talks with Kissinger *147*

Tuy Hoa *183*

U

U Minh Forest: VC base 108, 115

U Tapao, Thailand *187*

Ubon Royal Thai Air Base 90, 172

Udorn, Thailand *95*

underground press (U.S. forces) **146**

uniforms: for patrolling *79*; Australian *61*, *69*; French paratrooper *21*; NVA Infantryman *157*; U.S. Marine *124*; Viet Minh Infantryman *21*

Union Indo-Chinoise 12

United Nations: support for South Korea *23col*; Vietnamese refugees *190*

United States, and Southeast Asia **8–11**, *23*, 24, 27; "Domino Theory" *27*; war policies condemned by de Gaulle *83col*; at close of war 172, *179col*, *183*; *see also* Cambodia; Laos

United States, and Vietnam (1945–54) 12, **22**, 23, 24, *31*

United States, and Vietnam War policy:
under Kennedy 26, *26*, 27, 28, 29, 30–1, *30*, *31*, 42; full-scale commitment 31, National Security Action Memorandum 273 (1963): 32

under Johnson 27, 32, *42*, *48*, 72, *124*; Gulf of Tonkin Incident **32–9**, Gulf of Tonkin Resolution 35–8, 159, *159*; Starlite: (Da Nang) 38, 40, *47col*; main-force war begins 40, 43, *47col*, *59col*, Marines sent in 38, 40, 43, *47col*; other "flags" sought 60; pressure to "quantify" the war (body count etc) *75*, *83col*; Rolling Thunder **84–95**, military wants command 84, 86, pauses *59col*, 86, 95, end *134*, 139, *139*; Coast Guard patrols *114*; Khe Sanh 124, 125; Embassy building attacked in Saigon 128; Tet Offensive *130*, *130*, *134*

under Nixon, and continuing war: renewed attacks on NV *90*, *95*, 162–6, *167*, *167*, *171col*, Linebacker **175–9**; action in Cambodia 148–51, *155*, *156*, **159**; withdrawal of involvement (1969 +) *143*, 147, *147col*, Vietnamization *see separate entry*; president's powers curtailed 150–1, War Powers Act (1973) *179col*, 180; peace negotiations and agreement *see separate entry*; after Peace Agreement (1973) "aid" to SV 180–2; fall of the South *182*, **183**, 187; refugees *190*; superpower talks: China *159col*, 162, **162**, *171col*; Soviet Union 160, *171col*, 172; *see also* public opinion, reactions, in U.S.

United States forces: black, Hispanic and other races **147**; conventional techniques against NVA area warfare 8–10, 72; crimes, murders *143*; DEROS *107*; military commitment and combat deaths **178**; morale in decline *143*; R and R *104*, *147*; tour of duty *107*; first VC attacks on U.S. targets 38; withdrawal of troops 147, *147col*; *see also* draft; veterans

United States Air Force (USAF) 84; aid to ARVN: Ap Bac 25, 26–31; FACs *81*; PoWs 86, **94**; rescue of downed pilots by helicopter **90**, 94; Rolling Thunder *see separate entry*; Easter Offensive (An Loc) 90, **162–71**, *167*; Freedom Dawn 172–9; *Mayaguez* Incident *187*; 8th TFW ("Wolfpack") **89–92**, 172–9; 308th TFS *74*; 158th Aviation Btn **155–9**; 223d Combat Aviation Btn 155–9

United States Army: first helicopters in 48, **50**; numbers reinforced 72

Units: II Field Force 82–3, 98–107; 173d Airborne Brigade *47col*, 48, 60, 82–3, insignia *97*, Junction City 96–103, **102**, *102*, *105*, *107*; 196th Infantry Bde (Light) 72, 78–9, 96–8, 102, insignia *73*; 199th Infantry Bde (Light) 72; 11th Air Assault Div (Test) 48, **50**; 101st Airborne Div, (Separate) 1st Bde 48, *59*, *59col*, 74, 134, 137, **140–7**, 151, insignia *141*, 2d Bde 140; 3d Airborne Btn *157*; 1st Air Cavalry Div (Airmobile) **48–59**, *59col*, 71, 74, *127*, 137, 140, *143*, founded 48, *50*; 1st Bde *59*, 3d Bde 126

Infantry Divisions: 1st *73*, 74–9, **96–107**, 1st Bde 102, *105*, 3d Bde 102; 2d 48; 4th 72, 82–3, 3d Bde 102; 9th 72, *75*, 101, 105–7, **108–17**, *147col*, insignia *109*; 25th ("Tropic Lightning") 35, 72, *73*, 74, 82–3, 96–8, *98*, 2d Bde 102; 27th ("The Wolfhounds") *73*, 76, 79–83; 5th (Mechanized) 151; 1st Air Cavalry Div *49*, 59; 5th Air Cavalry Regt, 2d Btn *59*; 7th Air Cavalry Regt, 1st Btn 55–9, *55*, 2d Btn *59*; 11th Armored Cavalry Regt 72, *74q*, 96–8, 102

Artillery Regiments: 9th, 7th Btn *105*; 32d *97*; 33d, 2d Btn 103; 108th Artillery Group 151; 319th, 3d Btn 102, *102*; Cavalry Regiments: 4th 78; 7th 140, 5th Bde *123*; 9th 51–5, 126, 3d Bde ("Garry Owen") 55

Infantry Regiments: 1st, 2d Btn **77–83**; 2d, 1st Btn 78, 2d Btn 78, 103; 16th, 1st Btn 102; 18th, 2d Btn 78; 20th, 1st Btn *137*; 21st, 3d Btn 78; 26th, 1st Btn 96; 27th *105*, 1st Btn **72–83**, 2d Btn 81; 28th, 2d Btn 78; 31st, 4th Btn 77, 78, 81–3; 47th, 3d Btn 108, 110, 114, 4th Btn 108; 60th, 3d Btn 110–15, 5th Btn 110; 187th 3d Btn 143–7; 501st 2d Btn 140–7; 502d, 1st Btn 140; 503d, 2d Btn 102, *102*; 506th, 1st Btn 140–7, 2d Btn 147; 65th Engineer Battalion 99; 168th Engineers 103, 105; Mobile Riverine Force (MRF) *107*, **108–17**; River Patrol Force *110*; Task Force X-Ray 130–4

Marines 72, 74, **124**; BLT *192gl*; Dewey Canyon *139*, 140; DMZ 74, *95col*; Easter Offensive (An Loc) *167*; Khe Sanh *115col*, 116–27; *Mayaguez* Incident **187**; attacks on NV 172–9; Starlite 38, **40–7**;
Units: 1st Div 72, 74; 9th Expeditionary Bde 40
Regiments: 1st, 1st Btn 134; 3d, 1st Btn 40, 3d Btn 43, 46, 47; 4th, 2d Btn 43, *44*, *45*, 46, 47; 5th, 1st Btn *133*, 138, 2d Btn 134–7, 3d Btn 138, 9th *139col*, 1st Btn 122, 124, BLT (3/9th) 40–1; 26th **116–27**, 3d Btn 116–8, 123, 126; 3d Marine Tank Btn 134; Task Force X-Ray 130–4

Navy (USN): aircraft *90*; Gulf of Tonkin Incident **32–9**, De Soto patrols 32; insignia *33*; Mobile Riverine Force (MRF; Task Force 117) 108, Rach Ba Bai River **108–17**; Task Force 115 ("Market Time") *114*; NV attacked by aircraft 172–9; PoWs *94*; River Patrol Force (RPF; Task Force 116 "Game Warden") *110*; Rolling Thunder 84–6; NV coast shelled *83col*; Starlite *45*, 47, *47col*; SEALORDS 115; Seventh Fleet Task Force 166, *167*, *171*, aircraft carriers *90*, evacuation of Saigon **182**; Swift boats *114*, *115*

Special Forces (Green Berets) 8–10, 26, 32, *47col*, 48, *58*, *71col*, *147*, 148; 5th Special Forces Group, activated *31col*; with ARVN 72, 108; with Australian SAS *66*, *71*; control CIDGs for MACV *58*; counterinsurgency 42, *42*, *71*; intelligence gathering 79, *83*; A Shau valley and Hamburger Hill **140–7**; Attleboro 79–84; Ia Drang 48–59; Junction City 98, 105; Khe Sanh Combat Base 116, 123; Lang Vei camp 116, 122, 123, *127*; Son Tay raid 94, *95*

U.S./South Vietnamese Campaign Plan (AB-141) 72

Utah, Operation 74

V

Vam Co Dong River 96–8

Van Tuong village complex:

Starlite **43–7**
Vann, John Paul **26–31**, 169
veterans, U.S. *178*, *191*; Memorial,
  in Washington *189*, *191*, *191col*;
  Vietnam Veterans Against the
  War *136*, *159col*
Viet Bac 14, 20
Viet Cong (Vietnamese
  Communists; previously Viet
  Minh) 148, 160; Ap Bac **24–31**;
  areas of control 32, 42, 48, 60,
  108, Mekong Delta 108, (Battle
  of Rach Ba Rai River) *107col*,
  108–15; attacks on U.S. targets
  38, Starlite **40–7**, 116; Attleboro
  72–83; booby traps 42, *78–9*, *98*;
  Cedar Falls 96–8; general
  strategies *30*, 47, 48, 74;
  Junction City *95col*, **96–107**;
  Long Tan **60–71**; public
  execution of VC suspect *130*;
  "stay behind" Viet Minh parties
  24–6, *26*; tunnels 96–8, *97*, *98*,
  102; *see also* Tet Offensive
VC units: 5th Div **60–71**, *68*, 71,
  171, D445 Btn ("Phuoc Tuy's
  Own") **60–71**, *68*; 9th Div
  72–83, 98–107, *163*, **166–71**;
  304th Div *122*; 325thC Div *122*;
  1st Regt 42–7, 60th Btn *46*; 272d
  Regt 102–3; 273d Regt *101*, 107;
  263d Btn 110; Saigon C-10 City
  Battalion 128
Viet Minh (*Viet Nam Doc Lap Dong
  Minh Hoi*; later Viet Cong) 8–10,
  20, 24–6, *26*, *30*; First Indochina
  War **12–23**, Geneva Accords
  (1954) *23*, 26; military
  organization *20*, *21*; *see also* Viet
  Cong
Vietnam 11; Democratic Republic
  of Vietnam 12, *23col*, 24;
  partition 8, *9* (*map*), **23**, 26; *see
  also* Indochina War, First;
  reunited: continuing war 10,
  188–91, invades Cambodia *186*,
  187col; Chinese attack 188–90
Vietnam Veterans Against the War
  136, *159col*
Vietnamese Air Force, South
  (VNAF) 26
Vietnamese National Army *167*
Vietnamese Nationalist Party 12
Vietnamese Workers' Party 24–6;
  see also Viet Cong
Vietnamization of SV forces 115,
  139col, *143*, 148, **159**, 160, *192gl*;
  after Hamburger Hill *143*, *145*,
  147; Lam Son 719: *149*, *152–3*
"Village War" (against VC) 72
villagers *see* peasants
Vinh Yen 19
Vung Tau *63*, *104*, *114*; Long Tan
  60–71
Vung Tau Charter 38

W
"Wagon train" position: Ap Bau
  Bang II *101*, 105–7
Wallace, William *72q*

Walt, Lewis W. *42*
war crimes: U.S. PoW trials
  proposed *94*; "International
  Tribunal" accuses U.S. *95col*
"War of the Posts" 14
War Powers Act *179col*, 180
War Zone C 42, *192gl*; U.S.
  offensives *71col*, **72–83**, Junction
  City *95col*, **96–107**
War Zone D 48, 60, *192gl*
Warnke, Paul *84q*
Washington: antiwar
  demonstrations 107, *136*, *159col*;
  Vietnam Memorial *189*, *191*,
  191col
Watergate *183*
Westmoreland, William Childs *34*,
  35, 38, 60; Starlite, Da Nang
  40–2; Ia Drang 48, *51*; U.S./
  South Vietnamese Campaign
  Plan for National Priority Areas
  72, Attleboro *76*; accepts joint
  riverine force 108, *108q*; Khe
  Sanh *116q*; Niagara *126*; hands
  over MACV command *127col*,
  143; Tet Offensive 128–30, *130*,
  139, 140, Delaware (A Shau
  valley) 140; wants to enter Laos
  and Cambodia *159*
Wetterhahn, Ralph 92
White Beaches 110, *113*, 114
Willoughby, Frank C. *127*
Wolfe, Hiram M. IV: 105–7
"Wolfhounds" 79–83
"Wolfpack" *89*, 90–2
Wood, Walter *187*
World War II: effects on Vietnam
  12, 19, 22, *23col*

X
Xom Bang 84
Xom Giua village 102
Xuan Loc *181*, 183, *187col*, 189

Y
Yankee Station *90*
Yen Bay uprising 12
Young, David *183*
"Young Turks" 38

Z
Zais, Melvin 147

PICTURE CREDITS
The following abbreviations have been used:

a	above	*r*	right	*c*	center
b	below	*l*	left		

AP — Associated Press
DOD — Department of Defense Still Media Records Center
IWM — Imperial War Museum
Page — Tim Page
RHPL — Robert Hunt Picture Library
SACU — Society for Anglo-Chinese Understanding
Topham — John Topham Picture Source
TRH — TRH Pictures

back cover AP; Cover Page; 1 DOD; 2 Don McCullin/Magnum; 4 DOD; 6a RHPL; 6b Page; 8 Roger-Viollet; 11a LL-Viollet; 11b Collection Viollet; 12a RHPL; 12bl Harlingue-Viollet; 12br RHPL; 13a ECPA Armées; 13bl La Musée de la Légion Etrangère; 13br SIPA PRESS; 14l IWM; 14ar ECPA Armées (MB); 14br Daniel Camus/Magnum; 15l Edimedia; 15r Daniel Camus/Magnum; 15a U.S. Marine Corps/Carina Dvorak; 18a Edimedia; 18b ECPA Armées; 19l IWM; 19r SACU; 20–22 Edimedia; 23 Roger-Viollet; 25 U.S. Dept of Military History; 26 DOD; 26–27 Topham; 27 Hulton/Deutsch Collection; 30 AP; 31l DOD; 31c AP; 31br Hulton/Deutsch Collection; 33a Naval Photographic Center; 33b DOD; 34a DOD; 34b Popperfoto; 35 DOD; 38 Popperfoto; 39l John Frost; 39r Hulton/Deutsch Collection; 41a Page; 41b AP; 42l Page; 42r Topham; 43l Page; 43r DOD; 47 Topham; 49a Page; 49b Page; 50 DOD; 51 AP; 54 DOD; 55 AP; 57 Page; 58 Page; 58r AP; 59 AP; 61a AP; 61bl Page; 61br Australian War Memorial; 62a AP; 62b Australian War Memorial; 63a Australian War Memorial; 63b AP; 66–68 Page; 70l Topham; 70r Page; 71 Topham; 73a AP; 73b DOD; 73c DOD; 74–5 DOD; 74 Page; 75 U.S. Naval Museum/Photo Kim Nielsen; 78 Page; 79l Topham; 79r DOD; 80–82 DOD; 83 J. Olsen/Life/Colorific; 85 TRH; 86 DOD; 87a Topham; 87b Hulton/Deutsch Collection; 90 DOD; 91a DOD/Carina Dvorak; 91b Magnum; 94a U.S. Naval Museum/photo Kim Nielsen; 94b Topham; 95 DOD; 97al AP; 97b DOD; 98 DOD; 99a AP; 99b DOD; 102 DOD; 103a AP; 103b DOD; 104 DOD; 105a Page; 105b DOD; 106 Hulton/Deutsch Collection; 106–7 Page; 109 Page; 110–111 DOD; 111a RHPL; 114 Page; 115 DOD; 117a Popperfoto; 117rb Corbis; 118 AP; 119a DOD; 119b Popperfoto; 125a AP; 125b Popperfoto; 126a RHPL; 126b DOD; 127a DOD; 127b Topham; 129l Popperfoto; 129ar DOD; 129ac Popperfoto; 130a AP; 130b DOD; 131a RHPL; 131b Magnum; 134bl Library of Congress; 134br Popperfoto; 135 AP; 136al Library of Congress; 136br Popperfoto; 137 Ron Haberle/Life/Colorific; 138 Philip Jones Griffiths/Magnum; 139 John Frost; 141 AP; 142l Topham; 142r AP; 143al RHPL; 143ar Hulton/Deutsch Collection; 143b David Burnet/Colorific; 146l Topham; 146r Ken Sams Collection; 147a Popperfoto; 147b Gamma/Frank Spooner Pictures; 149 AP; 150a AP; 150b Hulton/Deutsch Collection; 151 Hulton/Deutsch Collection; 154a RHPL; 154b Topham; 155l Popperfoto; 155r Hulton/Deutsch Collection; 156a DOD; 156b Page; 158 DOD; 159 DOD; 161 AP; 162a AP; 162b Popperfoto; 163 AP; 166–7 DOD; 167 RHPL; 170a DOD; 170b AP; 171 Gamma/Frank Spooner Pictures; 173a TRH; 173b RHPL; 174 DOD; 175l DOD; 175r Hulton/Deutsch Collection; 178 AP; 179 Rex Features; 181a Rex Features; 181b Nik Wheeler/Black Star/Colorific; 182 AP; 183 Hulton/Deutsch Collection; 186a Frank Spooner Pictures; 186b Rex Features; 187 DOD; 188 Page; 189a Tsuno/Gamma/Frank Spooner Pictures; 189b Page; 190 Sipa/Rex Features; 191a Page; 191b Gamma/Frank Spooner Pictures;

ACKNOWLEDGMENTS
Figure artwork — Richard Hook/Linden Artists
Profile artworks — Terry Hadler/Bernard Thornton Artists
Maps — Technical Art Services and Russell Barnet/Jillian Burgess Artists
Computer maps — Chapman Bounford & Associates
Index — Valerie Lewis Chandler